WOMEN IN MASS COMMUNICATION

SOME OTHER VOLUMES IN THE
SAGE FOCUS EDITIONS

WOMEN IN MASS COMMUNICATION
Challenging Gender Values

Edited by
Pamela J. Creedon

SAGE PUBLICATIONS
The Publishers of Professional Social Science
Newbury Park   London   New Delhi

To my mother, Louise;
my sister, Barb; and my brother, Jim

For information address:

SAGE Publications, Inc.
2111 West Hillcrest Drive
Newbury Park, California 91320

SAGE Publications Ltd.
28 Banner Street
London EC1Y 8QE
England

SAGE Publications India Pvt. Ltd.
M-32 Market
Greater Kailash I
New Delhi 110 048 India

Printed in the United States of America

Library of Congress Cataloging-in-Publication Data

Main entry under title:

Women in mass communication : challenging gender values / editor,
    Pamela J. Creedon.
        p. cm. —— (Sage focus editions ; v. 106)
    Bibliography: p.
    ISBN 0-8039-3447-5. —— ISBN 0-8039-3448-3 (pbk.)
    1. Mass media and women. 2. Mass media——Study and teaching.
3. Women in the mass media industry. I. Creedon, Pamela J.
P94.5.W65W67 1989
001.51 ′088042——dc19   89-4317
                                                              CIP

FIRST PRINTING, 1989

Contents

PART II. THE PROFESSION

Section A: A Close-Up of Women in, on, and Through
Mass Communication

Section B: A Voice and Vision for the Future

Preface

One of the most difficult aspects of editing a book is knowing when it is—and you are—done. This is very difficult because a book is a composite of people and ideas that change and grow, that are at once different and yet similar. It is the job of the editor to find the thread that will keep them together, yet be flexible enough to let them continue to change and grow.

It is also very difficult to know when you're done because each word choice reveals something about the book, the editor, and the authors. In every sentence, subtleties in the choices among words like *can, should, would, could, might, may*, and *will* become ideological and political decisions. Even more thought-provoking are the philosophical agreements and disagreements between the editor and the other authors.

In fact, this book, as you read it today, is in its fourth draft form. It started as a transcription of some talks about "feminization" in mass communication, and it ended as a humanistic philosophical discourse about values in mass communication, which concludes with a big dose of the "real" world for women in mass communication. Along the way, it also shifted from its original liberal feminist or reforming focus to its current transformation focus.

The contents of the first part of this book deal primarily with the gender switch in mass communication and its potential to challenge traditional values in the field. We begin by looking at the pedagogical base of mass communication. Many of the chapters in Section A of Part I call for significant changes in the way we think about gender in the context of mass communication. Some represent pioneering efforts to extend feminist theory in areas such as media law and media history, and each of them could easily be developed into a full-length book. This part of the book also provides an international perspective on many of these same issues and some additional perspectives on studying women of color in mass communication.

The concluding two chapters in Part I describe the status of women faculty and their impact on students in mass communication programs across the country. These chapters are important finishing touches to the call for re-vision in the way mass communication is taught and practiced today.

The focus of the book changes in Part II, and turns to the concept of sexism and economic equity in current mass communication practice. Chapters in this section provide a status report on employment, salaries, and other issues women face in, on, and through the mass media and the related disciplines of public relations and advertising.

The book concludes with two extremely important chapters. One discusses the alternative values presented by the women's movement media. The other paints a picture of re-visioned futures for mass communication based on various feminist theoretical positions.

SOME VERY IMPORTANT ACKNOWLEDGMENTS

I am indebted to a number of people for technical, professional, theoretical, philosophical, and personal help and insight during this book project. The book would not have been possible without the generous support of The Ohio State University School of Journalism and its director, Walter Bunge. The two Ohio State graduate associates who worked with me on the project also deserve special recognition: Sandra Little, who tirelessly transcribed the lectures that formed the original core of the book, and Lynne Cope, who spent countless hours in the library locating resources and double-checking references on the final draft. For technical editing assistance and support, I want to thank John McClelland, who looked over my shoulder and generously donated much of his time and expertise.

A great deal of theoretical direction for the book came from Leslie Steeves and Lana Rakow. The same amount of philosophical direction came from Ann West and Rebecca Rooney. In fact, without the kindness, help, understanding, and support of these four persons, this book never would have been completed.

Finally, I want to thank several other special people. First is Lee Becker, who took time to show me that there is more for a professional in academia than telling old war stories in the classroom. The others are my mother, Louise Creedon, my sister, Barb Morris, and my brother, Jim Creedon, who have supported every aspect of every project in which I've ever asked for their help, including this one.

—*Pamela J. Creedon*

PART I

The Academy

Section A. Perspectives on Re-Visioning Gender Values in Mass Communication

1

The Challenge of Re-Visioning Gender Values

PAMELA J. CREEDON

A quiet revolution of sorts is spreading rapidly throughout academia today. The impact is becoming so widespread and significant that feminist scholars have even developed a special word, *re-vision* to describe the revolution. Adrienne Rich (1979) offers this perspective:

> Re-vision—the act of looking back, of seeing with fresh eyes, of entering an old text from a new critical direction—is for women more than a chapter in cultural history; it is an act of survival. Until we can understand the assumptions in which we are drenched we cannot know ourselves. (p. 35)

The literary canon, for example, has been undergoing a careful re-visioning since the early 1970s. Scholarship in the field has moved beyond an examination of Shakespeare's sexism and the search for "lost" women writers. Literary history is now open to "more works by writers from unempowered segments of our culture [that] will change the values institutionalized in the canon" (Draine, 1988, p. A40).

One might expect careful scrutiny of assumptions, or re-vision, to be endemic to mass communication as well. We teach budding journalists to approach every story "with fresh eyes," that is, critically, but fairly, because we have been taught that journalists, who pen the first rough draft of the American version of world history, should be especially sensitive to and cautious about assumptions. But, for reasons that will become clear in the next few pages, assumptions about gender and gender values, which are institutionalized *within* the mass communication canon, are only beginning to be re-visioned.

AUTHOR'S NOTE: I wish to thank Leslie Steeves, Lana Rakow, Rebecca Rooney, Molly Merryman, Lynne Hobstetter, and John McClelland for their comments and suggestions on this chapter.

This lack of scrutiny is especially puzzling in light of the gender switch now clearly observable in mass communication. The gender switch comes as no surprise, however. Since 1977 the majority of students enrolled in journalism and mass communication programs have been female. In the early 1980s, national enrollment patterns stabilized at about 60% female to 40% male, and a similar ratio also became the norm for graduates of mass communication programs (Peterson, 1982). Recently, these students entering mass communication practice have tilted employment statistics toward the female gender in many entry-level categories. Further, some researchers predict that in the United States, in less than a decade, the mass media and related communication fields such as public relations will be predominantly female.

The increasing number of women in mass communication careers is a significant change, presumably with potential for bringing about some changes in the dominant value system. Exploring the potential of the gender switch to energize a widespread re-vision of values in mass communication is the purpose of this book. To do so, the book examines the potential for change that a re-vision of values could have in mass communication. But, since an examination of values embedded in all of the rules and principles in mass communication would have been too overwhelming, for both authors and readers, the task was reduced to a broad critique of gender assumptions in mass communication and how these assumptions are revealed through media coverage of and communication about gender and the gender switch.

The book has first a dimension of singularity. This singularity is feminist, and thus provides an opportunity to re-vision mass communication and its value system from an alternative viewpoint. However, the re-vision is not confined to only *one* feminist theoretical position. Instead, the authors re-vision mass communication in a way that exposes multiple visions—a variety of feminist perspectives—which allow the reader to examine assumptions in mass communication through various humanistic lenses. The re-visioning process also expands one's consciousness about the way assumptions affect individual women and men, as well as various groups of people, differently. Therefore, the re-visioning process described in this book is also connected to, or can be applied to, assumptions about race, class, and sexuality.

The book has selected the first rough draft of a new chapter of mass communication history, the chapter about the gender switch, as the microcosm for analysis. The analysis is fresh in that it suggests a re-vision or new vision of the construction of the gender switch in mass communication.

The analysis suggests that dominant values have dictated news values. To demonstrate this point, the abundance of copy that has been written about the gender switch so far is assembled and analyzed, and the apparent failure of mass communication media to cover the core issue, their own role in constructing values in this culture, is challenged.[1]

But, beyond the book's singular (feminist) and fresh (gender switch) perspectives, there is a unique thread that ties the chapters together. The thread is the philosophical approach that makes this volume different from any other on gender in mass communication. That philosophical approach involves a re-vision of assumptions.

USING RE-VISIONING* "SOFTWARE"[2]

Perhaps an analogy will best illustrate how the re-visioning approach keeps the book together. If one thinks of this book as the *User's Guide to Re-Visioning* Software*, one can see that learning to re-vision is similar to learning the use of a new computer software program. The next few pages in this chapter essentially serve as the introduction to the user's guide. They are intended to explain the fundamental principles underlying Re-Visioning* Software to people with different backgrounds, interests, and knowledge. Therefore, they start by examining some fundamental assumptions about reality, specifically, assumptions about the social construction of reality. They review assumptions about facts and about how facts are given meaning. They cover the role of language in constructing the meaning of gender and of values associated with gender, followed by an exploration of the meaning of gender values from various feminist theoretical perspectives. The chapter also concludes with a case study of the liberal feminist's experience with Re-Visioning* Software.

The other authors approach the process of re-vision in mass communication by acting as editors and applying their blue pencils to the copy written thus far about the gender switch. They analyze the coverage to see if all points of view—all sides and angles of the story—have been adequately covered. They question what appears to be, at the least, a lack of originality in this first draft of the gender chapter of mass communication history. Several even suggest that the draft appears to have been plagiarized from other formerly male-dominated fields, like teaching, library science, and certain areas of banking. They question the apparent decision to treat gender as a separate chapter in the history book, rather than integrating it into each chapter, page, paragraph, sentence, and word. They call for an investigation of what appears to be a conflict of interest, since much of the copy has been edited by those with a vested interest in directing its outcome. They ask how the coverage of conflicting gender values would differ, or possibly improve, if it were viewed more as an ongoing, in-depth issue than as "spot news."

The authors also show how the software can be used to re-vision issues related to the gender switch in specific media industries such as newspapers, magazines, television, radio, public relations, and advertising. The book ends with a chapter by Lana Rakow that demonstrates the pioneering graphics capability of Re-Visioning* Software to draw alternative futures for mass communication.

FACT, MEANING, AND REALITY: DEVELOPING A SHARED LANGUAGE ABOUT GENDER

Understanding gender is at once very simple and very complex. The deeper one probes into political, economic, or other cultural interpretations of gender, the more complex and diverse the ranges of opinion prove to be. It quickly becomes a case of "The more you learn, the more you realize how little you really know."

Applying this aphorism to the relationship between gender and mass communication is simple. First, it is impossible to examine gender as news without placing it in some context. As news, gender becomes part of a culture described by a particular writer, class, power structure, or the like at a particular point in history (Carey, 1975, p. 8). Also, as news, gender is likely to be treated as an event occurring at a discrete time, rather than as an issue of ongoing significance (Tuchman, 1978, p. 138). To illuminate the two preceding points, this introductory chapter begins with an exploration of the context in which meaning is developed through and created by mass communication. This exploration starts by discussing the way meaning and reality have developed, have been created, from the facts about the gender switch in mass communication.

A review of the facts of this story. Fact: For more than a decade, women have made up the majority of students enrolled in American schools of journalism and mass communication. Fact: These female graduates are finding employment, and, due to this influx of women, mass communication is becoming a female-intensive occupational category.

The meaning of these facts. Facts are given meaning at various levels. The levels are formed by the number of people involved and their relationship to the communication. They include societywide, institutional/organizational, intergroup or association, intragroup, interpersonal, and intrapersonal levels (McQuail, 1987, p. 6).

Differing interpretations of the *meaning* of the facts about the gender switch are found at these various levels. Depending upon the level of communication and the people involved in determining meaning, some interpretations are more traditional—and some more radical—than others. Some interpretations are more positive—and some more negative—than others. Some interpretations are more powerful—and some less powerful—than others.

Feminist scholars offer convincing evidence that these perceptions of gender can matter more than facts (Benderly, 1987; Lenz & Myerhoff, 1985; Rakow, 1986). In terms of the gender switch in mass communication, the prevailing meaning attached to the facts has suggested that a female majority in the field does not translate into superior power or influence for women; instead, it has been translated to mean a decline in salaries and status for the field.

This meaning is reinforced, more often than not, when stories about the gender switch appear in rather sensationalized spot news stories in the mass media. "Velvet ghetto," for example, is the term that has been used to describe the impact of women in public relations, while the "pink-collar ghetto" label is attached to predominantly female news editorial positions. Both terms certainly undercut a positive construction of the meaning of women entering the field.

Feminists argue that this type of coverage fits rather nicely with George Gerbner's (1978) description of cultural resistance. According to Gerbner, when the dynamics of a social movement threaten or promise to overpower or restructure a particular set of social relations or values, the dynamics of cultural resistance come into play. He describes the three main tactics of resisting change as discrediting, isolating, and undercutting (p. 48).

Epithets such as those mentioned above not only serve a discrediting function, but they are great for headlines—they are short and provide concrete images—and they are bandied about freely in the media. Then, when readers attempt to construct the meaning of the trend from the language used in media reports, they find themselves in a "bad news" ghetto. These headlines from professional journals reporting about the trend demonstrate the point: "Public Relations: 'Velvet Ghetto' for Women" (*Ragan Report*); "Is the PR Field Being Hurt by Too Many Women?" (*Advertising*

Age); "Women Execs Call Gender a Career Obstacle" (*Communication World*); "A Concern: Will Women Inherit the Profession?" (*Public Relations Journal*); "Pink Collar Ghetto" (*Editor & Publisher*). By 1986, headlines like these had moved from the professional and trade press into the popular press and continued to construct a "bad news" ghetto image for the trend.

The reality of these interpretations of the gender switch. In her book *Making News*, Gaye Tuchman (1978) describes the ways news helps to shape the reality of an event:

> News stories not only lend occurrences their existence as public events, but also impart character to them, for news reports help to shape the public definition of happenings by selectively attributing to them specific details or "particulars." They make these selected details accessible to news consumers. (p. 190)

Some mass communication theorists also suggest that the dominant or most powerful interpretation often shapes what is called the *consensus* interpretation of a situation or set of facts (Carey, 1988; McQuail, 1987; Parenti, 1986). Further, because it reflects the most powerful interpretation, the consensus interpretation is what is most often repeated and recorded (by journalists, historians, and the like). Moreover, since repetition at least enhances recall, a consensus interpretation repeated often enough becomes believable, eventually taking on the dimension of "reality."

To define reality, I turn to Jane Wagner. In her play, *The Search for Signs of Intelligent Life in the Universe* (1986), Wagner's narrator, a mad bag lady who communicates with aliens from outer space, offers this view: "What is reality anyway? Nothin' but a collective hunch. My space chums think reality was once a primitive method of crowd control that got out of hand" (p. 18).

Mass communication theorists who take a cultural approach to communication also argue that reality is nothing more than—and nothing less than—a "collective hunch." They suggest that when countless personal and interpersonal interpretations are communicated via mass channels, meaning tends to become homogenized and consensus values prevail. James Carey (1988) describes this process of creating consensus meaning as follows:

> It is not only that societies are drawn together around some form of consensus narrative that is variable as to style and technique but the consensus narrative

is about something; in fact, it is about itself—the continuous reweaving of given patterns of action and signification. (p. 16)

Thus, by continuously reweaving patterns, consensus meaning almost exists outside of, or in spite of, the story or event being communicated. In such a way, these consensus patterns are woven and rewoven first to become, and later to reinforce, the dominant value system's "reality" in a society or culture.

A significant number of other media scholars agree with this notion of a collective or consensus construction of reality. For example, Tuchman's (1978) hypothesis is that news helps to construct social reality.

News does not mirror society. It helps to constitute it as a shared social phenomenon, for in the process of describing an event, news defines and shapes that event, much as news stories construed and constructed the early period of the modern women's movement as the activities of ridiculous bra burners. (p. 184)

Michael Parenti (1986) further argues that journalists can't report facts "objectively" because the raw material of news (e.g., sources) represents the dominant interests in society. Thus he describes the "myth of objectivity":

Opinions that support existing arrangements of economic and political power are more easily treated as facts, while facts that are troublesome to the prevailing distribution of class power are likely to be dismissed as opinionated. And those who censor dissenting views see themselves as protectors of objectivity and keepers of heterodoxy when, in fact, they are the guardians of ideological conformity. (p. 50)

Not surprisingly, the use of consensus news values results in news stories that sound strangely similar across the media channels. But, while media scholars are actively studying the relationship between "facts" and "stories about facts," the practice (of journalists who write the first draft of history) has been perceptibly slower in considering the possible implications of Tuchman's and Parenti's analyses of the nature of news. Journalists maintain that they report the "facts" in an "objective" manner. However, Bird and Dardenne (1988) respond that " 'news values,' which journalists often imply are something intrinsic in events, to be deduced as 'news sense,' are culturally specific story-telling codes" (p. 73).

Fact, meaning, reality, and the gender switch. What does this all mean? If we accept that news values are culturally specific story-telling codes, then "objective" reporting is simply a matter of accurately reflecting the consensus interpretation. *Ergo, any challenge (e.g., the gender switch) that is vital and significant enough to become a threat to the ideology of the dominant value system should be expected to be presented as having negative, rather than positive, potential for change.*

This interpretation should sound very familiar to graduates of journalism programs who were disillusioned when they learned the old axiom, "News is anything the editor says it is." Many went along with, and continue to go along with, this principle when they entered the work force, as long as they were not asked to do anything terribly unethical. In a sense, they accepted the principle by rationalizing that the editor (or manager or president) has a higher level of authority and thus a better understanding of news or organizational values. However, this axiom may need to be examined more carefully. It may be that it means something extremely significant in this particular study of the challenge that the gender switch presents to values in mass communication. It may really say that reality (news) is anything the dominant value system (editor) says it is.

Comparatively little has been done to address the media construction of "reality" about the gender switch or to incorporate feminist theory into the analysis. For example, many feminists suggest that, if not met by resistance, women's culture could act as a catalyst for positive change by pushing the cultural norms of feminized fields against existing boundaries (Lenz & Myerhoff, 1985). Some also argue that the gender switch, sometimes described as "feminization," could be constructed as a way to achieve balance in values and an appreciation of differences.[3]

In a broader context, feminists often do not agree with the "facts" or the "stories about the facts" found in most Western history or science books. They suggest that there can be differing interpretations of what has come to be accepted as "fact." Riane Eisler (1987), for example, cites new archeological findings and interpretations that suggest that there were "many thousands of years when the basic technologies on which civilization is built were developed in societies that were not male dominant, violent and hierarchic" (p. xvi). Beryl Benderly (1987) looks closely at the "hard" sciences and abandons her belief in their social neutrality after she finds countless examples of misinterpretation of physiological differences between men and women.

The point of the preceding paragraphs is to propose that media stories about women in this culture—not simply those about the gender switch in mass communication—have been written under a cloud of assumptions about the facts, the meaning of the facts, and the reality of the facts about gender in general. There is precious little evidence to suggest that journalists have examined the cultural assumptions that lie beneath their own, their sources', or the consensus interpretation of gender values and the gender switch in mass communication.

LANGUAGE AND GENDER

What can be done to re-vision gender and the gender switch in mass communication? One starting point for communicators could be to examine the role of language in constructing reality. Many argue that language is a key ingredient in the consensus construction of meaning and reality. One way to understand the basis for this argument is to analyze Latin, a language that we are taught is "dead." Examination of the words and structure of Latin shows us that the Roman culture existed at the time of the "death" of the language. Certainly, we would not expect to find Latin equivalents for terms such as *IBM PC* or *videotext* because the products did not exist in that culture.

In contrast, a living language is one that changes to reflect the evolution of its culture. A living language weaves or communicates the consensus meaning of culture and cultural norms as perceived by those who make the rules.[4] In one sense, this process constructs a language boundary for socially acceptable reality. If a word is not in the dictionary, or if a sentence is not in proper grammatical form, it is not acceptable. Unacceptable words and constructions violate rules, which are guarded by those who "enforce" our language.

For example, some language enforcers still maintain that the English language can be gender neutral, in spite of the fact that their relentless defense of masculine pronouns as harmless "generics" is challenged by numerous research studies.[5] Recognizing that "enforcer" roles exist in a living language and that persons in those roles can affect (and effect) the construction of reality is an important step for communicators who make their living by using the words and symbols of language.

An investigative journalist would, of course, have one key question: Who are the enforcers? Who determines what new words, thoughts, and phrases should be added to the language and what meaning will be given to them? For example, to help American English teachers with the determination, the Modern Language Association (MLA) was created. It has been described as the marketplace and funeral parlor for American English. The

MLA can give birth to new words that describe "reality," bury archaic words and uses that no longer describe "reality," barter over the meanings of old and new words to make certain that they reflect "reality," and argue about changes in the structure of the language that enforce "reality." In essence, the MLA and other opinion leaders in language, such as etymologists and dictionary staff, decide what is acceptable, perhaps normative, and what is not in language. In the mass media, the United Press International and Associated Press stylebooks perform somewhat similar functions.

Studying the nature of language inevitably leads to the discussion of the widely shared feminist position that power exists in the form and structure of language.

> Feminists have examined language as a symbolic system closely tied to patriarchal social structure. They argue that language is deeply patriarchal, that the "theft of the language" is part of women's condition of relative powerlessness and that women need to rework traditional forms in order to create women-centered language and meaning. (Thorne, Kramarae, & Henley, 1983, p. 11)

Some feminists have attempted to recapture power from language. One example is found in the word *re-vision*, introduced earlier. To create this word, Adrienne Rich symbolically seized power over the language when she violated a rule without checking with the MLA or with anyone at *Webster's*.[6] She took the word *revision* and consciously seized the language license necessary to allow it to lead a double life as a noun and verb with a new meaning as *re-vision*.

The symbolic aspect of language also plays an important role in the social construction of concepts like gender. Many feminists argue that the term *gender* is drenched with symbols that expose cultural assumptions about masculinity and femininity. They suggest that, since the meaning of *gender* can and does change as culture changes, it is problematic to describe it in terms of current constructions of socially acceptable roles. In a broad sense, American culture is composed of a rigid, bipolar gender system with numerous accompanying assumptions—including that this is a natural system—for appropriate masculine behavior and for appropriate feminine behavior. However, the dividing line between these constructs can shift over time and from place to place. For example, increased participation in and media coverage of women's sports is at least partially responsible for a greater general acceptance of female athletes in American culture. Yet certain sports continue to be considered more sex-appropriate for women (e.g., tennis, gymnastics, and golf) than others (e.g., basketball, football, wrestling) by the culture (Kane, 1987).

As mass communication researcher and feminist scholar Lana Rakow (1986) explains, gender is

> both something we do and something we think with, both a set of social practices and a system of cultural meanings. The social "doing" of gender—and the cultural meanings—"thinking the world" using the categories and experiences of gender—constitute us as women or men, organized into a particular configuration of social relations. (p. 21)

Other feminists, including Bell Hooks (1984), also argue that gender, race, and class share the outcomes of being denied power through language and language symbolism. To acknowledge the point in this book, a conscious decision was made to violate another convention of style (including AP and UPI style) in order to recognize racism in the language. *Black* is capitalized throughout this book when referring to race for two reasons. One is that *Black* is often used in place of the term *Negro*, formerly used to designate race or ethnicity. Second is to recognize and to draw attention to the political ramifications of issues involving race. Conversely, the term *white* is not capitalized in this book in order to symbolically deny political power to the term. (A note of interest—the fourth edition of the American Psychological Association's publication manual will reportedly call for capitalization of both *Black* and *White* in reference to race.)

Beyond examples of specific words, many feminists also find ample evidence that language rule enforcers perceive their role as aiding and abetting the dominant value (consensus) system. Even a system of references and notations has some implicit assumptions. As another symbolic gesture, the guidelines of the *Publication Manual of the American Psychological Association* (APA), third edition, have been modified in this book. The modification is rather simple: Chapter reference sections include first names of authors rather than just initials, as APA dictates. The impact of the modification is important, however. By adding the first names of the authors, which will most likely reveal whether the author is male or female, we provide readers with another clue about the perspective, and perhaps assumptions, of an author's theories.

The preceding pages have discussed how avoiding assumptions built into our language about gender (or any value) requires constant personal and collective vigilance. They demonstrate that the role of language in shaping the meaning of values has not been adequately covered or recognized by mass communicators. Further, while news coverage of the women's movement has been and still is criticized, largely legitimately, for presenting trivial images of bra burners, women's libbers, and "person-hole" covers, the potentially blockbusting investigative stories about feminist charges of language theft and insider manipulation of language are never assigned to reporters. Language is the exact spot where the preliminary jousts by challengers to the dominant value system take place, and it is a story that has been largely ignored by the mass media.

FEMINIST THEORY AND GENDER VALUES

Another active re-vision of values in mass communication would involve incorporating feminist theory into the analysis of gender and the gender switch. Brenda Dervin (1987) describes three stages in the general evolution of feminist scholarship:

> Feminist scholarship has evolved over time... from a focus on sex differences (the traditional approach), to a focus on improving society and making women more like men (the reformist or liberal approach), to the current focus on giving voice to women (the radical feminist approach). (p. 110)

A critical analysis by feminist scholar and mass communication researcher Leslie Steeves (1987) further distinguishes feminism by several broad categories—biologistic, individualistic, social psychological or sociocultural, and economic. Steeves uses these categories to describe different theoretical positions that various feminists have taken about the role of women in society.

The differences between the perspectives are significant. According to Steeves (1987), liberal feminists assume that rational argument and legal efforts can move women away from the private sphere of the home and toward equity with men in the public world of objectivity and rationality (pp. 100-101). Applied to the mass media, scholars assume that persuading media organizations (via argument and legislation) to hire women, increase representations of women, and avoid stereotypes is the solution to women's disadvantaged status.

In contrast, radical feminists do not believe that "masculine" values such as objectivity and rationality are superior to "feminine" values. Rather, they assume that feminine values are superior and need to be celebrated and encouraged. Since "patriarchy" (the many ways in which men oppress women) is so powerful, most radical feminists believe that separatist activities are an important means by which women can achieve strength. In regard to mass communication, radical feminists encourage alternative feminist media in which women can freely express themselves in their own language (Steeves, 1987, pp. 97-100).

While Steeves believes that all forms of feminism are important, she argues that neither radical nor liberal feminism has significantly challenged the public-private dichotomy on which patriarchy depends; nor has either come to terms with crucial contextual considerations of class and race. She feels that socialist feminism—a combination of radical and Marxist perspectives—currently offers the greatest potential as a comprehensive framework for addressing women's oppression in mass communication, though much more theoretical and empirical work is needed (p. 95).

These differences—about how women's interests can best be served or how much change is needed—among liberal, radical, socialist, and other feminisms are viewed by many feminists as evidence of strength within the feminist movement. In essence, difference is viewed as strength because homogeneity often results in the domination of one set of values. However, the media have typically covered the diversity within feminist theory as a sign of fragmentation, discord, and weakness within the feminist movement.

Bird and Dardenne (1988) offer a way to re-vision the narrative of news stories:

> We might think how journalists could learn to create stories that can be processed by their readers, but that speak in other narrative voices. Journalists do tend to tell the same stories in similar ways; the telling of one story by nature excludes all the other stories that are never told. (p. 83)

A re-vision of the media coverage of feminism would include the various voices of the movement, without presenting one as superior to the others and without creating an image of weakness out of diversity. A re-vision could help construct an alternative and positive interpretation of the gender switch.

A LIBERAL FEMINIST CASE STUDY

Nearly a quarter of a century has passed since the first Conference on Equal Opportunity was held at the White House in 1965, and the passage of time has exposed the implicit assumption of equal opportunity. The implicit assumption was that white women and people of color would have equal opportunity to compete within, and thus to conform to, the *existing* system. It was an easy assumption for female baby boomers like me to buy into because the system also rewards those who conform.

In the early 1970s, laden with baggage about women's place and proper behavior, and convinced that rejecting "women's" values would gain us respect and promotions in our careers, we entered the job market. We were constantly proving our equality, proving that we were "as good as" or better than men, proving that we could compete with men, and proving that we could fit into the dominant value system.

A created media event even helped to symbolize our potential for success in that value system. On September 30, 1973, Billie Jean King took the tennis court in the Houston Astrodome and defeated Bobbie Riggs on prime-time television. The media coverage was "sensational." It was billed as the "Battle of the Sexes"—a winner-take-all duel, between a 29-year-old woman at the top of her form and a more than 50-year-old pre-World War II Wimbledon champion.[7]

The media also caught "first woman fever" about then and kept us supplied with role models. Columns and news shows were crammed with filler about women gaining access to police and military academies, participating on college athletic teams, and climbing the corporate ladder. Quickly, a few tough women were visible as editors, anchors, account executives, managers, and directors. Some, like me, who eventually entered the "big time," the corporate world, wore the look-alike outfits—Evan Picone navy blue pin-striped suits, red paisley silk scarf ties, and wingtip pumps. We were obviously succeeding within the system, on its terms.

But what this dress-alike, act-alike contest really produced were women who functioned something like a Barbie-and-Ken Transformer Doll. It could be switched from boy to girl, from man to woman, from lady to gentleman, with some careful manipulation. At the touch of a button, the doll could even perform gender-specific activities, such as spitting or spraying perfume.

Furthermore, when we baby-boom Transformer dolls started to expect our little victories to add up to some sort of major social change, we had a rude awakening. We found out that life in the Land of Equal Opportunity simply meant an opportunity to devote an entire life and career volleying with each and every "Bobby Riggs" at *his* game, on *his* court, using *his* balls, *his* umpires, and *his* line judges. One homespun philosophy calls this the "drip-drip theory of social change: if you drip water on a rock long enough, one day it will be eroded" (Huber, 1983, p. 335).

Echoing these thoughts in an article in the new Australian-owned, for-profit version of *Ms.* magazine, Shana Alexander (1988) writes:

> As for the Women's Movement, I often think we may have opened Pandora's box. We wanted to be equal. We insisted. We did it. But we forgot we were in a man's world; everything we saw, and felt, and raged against was seen through that perspective. We were like the Eskimos who don't see snow, who have no word for snow, because they live in a world of snow. They have different words for falling snow, frozen snow, melting snow, sleeting snow, drifting snow, but no common linguistic root: snow. So when we decided to be equals, we meant, without thinking of it, *equals in a man's world.* We were still playing by their rules, or defining equality in their terms. We forgot that we are different from men; we are the *other*, we have different sensibilities. Today younger women across America are paying for our error. (p. 44)

We early liberal feminists did not see the snow that Alexander describes in our careers. We assumed that the values of the dominant system were somehow a primordial workplace norm. Many of us no longer believe that a world of snow is superior to a world of rain, or sunshine, or cloudiness, or whatever. Instead, we recognize the need for a system that values diversity in its people, language, culture, research, etc.

After looking back on nearly two decades of a Sisyphean liberal feminist career pattern, I am drawn toward the re-visioning approach, which rejects reform and equal opportunity as absolute values. The re-visionist position to which I now subscribe holds that real, positive change will, as Steinberg (1987) says, "require *both* improving women's position within the existing system *and* changing the terms of the system itself" (p. 470).

This book describes how both of these goals must be priorities on the agenda in mass communication as well.

A CONCLUDING COMMENT ABOUT METHODOLOGY
AND ASSUMPTIONS

Two assumptions shape the following discussion: (1) All research has a political dimension, and (2) when the political dimension of research challenges the orthodoxy, it creates controversy. The content of this volume challenges the orthodoxy (dominant values), so it is vital to acknowledge some of the anticipated controversy explicitly.

First, the chapters in this book represent a rich blend of qualitative and quantitative research and a variety of approaches, including ethnomethodology and personal testimony—often considered the hallmark of feminist scholarship and openly rejected by some scholars. Further, this book's mixture of methodologies may trouble those who believe that there is one superior and preferred methodology and research orientation. Adrienne Rich, Marilyn Frye, Riane Eisler, and other scholars have pointed to the process of devaluing nontraditional approaches that takes place in academia and, how, "under the protective mantle of 'objectivity' and 'field-independence,' science has often negated as 'unscientific' and 'subjective' the caring concerns considered overly feminine by the traditional view" (Eisler, 1987, p. 191). This book purposely features alternative methodologies for approaching the study of gender. This sharing and acceptance of various methodologies will serve to support a variety of approaches to gender research by not modeling conformity to a dominant pattern.

Similarly, some empiricists may find portions of the content of this book to be scientifically unacceptable. They will find these portions unacceptable because the empirical approach to knowing and knowledge does not allow one to draw conclusions based on impressions and experiences. The empirical approach requires clear evidence that the scholar approached the subject with a hypothesis that specifies an expected finding and then tested this hypothesis. In Chapters 12 and 13, for example, the authors have combined descriptive data on the status of women in a particular medium with a survey clearly featuring stated hypotheses, followed by data analyses, followed by an analysis of which hypotheses were proven and which were not.

But the approach taken by authors in other chapters does not conform—and is not intended to conform—to the traditional scientific method. In this second approach, the focus is on the validity of subjective rather than "objective" reality (Yllo, 1988, p. 38). For example, Chapters 5, 14, and 16 primarily recount a subjective reality of mass communication for those who are experiencing it. Whether or not this testimony is objectively verifiable or reliably reproducible is not integral to this approach. While these chapters represent perhaps the most controversial research in this volume, some scholars within the mass communication research cloister are beginning to listen to the arguments of gender researchers who propose transforming or re-visioning research consciousness by accepting subjective truth as something that has value.

This approach is part and partial to changing the terms of the system and improving women's (and ultimately people's) position in it. For, when women and people of color are permitted and encouraged to speak for themselves, by themselves and from themselves, it is their language that shapes reality. If such diversity is communicated freely, through the mass media for example, it would empower a shift in values on many levels. So this book is both a theoretical and practical example of the essence of re-visioning.

Another approach taken by many of the chapter authors is to provide a qualitative review of literature and studies in a particular area. While qualitative research also has its critics, it has champions in many disciplines. It is especially valuable where the existing body of knowledge has not been systematically examined and organized from a theoretical perspective. Scholars can then use these descriptive reviews as a springboard for analysis, conclusions, and recommendations based on interpretation of the available secondary research. Chapters 2 and 3 are among those that approach the subject of the book in this manner.

Much as this book intentionally does not advance one superior (preferred) research methodology, this introductory framework for viewing gender in mass communication should not be construed as an argument about a superior (female) value system. Further, while the terms *patriarchy* and *dominant white male value system* are used throughout the book, it is not a book about blame.

Overall, the concept of re-visioning advances the need to value diversity—not any one particular set of values. Riane Eisler (1987) suggests that "if we free ourselves from the prevailing models of reality, it is evident that there is another logical alternative: that there can be societies in which difference is not necessarily equated with inferiority or superiority" (p. xvii).

This book does not purport to answer all the questions that have ever been raised about gender. The Re-Visioning* Software in this book is a first-generation version that focuses on gender values. Undoubtedly, it will need to be upgraded and improved. But if it causes the reader to pause and re-vision a personal assumption about values—about gender, race, class, or sexuality—then it will have accomplished a great deal. As Tom Robbins (1980) puts it: "Equality is not in regarding different things similarly; equality is in regarding different things differently" (p. 97).

It follows that the single most important thing to remember when using Re-Visioning* Software is that nothing should be taken as a given. In other words, the user must be constantly vigilant for assumptions about values subtly woven into and quietly existing throughout a system like mass communication. A set of shared assumptions creates something close to what is known as a "culture." And, unfortunately, whether personal or collective, cultural assumptions often behave like a computer virus that has been programmed to confuse or fool the computer and control behavior in the user's system.

Finally, the first generation of Re-Visioning* Software found in this book can serve as a catalyst to advance the discussion and research that will be necessary to critically, but fairly, expose other assumptions about gender values embedded in the mass communication canon.

NOTES

1. Leslie Steeves offers a compelling analysis that women's values do not equate with feminism. She argues that the analysis must include class, race, and sexuality. For the purpose of this chapter, I envision the potential of the gender switch as empowering alternative values, not exclusively women's values.

2. I have taken literary license in using an asterisk to stand in for the symbol for a registered trademark, to give the concept of Re-Visioning* Software special status as a protected idea. The idea is not, however, registered, and there is no intent ever to do so, because, if it were registered, Re-Visioning* Software would be required to conform to the rules and regulations of the dominant system, and it would presumably be overcome by what is described below as the fatal flaw of liberal feminism—assuming the values of another system.

3. We need to look at two terms: *feminization* and *balance*. Strictly speaking, the U.S. Department of Labor says that occupational feminization occurs when a labor force can be termed female intensive because 60% or more of the workers in the field are women (Rytina & Bianchi, 1984). However, *feminization* is not such a simple word to define. According to *Webster's*, *feminize* can be used as either a transitive or intransitive verb that means "to make or become feminine or effeminate" and *feminization* is listed as the noun form (Neufeldt, 1988, p. 498). Unfortunately, this denotative dictionary definition raises myriad connotative cultural concerns. The concerns, of course, center on what happens to a field when it is "dominated by women," and presumably adopts female values and supposedly becomes an "effeminate job" category for males.

Balance is also an interesting term. Some contend that a balance in values is the opportunity presented by feminization; others have seized the opportunity to argue for a balance in numbers. In fact, one argument advances the seemingly contradictory concept that attracting men back into the field is something to strive for "so that gender is not viewed by anyone in management as an important determinant of the character of the field or the promotability of its practitioners" (Hunt & Thompson, 1988, p. 50).

4. The validity of the feminist critique that language plays an ideological boundary role was proven to me during the development of this book. In attempting to ensure that the text was free from sexist language, I suggested that we consider using plural possessive pronouns with singular noun or pronoun antecedents—if other constructions proved inappropriate or awkward. This suggestion was flatly rejected by editors at the publishing company, who professed to be "shocked" at the suggestion of such a flagrant violation of grammatical principle. I view the response as evidence that the request touched off the automatic sensing devices that stop us from approaching too close to the value system that is protected by

language. I do not, however, use this example to chastise the publisher's editors. They simply reflect the "enforcer" role and the hegemonic nature of our linguistic tradition.

5. I have never been able to forgive Apollo 11 astronaut Neil Armstrong for beaming down to earth the first recorded sexist language from outer space. On July 20, 1969, during what can arguably be called one of the first "global village" television transmissions, Armstrong told masses of viewing earthlings that his walk on the moon was: "One small step for (a) man; one giant leap for mankind." I've listened to that famous garbled transmission at least ten times over the years and I've never heard the mysteriously inaudible indefinite article that NASA officials promptly told us had been lost in the radio transmission from space. Did he say "one step for *a* man" or "for man"? Or, did he mean to say it, but simply forget, overcome with the excitement of knowing that what he said was destined to be recorded verbatim for a new chapter of the standard American history textbook? Many daily newspaper reporters had it in their notes, stories, and headlines sans indefinite article. NASA's prompt clarification and insertion of the missing article didn't completely clean up the first mass-mediated sexist language from outer space, but it did show that someone at NASA knew that someone on Earth would notice.

6. I ascribe male gender specifically to *Webster's New World Dictionary of the American Language: Second College Edition* (1984), published by Simon and Schuster. I feel justified in doing so since a male, David B. Guralnik, was the volume's editor in chief, and since it has been argued that entries in the edition lack a feminist perspective. The *Third College Edition* (1988) lists Victoria Neufeldt as editor in chief, with Guralnik as editor in chief emeritus. While some evidence of a change in perspective can be found in entries in the third edition (e.g., *gender gap* and *gender-specific* are included for the first time), the lack of sensitivity to a feminist perspective remains (e.g., *gender* is explained simply as a colloquial equivalent for a person's sex.)

7. See John Lucas and Ronald A. Smith (1982, p. 258). Here, for example, are a few lines from this male chronicle titled *Her Story in Sport*: "Riggs represented the reactionary male chauvinists, while King symbolized the feminist movement. It is ironic that an athletic event *should have been chosen by the American people* to signify the merits of the two sexes, since for physiological reasons women are not equal to men in those athletic performances where strength and speed are important." The emphasis is added here to expose the assumption that the American public had any role in "choosing" this contest to symbolize equality. The media system and the event promoters chose it for us. I would also point out the assumption that *all* women are unequal to *all* men in strength and speed.

8. To support a continued emphasis on re-visioning and transformation, all of the authors have agreed that royalties from the sale of this book will go to the Committee on the Status of Women of the Association for Education in Journalism and Mass Communication to fund future research that builds on the findings reported here.

REFERENCES

American Psychological Association. (1983). *Publication manual of the American Psychological Association* (3rd ed.). Washington, DC: Author.

Alexander, Shana. (1988, September). A woman undone. *Ms., 17*(3), 40-45.

Bates, Don. (1983, July). A concern: Will women inherit the profession? *Public Relations Journal*, pp. 6-7.

Benderly, Beryl Lieff. (1987). *The myth of two minds: What gender means and what it doesn't mean.* Garden City, NY: Doubleday.

Bernstein, Jack. (1986, January 27). Is pr field being hurt by too many women? *Advertising Age*, pp. 66-67.

Bird, S. Elizabeth, & Dardenne, Robert W. (1988). Myth, chronicle, and story: Exploring the narrative qualities of news. In James W. Carey (Ed.), *Media, myths, and narratives: Television and the press* (pp. 67-86). Newbury Park, CA: Sage.

Carey, James W. (Ed.). (1975). A cultural approach to communication. *Communication, 2,* 1-22.

Carey, James W. (1988). *Media, myths, and narratives: Television and the press.* Newbury Park, CA: Sage.

Dervin, Brenda. (1987). The potential contribution of feminist scholarship to the field of communication. *Journal of Communication, 37,*107-120.

Draine, Betsy. (1988, August 10). Academic feminists must make sure their commitments are not self-serving. *Chronicle of Higher Education*, p. A40.

Eisler, Riane. (1987). *The chalice and the blade.* San Francisco: Harper & Row.

Frye, Marilyn (Ed.). (1983). *The politics of reality.* Trumansburg, NY: Crossing.

Gerbner, George. (1978). The dynamics of cultural resistance. In Gaye Tuchman, Arlene Kaplan Daniels, & James Benet (Eds.), *Hearth and home: Images of women in the mass media* (pp. 46-50). New York: Oxford University Press.

Guralnik, David B. (Ed.). (1984). *Webster's new world dictionary: Second college edition.* New York: Simon & Schuster.

Hooks, Bell. (1984). *Feminist theory: From margin to center.* Boston: South End.

Huber, Joan. (1983). Ambiguities in identity transformation: From sugar and spice to professor. In Laurel Richardson & Verta Taylor (Eds.), *Feminist frontiers* (pp. 330-336). Reading, MA: Addison-Wesley.

Hunt, Todd, & Thompson, David W. (1988, Spring). Bridging the gender gap in PR courses. *Journalism Educator, 43*(1), 48-51.

Jaggar, Alison. (1983). Political philosophies of women's liberation. In Laurel Richardson & Verta Taylor (Eds.), *Feminist frontiers* (pp. 322-329). Reading, MA: Addison-Wesley.

Kane, Mary Jo. (1987). The "new" female athlete: Socially sanctioned image or modern role for women? In Marlene J. Adrian (Ed.), *Sports women* (pp. 101-111). Basel, Switzerland: S. Karger.

Lenz, Elinor, & Myerhoff, Barbara. (1985). *The feminization of America: How women's values are changing our public and private lives.* Los Angeles: Jeremy Tarcher.

Lucas, John A., & Smith, Ronald A. (1982). Women's sports: A trial of equality. In Reet Howell (Ed.), *Her story in sport: An anthology of women in sports* (pp. 239-265). West Point, NY: Leisure.

McQuail, Denis. (1987). *Mass communication theory: An introduction* (2nd ed.). Newbury Park, CA: Sage.

Neufeldt, Victoria. (Ed.). (1988). *Webster's new world dictionary: Third college edition.* New York: Simon & Schuster.

Parenti, Michael. (1986). *Inventing reality: The politics of the mass media.* New York: St. Martin's.

Peterson, Paul. (1982). *Today's journalism students: Who they are and what they want to do.* Columbus: Ohio State University School of Journalism.

Pink collar ghetto. (1985, November 2). *Editor & Publisher*, p. 34.

Public relations "velvet ghetto" for women. (1983, October 17). *Ragan Report,* supplement.

Rakow, Lana. (1986). Rethinking gender research in communication. *Journal of Communication, 36*(4), 11-26.

Rich, Adrienne. (1979). When we dead awaken: Writing as re-vision. In Adrienne Rich (Ed.), *On lies, secrets, and silence*. New York: Norton.

Robbins, Tom. (1980). *Still life with woodpecker*. New York: Bantam.

Rytina, Nancy F., & Bianchi, Suzanne M. (1984, March). Occupational reclassification and changes in distribution by gender. *Monthly Labor Review*.

Steeves, H. Leslie. (1987). Feminist theories and media studies. *Critical Studies in Mass Communication, 4*(2), 95-135.

Steinberg, Ronnie. (1987, December). Radical challenges in a liberal world: The mixed success of comparable worth. *Gender & Society, 1*(4), 466-475.

Thorne, Barrie, Kramarae, Cheris, & Henley, Nancy. (Eds.). (1983). *Language, gender and society*. Rowley, MA: Newbury House.

Tuchman, Gaye. (1978). *Making news*. New York: Free Press.

Wagner, Jane. (1986). *The search for signs of intelligent life in the universe*. New York: Harper & Row.

Women execs call gender a career obstacle. (1983, May). *Communication World*, p. 14.

Yllo, Kersti. (1988). Political and methodological debates in wife abuse research. In Kersti Yllo & Michele Bogard (Eds.), *Feminist perspectives on wife abuse* (pp. 28-50). Newbury Park, CA: Sage.

2

Changing Media History Through Women's History

SUSAN HENRY

Women's participation in American journalism is as old as the field itself. We know, for example, that the first press in the American colonies (established in Cambridge, Massachusetts, in 1638) was owned by a woman, and that at least 17 women worked as printers in colonial America before the ratification of the Constitution in 1788. Still more women labored in print shops as compositors, binders, writers, and press workers during this period.[1]

Yet, although the work of American women journalists can be traced as far back as the field's origins, the historical study of women journalists, of women's images in the mass media, and of their presence as members of mass media audiences has a much shorter lineage. Women began to move up "from the footnotes" of journalism history texts only about a decade ago, and substantial research by journalism historians on topics related to women began less than a decade before that.[2]

In this brief time, however, such research has progressed rapidly. The new stories of at least 100 women journalists have been told, many historical studies of media consumed primarily by women have been carried out, women's media images during different periods have been studied, and the roles played by the mass media in advancing or retarding social, political, and economic developments of particular importance to women increasingly have been examined.

As a result, unlike historians studying women and journalism only a decade ago, today's researchers have a substantial body of scholarly literature on which to draw. These scholars no doubt will be influenced by the methods and subjects chosen as well as by the conclusions drawn in these earlier works. Thus this is an appropriate time to begin an evaluation of the state of this literature, to examine the effects this research has had on the

larger field of journalism history, and to suggest directions that future research might take.

NEW RESEARCH, NEW INTEGRATION

Certainly one of the most striking aspects of the historical research on
women and American journalism is its quantity. The field has attracted a
large number of productive, imaginative scholars. One indication of the
quantity of published articles on women is found in the first 10-year index
(covering 1974-1983) of *Journalism History*, the oldest journal in the
field. Here "women," with 26 entries, is the third largest topic category,
preceded only by the large, miscellaneous categories labeled "general" and
"biographies." In addition, 12 of the 35 entries listed under "biographies"
refer to studies of women ("Cumulative Index, Vols. 1-10, 1974-1983,"
1983).

Similar evidence of the proliferation of this research is found in an article by Donald Shaw and Sylvia Zack (1987) analyzing the last decade of
historical articles published in *Journalism Quarterly*, the main professional journal for research in mass communication, and in *Journalism History*.
Citing work that has, in their opinion, contributed "new evidence and perspectives" to the field, Shaw and Zack single out 108 individual articles.
Of these, 26—almost a quarter of the total—are on topics related to wom-
en. The authors make no attempt to count or categorize all articles appearing in these two journals during this time, yet the fact that they cite such
a larger number about women is an indication of the amount of strong published work available.

Recent articles on women in journalism history are notable for more
than just their quantity; they also are varied in the subjects covered. A substantial amount of this research is devoted to "retrieving" previously unrecognized women journalists and placing them within the historical record, but, in addition, excellent studies have been done on topics such as
suffrage and birth control publications, the effects women journalists'
"marginal" professional status has had on their journalism and their careers, how women and particular women's issues have been covered by
both specialized and mainstream media, and methodological and conceptual issues growing out of the study of women.

In contrast, most books on women and journalism history published in
the 1970s and 1980s have been biographies of individual women rather

than studies of wider trends and issues. Still, many of these in-depth studies
constitute significant contributions to the literature, particularly in light of
the many hundreds of biographies and autobiographies of male journalists
crowding library shelves. It also should be noted that these books have tak-
en as their subjects a range of women and types of journalism. For example, recent well-received biographies include studies of Freda Kirchwey,
owner, editor, and publisher of *The Nation* (Alpern, 1987); of suffragist
editor and activist Abigail Scott Duniway (Moynihan, 1983); of Dorothy
Day, publisher of the radical *Catholic Worker* (Roberts, 1984); and of *Life*
magazine's renowned photographer, Margaret Bourke-White (Goldberg,
1986). At the same time, recent group biographies have examined, in less
depth, still more women journalists' lives.[3]

In addition to their progress in studying the individuals, publications,
and issues previously unknown or unrecognized within journalism history,
historians of women have begun to succeed in another important area: the
integration of their research into the overall picture of American journalism history, especially as it is being taught in colleges and universities. A
rough indication of their success can be found by examining the table of
contents of the dominant text in the field,[4] Edwin Emery and Michael
Emery's *The Press and America*. The third edition, published in 1972, and
the sixth edition, published in 1988, are very different in their inclusion of
material related to women. These differences are evident beginning with
the first sentence of each edition's foreword—which announced in 1972,
"Journalism history is the story of man's long struggle to communicate
freely with his fellow man" (Emery, 1972, p. iii) and was revised in 1988
to read, "Journalism history is the story of humanity's long struggle to
communicate" (Emery & Emery, 1988, p. v). They continue to the last
page of each index, where the heading "women in journalism" references
a total five pages in 1972 and 103 pages in 1988. These additional pages
primarily reflect the legions of women's names now included in the sixth
edition's voluminous lists of printers, reporters, editors, publishers, broadcasters, photographers, and advertising and public relations practitioners.
A dozen and a half illustrations showing women journalists also have been
added during the 16 years, while the expanded 1988 annotated bibliographies accompanying each chapter contain many new sources on women
and journalism history.

REASONS FOR THE NEW RESEARCH

It is now possible, then, to identify a substantial and varied body of published work on women and journalism history, and to note a systematic integration of material about women into the key journalism history text. What accounts for this progress? The most obvious answer is that the number of scholars doing historical research on women in journalism has increased markedly.

While there is no reliable way to determine how many journalism historians have studied topics related to women during any period (and whether good work was produced that was not accepted for publication), it certainly is notable that since the early 1970s the journalism faculties of American colleges and universities have included growing numbers of the professors most likely to study women—that is, women. Just as many more women have become professional journalists in the last decade and a half, so have many more become journalism professors.

The most recent study to bring together detailed data on journalism educators found that in 1988 women made up 24% of higher-education journalism faculties, compared with only 7-8% in 1972 (see Schamber, Chapter 7, this volume). While this still shows a serious imbalance between men and women (and the imbalance is compounded by significant rank and salary differences), it more than doubles the percentage of a decade earlier. A related earlier study examined the authorship of full-length *Journalism Quarterly* articles by women, noting an increase from 7% during the 1960-71 period to more than 16% for 1979-83 (Sharp, Turk, Einsiedel, Schamber, & Hollenback, 1985, p. 3).

Certainly not all women teaching journalism are also doing research on women, and only a minority of those who are studying women also are historians. But there is little doubt that the increase in the number of female journalism professors has coincided with a marked increase in the amount of scholarly work on women in journalism history—much of it authored by women—being published. And, as more work has been published, additional researchers have been drawn to the study of women and journalism history.

Yet this small influx of women journalism historians cannot by itself explain the progress made in research on women, for few historians would risk studying women in journalism if they thought there was little chance their work would be accepted or valued by others in the field. Professors just beginning their careers—as was the case with many female scholars researching women during the 1970s—need to be particularly sensitive to the publishing potential of their research.

Understanding their success thus also requires recognizing what I believe is another important factor: the interest in and openness to research on women shown by a number of important male journalism historians. For more than a decade, some of the field's most respected men have given particular encouragement to scholars studying women in journalism history. Their personal enthusiasm for—and public recognition of—this research has meant that those who pursue it generally have not had to fight the kinds of hard battles to establish the value of their work that, for example, many well-known American historians studying women face even today.[5]

Evidence of such support has been noted above. It includes the increasing references to women in *The Press and America*, the many articles related to women singled out in an article on important research in journalism history coauthored by Donald Shaw, *Journalism Quarterly*'s associate editor for history, and the three dozen articles on women published during *Journalism History*'s first decade, when it was edited by Tom Reilly. By calling attention to research on women in these varied ways, male journalism historians have helped to legitimate this work and to encourage its production.

Admittedly, scholars studying women in journalism history do face serious problems, such as a scarcity of both primary data and useful analytical models. But as a rule they have not had to overcome opposition to their work by established, influential male journalism historians and journal editors; indeed, the support of such people likely has provided important encouragement for these research efforts. Many things help account for their support, including the high quality of a great deal of this published work and the very capable scholars responsible for much of it. But I believe two less obvious factors also are important in explaining why major male journalism historians have encouraged research on women. These factors particularly deserve consideration because, to my mind, they bear directly on the future of historical research on women in journalism.

The first factor arises from the status of journalism history within the larger field of mass communication research. Simply put, the larger field exhibits a marked social science bias—which favors methods utilizing quantification—as well as a preference for research that examines current media issues.[6] Since most journalism history does not use social science research methods (although these methods have been applied, with very revealing results), and history, by definition, examines the past, this work tends to have a kind of undeserved secondary status as mass communication research. Thus journalism historians seldom are included as part of university communication research centers, just as their work usually is less well funded than that of social science mass communication researchers. Similarly, *Journalism Quarterly* prints far more articles utilizing social science research methods than traditional historical methods.[7]

Yet, ironically, this situation may well have made established male journalism historians more receptive to research on women than would have been the case if history were seen as more central to mass communication research overall. These historians can recognize the benefits of encouraging all scholars who are producing good history, no matter what its subject, since this will further strengthen a field that sometimes is unfairly viewed as peripheral. Indeed, new researchers as a whole tend to be encouraged, since they can help revitalize the field, both with their numbers and with their scholarship. This same secondary status seems to have made journalism historians less rigid than journalism social scientists in defining "acceptable" research subjects. As a result, new historians may be discouraged from exploring nontraditional research areas less frequently than are their social scientist colleagues.

A second factor also helps explain the support given journalism historians studying topics related to women. It is important to note, I think, that most of this research is substantially conservative: Research on women and journalism history has seldom challenged accepted ideas about such matters as how individuals should be studied or what criteria should be used in determining the significance of different media or journalists. Thus the specific topics examined in this research—for example, women journalists or the media coverage of women at different times—are new, but the scholars carrying out this research generally have studied their subjects within the accepted, male-developed framework of journalism history. As a result, their findings can easily be integrated into the field's existing literature, further strengthening the established framework because it is applied to women as well as to men.

This is not to say these scholars purposely have avoided developing radically different ways of thinking about their subjects, or that resistance necessarily would arise if they did. It is much more likely that, in the struggle to locate and analyze data needed for research on women, assumptions about journalism history simply have not been questioned. Similarly, solving the many practical problems often involved in studying women may have left researchers with little energy to pursue some of the more interesting implications of their studies, or to take advantage of useful literature outside of the field that might lead them to quite different subjects and analytical frameworks.

NEW DIRECTIONS FOR RESEARCH
ON WOMEN AND JOURNALISM HISTORY

As understandable as this conservatism is, it must be overcome, and alternative approaches to the study of women in journalism history must be developed. A logical starting point for this development is with the comments of those who have thought about this field and its future. Although no full-fledged critique of the existing research has yet been published, several scholars have made important points that can be utilized in finding new approaches.

The first point has been suggested independently by two well-known journalism historians. MaryAnn Yodelis Smith (1982) advises that historical studies of women "media processors" must be better developed so that they move beyond the traditional narratives that have dominated the literature. She stresses the need to analyze the lives of women journalists rigorously, and especially to provide sociocultural context for them (pp. 149-150). Similarly, Zena Beth McGlashan (1985) warns against the "positivist trap of creating but not critiquing heroes." Rather, she explains, the work done by women journalists must be critically examined, and differences between women should be carefully noted (p. 59).

Second is the observation by communication theorist Leslie Steeves (1987) that most research on women and journalism history rests on "liberal feminist" assumptions that do not question the established mainstream American media system, instead studying—and applauding—the "notable" women who were able to succeed within that system. Steeves also notes that these studies seldom examine how such factors as class, race, and sexual preference have affected the work done by these women (p. 103).

Third is feminist communication scholar Lana Rakow's (1986) recommendation of a "recovery and reappraisal approach" to the study of contemporary popular culture produced by and for women. She explains that this approach "calls not for adding women artists to a literary or artistic canon but for a re-evaluation of the criteria that establish canons and determine the artistic and social merit of creative expressions." Although she does not apply this concept to journalism history, Rakow praises historical studies of popular culture—especially of popular novels written by women for women readers—that avoid the kind of analysis usually applied to male-oriented popular culture and instead explore, within a true female context, the reasons such works were created and the functions they performed (pp. 28-32).

Social scientist Brenda Dervin (1987), like Lana Rakow, does not specifically address the study of journalism history, but she takes Rakow's advocacy of a female point of view in research on popular culture a step further when she explains that the "essential mandate" of all feminist communication research is to "invent approaches that allow us to hear the meanings of women on their own terms, including their observations of the structures that constrain them." We must, in short, focus on "giving women voice so that we may hear their reality" (p. 12).

A final useful observation comes from journalism historian Catherine Covert (1981). In an extremely perceptive article identifying and questioning the assumptions that male journalism historians have imposed on their field, she describes the male assumption that "history is about autonomy":

> Journalism history has classically celebrated independence and individual autonomy rather than subordination and dependence. The actions of strikingly autonomous individuals have been chronicled. "Freedom" has been valued as an existential state. (p. 4)

As a result of this assumption, she says, historians have paid little attention to the influences of family, friends and professional networks on journalists' careers. Similarly, the histories of small-town newspapers and other media that do not fit the "conflict" model of journalism and government—media that were devoted more to building community than to maintaining an adversary relationship with the power structure—seldom have been carefully studied (pp. 4-5).

The observations of these six writers are both complementary and cumulative; taken together, they form a kind of general outline for future research on women and journalism history. This research, they suggest, should be analytical and critical, moving beyond description to an understanding of why things happened and what they meant at the time to the women involved in them as media creators or audiences. This process may well require challenging and revising previously accepted precepts of journalism history that are not applicable to women. And it surely will lead to the discovery of new research subjects, as well as new ways of looking at old ones.

USING FIVE CONCEPTS FROM WOMEN'S HISTORY

Valuable ideas for carrying out the recommendations made by these communication scholars can be found in a large body of work that has received little attention from most journalism historians: the literature of women's history. The observations of women's historians can be particularly useful, for, far more than journalism historians studying women, they have noted the limitations of so-called contribution history, in which "man becomes the measure of significance" by which women's lives are judged and women are added to the existing historical scholarship only if they meet the male standard—as has been the case in much of the work done on women in journalism history. Contribution history is a first step in building women's history, these scholars say, but it should be only a transitional development on the road to new ways of studying women, new criteria for choosing subjects of study, and new questions being asked.[8]

Many different techniques for moving forward have been suggested by women's historians,[9] but one approach seems especially useful in directing future research on women and journalism history, for it helps solidify the six scholars' ideas briefly described in the previous section. This approach calls for replacing male-defined research with scholarship in which, in the words of historian Carroll Smith-Rosenberg (1980), "the events and processes central to women's experience assume historical centrality, and women are recognized as active agents" (p. 57). Joan Wallach Scott (1983) calls this an effort to "construct women as historical subjects," and she explains that it goes "far beyond the naive search for heroic ancestors of the contemporary women's movement to a re-evaluation of established standards of historical significance" (p. 145).

Just as women's historians have perceptively analyzed the problems of contribution history, so have they produced an extensive body of analytical research that is applicable to journalism history. Yet little of this research has yet been taken advantage of by historians of women and journalism, and I believe this is one reason the work most of these historians have produced remains largely descriptive and unquestioning of traditional, male-defined standards of journalism history.

As a first step toward utilizing this research, I have identified five concepts developed by women's historians that I believe can be used to help create new kinds of research on women and journalism history. These concepts are discussed, in turn, below. I also have utilized research conducted by women's historians to describe specific topic areas deserving of study that do not fit within conventional journalism history standards of significance, and thus may lead to a redefinition of these standards. In the process, I hope to show how historical research on women and journalism can change along the lines recommended by the communication scholars cited earlier.

Women's Culture

One area in which women's historians have contributed substantial useful research is that of the study of nineteenth-century American women's culture—the separate, self-created culture apparently shared by many middle-class women in which concerns of domesticity and morality were especially important. By creating this culture, it is thought, women were able to redefine and take control of the "separate sphere" into which they had been forced by the dominant male society. Here they developed shared, female-identified values, rituals, relationships, and modes of communication that were sources of satisfaction and strength. Although historians disagree about some of the details of this culture and about the extent to which it tended to be either confining or liberating, they do generally agree that it was an important, sustaining part of the lives of many bourgeois women of the period (Berkin, 1985, pp. 209-210; Scott, 1983, pp. 148-149).[10]

Research on women's culture provides a valuable context for studying particular forms of nineteenth-century journalism that have previously received little attention. Such a study might begin with an examination of the journalism produced by the women who lived and believed most fervently in the values of this culture. One excellent example of this journalism is *The Advocate of Moral Reform*, the weekly newspaper produced by the American Female Moral Reform Society.

Carroll Smith-Rosenberg (1985) describes her first attempts to understand the Society:

> [It] was so self-consciously female, so militantly antimale that it resisted all my efforts to subordinate it to a male schema. The rhetoric and programs of the American Female Moral Reform Society forced me to recognize it as a uniquely female institution, radically different from male philanthropies and reforms. (p. 20)

Her surprise is understandable, for the Society, formed in 1834, zealously attacked two problems that could barely be discussed in polite society of the time: prostitution and the sexual double standard that permitted middle-class males free sexual license. Its tactics included stationing members in front of brothels, where they would pray and sing hymns, and legislative lobbying campaigns, but its most important and effective work took place in the pages of *The Advocate* (Smith-Rosenberg, 1985, pp. 109–118).

Through *The Advocate*, the Society was able to carry its message beyond New York City, where it was founded, throughout the East Coast. By 1838 *The Advocate* claimed 16,500 subscribers, making it one of the country's most widely read evangelical newspapers, and in rural areas—where it circulated extensively—it may well have been the only newspaper a family received. Indeed, *The Advocate* was full of letters from rural readers describing their feelings of frustration over their confined lives and their gratitude for the connections they felt with other women through involvement in this moral reform effort. These letters often detailed the sins of male seducers and adulterers, as did the paper's editorials; lists of names of accused sinners also were printed. And one solution was proposed over and over: Women must control society's moral standards and behavior, and thus male licentiousness (Smith-Rosenberg, 1985, pp. 115-122).

One other aspect of *The Advocate* is particularly interesting: By 1843, all positions on the paper were held by women. The two women hired as editors in 1836 were among the first female weekly newspaper editors in nineteenth-century America, while in 1835 a female subscription agent was hired, in 1841 a female bookkeeper replaced the male financial agent, and two years later all the typesetters were women. All of this was part of a conscious campaign by the Society to show that women could work successfully in traditionally male fields (Smith-Rosenberg, 1985, pp. 122–123).

The Advocate is waiting to be studied by a journalism historian who can analyze it within the context of women's culture of the period. In addition, research should be carried out on other media related to nineteenth-century women's culture, and especially on groups of these publications, since this would make it possible to see trends and draw broad conclusions. We know, for example, that between 1784 and 1860 close to 100 magazines dealing with women's interests were published (Degler, 1980, p. 377). Most of them have not been studied.[11] Both the advertising and editorial contents of these publications deserve analysis, since advertising aimed at women may well have been particularly powerful in reinforcing the boundaries of their separate sphere, and thus keeping women within it.[12]

We also know that during the same period the American Female Moral Reform Society was most active, another reform movement—abolition—was attracting still more middle-class women and bringing them further outside their domestic worlds, even as it drew on the values developed within those worlds. The important—and still largely unstudied—work done by abolitionist women included much of the writing published in antislavery newspapers (Degler, 1980, p. 303; Lerner, 1979, p. 153). A full understanding of the women's culture underlying this journalism might well lead to a valuable reevaluation of it.

These three kinds of studies might combine in particularly significant ways, for they would provide examples of journalism fervently produced within the confines of women's culture to bring its ideals to a wider world, journalism produced primarily by those outside the culture who helped to solidify it, and journalism produced by women formed by the culture but applying their values to a different, although related, cause. Research in all three areas could result in new conclusions about the cultural roles journalism can play. And these in turn might lead to new criteria for determining media influence and historical significance.

Women as Community-Builders

Women's historians also have carried out valuable research on women's previously unrecognized work as community-builders. They point out that this work often began with women's recognition of immediate community needs that were first addressed in practical, informal ways, then became larger efforts to raise funds and create formal institutions—libraries, orphanages, and kindergartens, for example. Once these institutions became fully established and licensed, men usually took them over. And on an individual level, women have historically supplied continuity to their communities by maintaining and passing on to their children important family, religious, and social values (Lerner, 1979, pp. 165, 179).

Traditional historians generally have ignored this kind of work by women, although they have recorded the histories of many of these institutions once they were run by men (Lerner, 1979, p. 179). Recently, however, women's historians have begun to study these activities, and much excellent research has been done on the post-Civil War work of the "social feminists" who, building on many of the values of women's culture, became activists in such social reforms as the temperance, settlement, and child-welfare movements (Degler, 1980, pp. 326-327; Smith-Rosenberg, 1985, pp. 167-175).

Included in this literature is valuable information on Black women's institution-building and reform work. Because for decades following the Civil War many Southern communities lacked any kind of social welfare organization—or did not permit Blacks access to those organizations that did exist—Black women were particularly active in founding and sustaining such institutions as schools, orphanages, and old people's homes. In the cities, they organized settlement houses, child-care facilities, health clinics, and community improvement campaigns (Lerner, 1979, pp. 83-93). Similar work by urban immigrant women in the late nineteenth and early twentieth centuries also has been documented by women's historians.[13]

This varied scholarship on women as community-builders can be utilized by journalism historians in understanding the extensive work done by women in the medium that has most consistently welcomed their involvement: community journalism.[14] If this journalism—which has only infrequently been researched by journalism historians—were studied with a better recognition of women's roles in it, and better analyzed within the context of the historical literature on women's community-building, a new evaluation of its place in journalism history might result. And it should be kept in mind that community journalism includes many minority newspapers, where women no doubt also played important roles.[15] Indeed, one of the country's leading Black social reformers, Ida B. Wells, also edited or worked as a reporter for a number of Southern Black community newspapers (Lerner, 1979, p. 85; Scott, 1984, p. 347).[16]

Women's Formal and Informal Connections

Studies of women's culture and women's work as community-builders in the nineteenth-century United States have resulted in much new information about the close relationships these women often had with each other. Women's historians have shown that, beginning around 1800, women increasingly bonded together in formal, single-sex clubs and associations that were particularly popular in the last 30 years of the century, when millions of women joined (Degler, 1980, pp. 315-327; Scott, 1984, pp. 279-294). Among the members of these organizations were society's "new women," who, starting in the 1870s, began to move beyond conventional female roles to enter such previously male worlds as higher education, business, medicine, and the arts. Sometimes unmarried, these women found personal female support networks especially important (Smith-Rosenberg, 1985, pp. 176-177, 247-256).[17]

Historians studying women in American journalism should look for evidence of these kinds of formal and informal relationships in their subjects' lives and use the literature from women's history to help understand the importance of these connections. Knowledge of organizational memberships might well be particularly useful in studying women journalists of the last quarter of the nineteenth century, when such organizations proliferated and journalism initially was opened to women. Still, the total numbers of full-time female journalists in this period were small; according to U.S. census figures, they were 288 out of 12,308 full-time journalists in 1880 and had grown to 2,193 out of 30,098 in 1900 (Beasley & Silver, 1977, p. 38). As both distinct minorities in the profession and often "firsts" at their particular periodicals, these women must have needed the support of other women, and the connections made in the process may have influenced their work.[18]

I found that an understanding of these kinds of informal and organizational ties was key to my study of a late nineteenth-century American journalist, Helen Campbell. Campbell was a member of many organizations for professional women, including Sorosis, the first New York City women's club (which was founded by journalist Jane Cunningham Croly), and was an activist in the new home economics movement. Thus she spent much time with other women journalists and with women in business, the arts, and the professions. Divorced after 10 years of marriage, she also had an extensive friendship network composed of other women reformers, the most notable being feminist writer Charlotte Perkins Gilman. I have argued that these connections both influenced the contents of her writing—which often focused on the need for urban reforms—and helped provide her with personal support for her work as a journalist (Henry, 1984).

Strong connections to other women no doubt have been important for twentieth-century women journalists as well, so they too need to be examined. And, because the early twentieth century saw the establishment of many new professional organizations for women (Degler, 1980, p. 324), historians studying women journalists of this later period often may find that their subjects were members of women's press clubs with surviving archival records and publications that can provide useful insights about the professional networks of individual women.[19] Through such materials we may learn a great deal about how women journalists have been able to succeed in a predominantly male world.

Journalism historians who are able to collect data on these kinds of relations will find that these data also aid them in establishing valuable cultural contexts for their studies. At the same time, they may find that such information challenges the high value put on journalistic autonomy that Catherine Covert identified as underlying so much of our published journalism history. As a result, this kind of research may lead to a systematic question-

ing of that value and to new studies of the importance of supportive personal relationships for both female and male journalists.

Women's Work

Just as they have found new ways of interpreting and understanding the
personal lives of women, so have women's historians redefined the very
concept of work. These historians began by defining work the same way
male economists—and most other historians—did: as paid labor. They
soon discovered, however, that this excluded most of the work done by
women in the past, including carrying out extensive household, child-care,
and voluntary community tasks. Now, work is understood to include both
paid and unpaid labor done both outside and inside the home (Lerner, 1979,
pp. 178-179; Norton, 1986, p. 40).

Because so much of journalism history is the study of men and women
at work, this redefinition has a direct bearing on the field. This is particularly the case, I believe, when the new definition is combined with other observations about the unrecognized work of women. Among these observations is one made by a historian reviewing the biographies of the 1,359
women included in the three volumes of *Notable American Women*, who
was struck by the fact that numerous women had let men take credit for
their work. These women, she said, seem to have made themselves "purposely invisible" (Scott, 1984, p. 156). Similarly, a noted women's psy-
chologist has observed that married women's work often includes helping
their husbands do their work. Women may take great satisfaction in this,
she explains, since "women, more easily than men, can believe that any activity is more satisfying when it takes place in the context of relationships
to other human beings—and even more so when it leads to the enhancement of others." Yet, because "most of this activity has not been done in
direct and open pursuit of their own goals—therefore it is not activity in
the male definition of it" (Miller, 1986, p. 54).

Journalism historians who understand these different concepts of work
will begin to discover new examples of women's work in journalism. My
own research, for example, has resulted in the identification of a cohort of
American women in the 1920s and 1930s who worked with their better-
known husbands to produce journalism for which they received little public credit. The list so far includes Ruth Hale, wife of famed newspaper col-
umnist Heywood Broun; Jane Grant, wife of *New Yorker* founder Harold
Ross; Katherine White, wife of *New Yorker* writer E. B. White; and Clare
Boothe Luce, who developed the initial plan for Henry Luce's *Life* maga-

zine. But to me the most interesting couple in this cohort is composed of Doris E. Fleischman and Edward L. Bernays, who together formed the firm of Edward L. Bernays, Counsel on Public Relations, and who were wholly equal partners in the business from the time of their marriage in 1922 until Doris Fleischman's death in 1980 (Henry, 1988). No doubt other cohorts of journalists' wives who did similar work in their husbands' names can be found.

I also have been studying the work done by three generations of women in one newspaper publishing family, the Otis-Chandler *Los Angeles Times* dynasty. As I chart the largely unpaid and unrecognized work of publishers' wives, sisters, and daughters over more than three-quarters of a century, I am noticing both patterns and differences that establish a wide range of women's roles (Henry, 1987). Studies of women family members in many of the country's other publishing dynasties would allow similar opportunities to compare women's work over time and under changing social, political, and economic circumstances.

Uncovering women's contributions that have been hidden behind male accomplishments does more than add another dimension to our knowledge of the work done by women in journalism. It also calls into question the tendency of journalism historians to pay little attention to journalists who worked behind the scenes or lacked official titles. Equally important, it illustrates the importance of better recognizing the collaborative effort—some of it between husbands and wives—that may well have been behind a substantial amount of our journalism. And such recognition once again challenges the underlying value of autonomy in journalism history.

Women Media Audiences

Finally, I suggest that journalism historians can learn from one additional area in which women's historians have reexamined published American history. They have questioned the ways traditional historians have characterized particular historical periods or developments, pointing out that often these characterizations apply only to the men of a society. Indeed, they have shown that the events that have socially, intellectually, economically, or politically benefited men frequently have worked in opposite ways for women. For example, the Renaissance, which opened up many new opportunities for men, resulted in new restrictions upon women (Lerner, 1979, p. 175).

In the United States, the Jacksonian period has been reevaluated in a similar way. Women's historians have found that although for white men the 1830s and 1840s were a time of greatly expanded economic, social, and political opportunities, during that time women's positions deteriorated in many ways. They were, for example, no longer permitted to enter most of the business and professional occupations that had previously been open to them. Similarly, the "lady"—with all the restrictions on personal behavior that implied—became the feminine ideal. And in comparison with white males—large groups of whom gained voting rights during the Jacksonian period—women's political disenfranchisement seemed all the more extreme (Lerner, 1979, p. 18).

This new way of looking at one period in American history should be instructive to journalism historians, for it suggests that the labels and characterizations we have given media trends and developments also should be reexamined in light of women's experiences. The journalism of the Jacksonian era is a good place to start this reexamination, for this is the time of what is usually thought to be a seminal advancement in American journalism history: the beginning of the penny press. Emery and Emery (1988) label this inexpensive, readable, and entertaining form of journalism "the newspaper for the masses" and "the press of the common people" (pp. 115-119). Michael Schudson (1978) who has carefully studied the penny papers, explains that not only were they "spokesmen [*sic*] for egalitarian ideals in politics, economic life, and social life" (p. 60), but they "created a genre which acknowledged, and so enhanced, the importance of everyday life" (p. 26).

But were women among the "common people" to whom the penny press was meant to appeal? How egalitarian were these papers' expressed ideals related to women's concerns? Was the "everyday life" of women recognized in these papers? These are questions that have not been asked of the penny press,[20] even though it has been characterized as journalism that served the masses and in Schudson's words, "expressed and built the culture of a democratic market society" (p. 60).

Journalism historians do credit Horace Greeley's *New York Tribune* with advocating educational, legal, employment, and marriage reforms for women (although Schudson does not mention any of this). But such contents seldom are interpreted as adding to the democratic base of the penny press in any key way. Thus a systematic examination of the *Tribune* and other penny papers in terms of women readers still is needed.

The literature of women's history makes it possible to identify many of women's common concerns during this time (and research on women's culture is applicable here), just as it also makes it clear that most women had sufficient literacy skills to read the penny press (Degler, 1980, p. 306).

Urban areas attracted women who were interested in access to jobs and independent lives.[21] And, since married women of the period were responsible for their families' domestic well-being, the advertisers who financed penny newspapers would have benefited from appealing to women consumers. Clearly, then, although women were excluded from many areas of Jacksonian life, there is no reason they should have been excluded as penny press readers. If they were, then our accepted characterization of this journalism is inaccurate.

A systematic historical reexamination in terms of women readers would be useful for all American journalism that has been strongly characterized in terms of the size and composition of its audience. Certainly the metropolitan daily newspapers of the 1880s and 1890s, which have been heralded as the country's first truly mass-circulation press, deserve such analysis. Significantly, historians have noted that, for the first time, large, urban Sunday papers of the period began to carry special women's pages, with articles on such topics as fashion and family life, that were thought to appeal to middle-class women (Emery & Emery, 1988, p. 231; Schudson, 1978, p. 100). It may be that such articles were far more important in increasing circulation than has been thought.

But other questions about these papers also must be asked. For example, we are told that they attracted large numbers of working-class readers, but what in their contents would have appealed to working-class women? How popular with them were the women's pages that were considered such an innovation? And what kinds of coverage did these papers give the more substantial concerns of many urban women related to such topics as health, education, religion, and employment?

Because male journalism historians have studied most journalism primarily in terms of male audiences, these kinds of questions about the extent to which media audiences included or excluded women seldom have been asked. Thus we do not know their answers, or whether or not those answers will change our characterizations of different media at different times. The point is that until attempts are made to answer key questions about women audiences, such characterizations cannot be accepted uncritically.

CONCLUSIONS

There is no guarantee that any of the five concepts discussed above, taken from women's history and applied here to journalism history, will lead to a radical revision of that history. But it is clear that the development of these concepts by women's historians has not simply added new information to American history; it also has made it necessary to rethink previously accepted interpretations and information. Because of this, and because these concepts have such clear relevance to the history of journalism, their application is highly recommended.

There is little doubt that further research in these areas would expand our knowledge of women and journalism through the identification of new research subjects and the utilization of new analytical techniques. Indeed, one final lesson from this exercise is that the published scholarship of women's history offers journalism historians innumerable new research topics and approaches.

The solid base of the existing research on women and journalism history has placed the field in an excellent position to begin moving more rapidly out of its transitional stage. Scholars should be ready increasingly to bring to their work the kind of analysis, contextual interpretation, and questioning of assumptions that critics have said is needed. The rich literature of women's history provides a good starting point for that development, providing ideas that will sometimes challenge the field and often broaden and deepen it.

NOTES

1. Much of my early journalism research focused on colonial women printers. For published examples of this research, see Henry (1976, 1979, 1980, 1985).

2. Marion Marzolf published the first comprehensive history of women journalists and the media's treatment of women in 1977 (Marzolf, 1977). In the acknowledgments section of her book, Marzolf notes that when she began her research in 1972 she found women "mentioned mostly in the footnotes in standard journalism history texts" (p. ix). But, she explains, "I resolved to search for them and recover their lost history." An earlier book containing valuable information on women in journalism history is Ishbel Ross's *Ladies of the Press* (1936). Although Ross's work contains valuable information on some nineteenth-century women journalists, its emphasis is on her own contemporaries during the first third of the twentieth century. This makes it a valuable source for today's journalism historians studying women of this period.

3. The range of women journalists studied in recent group biographies is impressive, as indicated by the titles of three important histories: *Viewfinders: Black Women Photographers* (Moutoussamy-Ashe, 1986), *Brilliant Bylines: A Biographical Anthology of Notable Newspaperwomen in America* (Belford, 1986), and *Women of the World: The Great Foreign Correspondents* (Edwards, 1988).

4. A 1977 survey of journalism departments found that three-fourths used *The Press and America* as the text in their history courses (see Endres, 1978, p. 31).

5 For recent references to this problem by four well-known women's historians, see Joan W. Scott (1987, p. 1055), Mary Beth Norton (1986, p. 41), Carol Berkin (1985, p. 209), and Ann Firor Scott (1984, p. 366).

6. This bias is tellingly illustrated by a recent article in which the author reports a purported study of the "article productivity" of this country's journalism professors. He does this by collecting all research articles published in nine journals, then ranking schools and individual researchers according to the total number of articles produced. The nine journals include both general publications such as *Journalism Quarterly* and *Journal of Communication* and those covering narrower media topics such as *Journal of Advertising*, *Journal of Broadcasting*, and *Public Relations Review*. But no journal that carries a high proportion of historical research is included in the study, and as a result much of the journalism history being published in journals is excluded. In addition, no recognition of this inattention is given in the article; apparently it simply did not occur to the author that this key area of journalism research should be taken into consideration in his ranking of schools and individual scholars (see Schweitzer, 1988).

7. See "Special Supplement: Cumulative Index Volumes 51- 60 (1974-83)" (1984). The introduction to the index notes that 84 articles on "history and biography" were published in *Journalism Quarterly* between 1974 and 1983 (p. iii). By my rough estimate (attempting to count articles only once, even when they are listed in more than one topic category), approximately 1,000 articles were published in the journal during the period covered by the index. Thus less than 10% of the total were histories.

8. See, for example, Gerda Lerner (1979, p. 146) and Joan Wallach Scott (1983, p. 147). For an interesting argument advocating the continued production of contribution history, see Hilda L. Smith (1984).

9. For an excellent summary of ideas from the recent literature, see Joan W. Scott (1987). The best compilation of critical writing on women's history during the previous decade probably is a book edited by Berenice Carroll, *Liberating Women's History* (1976).

10. For a good overview of the debate among women's historians over the form, dimensions, and implications of nineteenth-century women's culture, see the combination of articles collectively titled "Politics and Culture in Women's History" in the Spring 1980 issue of *Feminist Studies*. For suggestions on how future research might best address the combined oppressive/liberating elements of separate spheres and women's culture, see Kerber (1988).

11. One historian who has made good use of some of this material is Ann Douglas; see her *The Feminization of American Culture* (1977).

12. Kerber (1988) notes that American advertising during the 1920s was used to help "redefine the housewife" and in the 1950s "to sustain that definition" (p. 28). Informed by an understanding of women's culture and separate spheres, journalism historians might well find it worthwhile to examine this advertising anew. Such an examination would be a significant addition to the field of women's history, particularly in light of Kerber's argument that more research needs to be done on women's separate sphere during the twentieth century (p. 18).

13. See, for example, Baum, Hyman, and Michel (1976, pp. 165-185).

14. Two good sources detailing women's participation in community journalism are Ross (1936, pp. 458-464) and Karolevitz (1985, pp. 125-131).

15. Some useful references to women's work in U.S. minority media are to be found in *The Ethnic Press in the United States: A Historical Analysis and Handbook*, an excellent collection edited by Sally M. Miller (1987).

16. Also see, in Penn (1891/1969), the chapter titled "Afro-American Women in Journalism" (pp. 367-427), which contains effusive profiles of 19 Black women journalists (including Ida B. Wells) working in the last half of the nineteenth century. Many of them were involved in social causes, especially temperance.

17. For a description of specific early 20th-century support and friendship networks, see Cook (1979).

18. Many educated Black women—who were "double minorities" in their professions—had an important support network in Delta Sigma Theta, a sorority founded in 1913 and now thought to be the country's largest Black women's group (see Giddings, 1988).

19. The Women's National Press Club in Washington, D.C., for example, has excellent archives that could be well utilized to chart relationships among journalists in that area of the country. For one study drawing on these materials, see Beasley (1986).

20. The other major scholar of the penny press, Dan Schiller, should be credited for commenting in a footnote: "The sex-biased character of the penny press deserves more study" (Schiller, 1981, p. 16). This is, however, the extent of of Schiller's comments on women and the penny press in his book—a not unexpected situation since even the major critiques of Schiller and Schudson's work do not note the lack of attention given to women as penny press subjects or audiences. See, for example, Eason (1984) and Nerone (1987); also, see the responses to Nerone's article by Schudson, Schiller, Donald L. Shaw, and John J. Pauly in the same issue of *Critical Studies in Mass Communication* (pp. 405-415).

21. One of the first historians to point out the advantages of urban life for women was David M. Potter in his classic 1962 essay, "American Women and American Character" (see Potter, 1973).

REFERENCES

Alpern, Sara. (1987). *Freda Kirchwey: A woman of the Nation*. Cambridge, MA: Harvard University Press.

Baum, Charlotte, Hyman, Paula, & Michel, Sonya. (1976). *The Jewish woman in America*. New York: New American Library.

Beasley, Maurine. (1986, August). *The Women's National Press Club: A case study in the professionalization of women journalists*. Paper presented at the annual conference of the Association for Education in Journalism and Mass Communication.

Beasley, Maurine, & Silver, Sheila. (1977). *Women in media: A documentary source book*. Washington, DC: Women's Institute for Freedom of the Press.

Belford, Barbara. (1986). *Brilliant bylines: A biographical anthology of notable newspaperwomen in America*. New York: Columbia University Press.

Berkin, Carol. (1985). Clio in search of her daughters/women in search of their past. *Liberal Education, 71*, 205-215.

Carroll, Berenice. (Ed). (1976). *Liberating women's history*. Urbana: University of Illinois Press.

Cook, Blanche Weisen. (1979). Female support networks: Lillian Wald, Crystal Eastman, Emma Goldman. In Nancy E. Cott & Elizabeth H. Pleck (Eds.), *A heritage of her own: Toward a new social history of American women* (pp. 412-444). New York: Simon & Schuster.

Covert, Catherine. (1981). Journalism history and women's experience: A problem in conceptual change. *Journalism History, 8*, 2-6.

Cumulative index, vols. 1-10, 1974-1983. (1983). *Journalism History, 20*, 73-83.

Degler, Carl. (1980). *At odds: Women and the family in America from the revolution to the present.* New York: Oxford University Press.

Dervin, Brenda. (1987). The potential contribution of feminist scholarship to the field of communication. *Journal of Communication, 37*, 107-120.

Douglas, Ann. (1977). *The feminization of American culture.* New York: Avon Books.

Eason, David L. (1984). The new social history of the newspaper. *Communication Research, 11*, 141-151.

Edwards, Julia. (1988). *Women of the world: The great foreign correspondents.* New York: Houghton Mifflin.

Emery, Edwin. (1972). *The press and America: An interpretative history of the mass media* (4th ed.). Englewood Cliffs, NJ: Prentice-Hall.

Emery, Michael, & Emery, Edwin. (1988). *The press and America: An interpretative history of the mass media* (6th ed.). Englewood Cliffs, NJ: Prentice-Hall.

Endres, Fred F. (1978). Philosophies, practices and problems in teaching journalism history. *Journalism History, 5*(1), 1-3, 30-31.

Giddings, Paula. (1988). *In search of sisterhood: Delta Sigma Theta and the challenge of the Black sorority movement.* New York: William Morrow.

Goldberg, Vicki. (1986). *Margaret Bourke-White: A biography.* New York: Harper & Row.

Henry, Susan. (1976). Colonial woman printer as prototype: Toward a model for the study of minorities. *Journalism History, 3*, 20-24.

Henry, Susan. (1979). Private lives: An added dimension for understanding journalism history. *Journalism History, 6*, 98-102.

Henry, Susan. (1980). Sarah Goddard: Gentlewoman printer. *Journalism Quarterly, 57*, 23-30.

Henry, Susan. (1984). Reporting "deeply and at first hand": Helen Campbell in the 19th-century slums. *Journalism History, 11*, 18-25.

Henry, Susan. (1985). An exception to the female model: Colonial printer Mary Crouch. *Journalism Quarterly, 62*, 725-733, 749.

Henry, Susan. (1987). "Dear companion, ever-ready co-worker": A woman's role in a media dynasty. *Journalism Quarterly, 64*, 301-312.

Henry, Susan. (1988, July). *In her own name? Public relations pioneer Doris Fleischman Bernays.* Paper presented at the annual conference of the Association for Education in Journalism and Mass Communication.

Karolevitz, Robert F. (1985). *From quill to computer: The story of America's community newspapers.* National Newspaper Foundation.

Kerber, Linda. (1988). Separate spheres, female worlds, woman's place: The rhetoric of women's history. *Journal of American History, 75*, 9-39.

Lerner, Gerda. (1979). *The majority finds its past: Placing women in history.* New York: Oxford University Press.

Marzolf, Marion. (1977). *Up from the footnote: A history of women journalists.* New York: Hastings House.

McGlashan, Zena Beth. (1985). Women witness the Russian Revolution: Analyzing ways of seeing. *Journalism History, 12*, 54-61.

Miller, Jean Baker. (1986). *Toward a new psychology of women* (2nd ed.). Boston: Beacon.

Miller, Sally M. (Ed.). (1987). *The ethnic press in the United States: A historical analysis and handbook*. New York: Greenwood.

Moutoussamy-Ashe, Jeanne. (1986). *Viewfinders: Black women photographers*. New York: Dodd, Mead.

Moynihan, Ruth Barnes. (1983). *Rebel for rights, Abigail Scott Duniway*. New Haven, CT: Yale University Press.

Nerone, John C. (1987). The mythology of the penny press. *Critical Studies in Mass Communications, 4*, 376-404.

Norton, Mary Beth. (1986, April 13). Is Clio a feminist? *New York Times Book Review*, pp. 1, 40-41.

Penn, I. Garland. (1969). *The Afro-American press and its editors*. New York: Arno. (Original work published 1891)

Potter, David M. (1973). American women and American character. In Don E. Fehrenbacher (Ed.), *History and American society: Essays of David M. Potter* (pp. 278-303). New York: Oxford University Press.

Rakow, Lana. (1986). Feminist approaches to popular culture: Giving patriarchy its due. *Communication, 9*, 19-41.

Roberts, Nancy L. (1984). *Dorothy Day and the* Catholic Worker. Albany: State University of New York Press.

Ross, Ishbel. (1936). *Ladies of the press*. New York: Harper & Brothers.

Schiller, Dan. (1981). *Objectivity and the news: The public and the rise of commercial journalism*. Philadelphia: University of Pennsylvania Press.

Schudson, Michael. (1978). *Discovering the news: A social history of American newspapers*. New York: Basic Books.

Schweitzer, John C. (1988). Research article productivity by mass communication scholars. *Journalism Quarterly, 65*, 479-484.

Scott, Ann Firor. (1984). *Making the invisible woman visible*. Urbana: University of Illinois Press.

Scott, Joan W. (1987). Gender: A useful category of historical analysis. *American Historical Review, 91*, 1053-1075.

Scott, Joan Wallach. (1983). Women in history: The modern period. *Past and Present, 101*, 141-157.

Sharp, Nancy V., Turk, Judy VanSlyke, Einsiedel, Edna F., Schamber, Linda, & Hollenback, Sharon. (1985). *Faculty women in journalism and mass communications: Problems and progress*. Syracuse, NY; report published with a grant from the Gannett Foundation. (Available from the Association for Education in Journalism and Mass Communication, College of Journalism, 1621 College St., University of South Carolina, Columbia, SC 29208-0251.)

Shaw, Donald Lewis, & Zack, Sylvia L. (1987). Rethinking journalism history: How some recent studies support one approach. *Journalism History, 14*, 111-117.

Smith, Hilda L. (1984, November). Women's history and social history: An untimely alliance. *Organization of American Historians Newsletter*, pp. 4-6.

Smith-Rosenberg, Carroll. (1980). Politics and culture in women's history. *Feminist Studies, 6*, 55-64.

Smith-Rosenberg, Carroll. (1985). *Disorderly conduct: Visions of gender in Victorian America*. New York: Alfred A. Knopf.

Special supplement: Cumulative index to volumes 51- 60 (1974-1983). (1984). *Journalism Quarterly, 61.*

Steeves, H. Leslie. (1987). Feminist theories and media studies. *Critical Studies in Mass Communication, 4,* 95-135.

Yodelis Smith, MaryAnn. (1982). Research retrospective: Feminism and the media. *Communication Research, 9,* 145-160.

3

Feminist Perspectives on Media Law

Or Media Law as if Women Mattered

CAROLYN STEWART DYER

What if women could incorporate their experience into the law, particularly that which governs speech and press? Would they consider freedom of expression the most vital liberty to preserve? What values would be central to a feminist conception of the law? Would they make different decisions from those the courts have made, or write different laws?

This essay ventures into the realm of speculation about a feminist vision of communication law. The course is largely uncharted because most of media law, with the exception of the law on obscenity, has so far escaped substantial feminist analysis. The arguments are tentative and incomplete, intended to open debate about media law as if women had a say. The objectives are to describe the law as it is relative to gender and to analyze it from feminist perspectives. The central questions are as follows: How does women's lived experience in this society relate to communication law? How would the law need to change to accommodate women's experience? To get to the point of addressing these questions, however, we must consider how the law is made and interpreted, and introduce the major premises of First Amendment law and feminist legal studies or feminist jurisprudence.

Communication law encompasses a broad range of topics, including interpretations of the First Amendment guarantees of free speech and press and other aspects of the law that involve the media of communication. To permit elaboration of alternative arguments, this chapter will focus a feminist light on only some of them: freedom of speech and press, libel, privacy, and obscenity.

LEGAL PROCESS AND PRINCIPLES

The law as we know it is whatever a majority of the U.S. Supreme Court says it is, what a coalition of interests in a legislative body think it should be, what members of a jury can agree it is. It is the product of people and institutions interacting about whatever subjects come before them or the construction of reality as decision makers see it. Although both men and women play roles in each of these and other relevant legal arenas today, the processes were established to serve the needs and to protect or advance the interests of a property-holding white male establishment when the Constitution and Bill of Rights were ratified in the eighteenth century.

The U.S. Supreme Court and the highest courts in the states have been central to development of communication law. To resolve controversies, the courts rely on principles and practices biased in favor of doing things the way the judges believe they have always been done. In this process, judges look to the decisions made in earlier cases to determine what the precedents, or previous rules of law, are and then apply them to what they consider to be the important facts of the current case.

The law changes over time, as judges sometimes decide that the situation in the present case is different in some way from precedent and so modify old principles. Occasionally, judges decide that a previous rule is wrong or obsolete and they overturn it, establishing a new rule in its place. When judges make new or modified law, they attempt to determine what traditional, accepted, everyday practice—known as the common law—is with regard to the subject at hand and use it to establish a new rule of law (Levi, 1949, pp. 1-2). Often, there are conflicting legal interests or rights in a case, each with its own precedent. To resolve cases involving such conflict, judges often attempt to balance the interests to reach a compromise or middle-ground resolution.

The process of making law by relying on precedent and common law is backward-looking and conservative of existing relationships among and between people and political, social, and economic institutions. The law depends to a considerable extent on the judges' interpretation of what facts are relevant, what the precedent is, what the common law or traditional practice has been, what conflicting rights and interests are, and how statutes and the Constitution apply (Levi, 1949, pp. 2-8). In this interpretation, judges, most of whom are male, rely on their vision and experience in society (Fund for Modern Courts, 1985).[1] To the extent that their experience differs in relevant respects from that of women, judge-made law is likely to fail to recognize and meet the needs of women.

American law rests on liberal principles of individual autonomy and freedom and the assumption that equally rational individuals exercise free will under conditions of limited government. The system recognizes a set of natural or fundamental human rights that provide freedom of action in some spheres and security in others. These rights are presumably available to all people (R. Dworkin, 1985, pp. 182-204). The liberal legal system favors empirical and objective methods for gathering evidence rather than phenomenological and subjective techniques. Rationality and logic are preeminent modes of thought in the law. In deciding cases, judges seek to neutrally apply abstract, generalizable, universal laws and, if not eternal, at least well-seasoned truths (Wechsler, 1959).

THEORIES OF FREEDOM OF SPEECH AND PRESS

In communication law, the courts test governmental actions and laws against the First Amendment to the Constitution, which provides for freedom of speech and press as part of fundamental American rights and liberties.[2] The traditional, liberal reading of these rights provides that speech and publication—or expression generally—should be shielded from prepublication or prior restraint by government and subject to penalties after communication in very limited circumstances. Although the Supreme Court and most legal theorists acknowledge some exceptions to absolute, unconditional protection for speech and press, the American media tend to presume that freedom of expression is legally unlimited. However, the courts have defined obscenity as unprotected speech (*Miller v. California*, 1973) and permit the balancing of national security interests against free speech (*Near v. Minnesota*, 1931; *New York Times v. U.S.*, 1971). Beyond these limitations, both individual and institutional expression are generally protected from government limitation. The First Amendment has been interpreted as providing protection for the organized press, the commercial and noncommercial print and broadcast media, making the press the only business specifically protected by the Constitution (Stewart, 1975).

The right to freedom of speech and press is usually understood as negative freedom, that is, freedom *from* government interference. Some believe these rights are empty, however, especially for those who do not have easy access to the mass media through which to speak. As a remedy, legal scholar Jerome Barron (1967) has argued that the government should take a positive role and provide freedom *for* speech and press through a court-enforced right of access to the media for those who are without adequate access to an audience.

For many theorists, freedom of expression is more important than, or preferred over, other rights guaranteed in the Constitution (McKay, 1959). Central to many First Amendment theories is the belief that the Constitution protects a *system* of freedom of expression such that if the freedom of expression of one entity—person, media institution, political group—in the society is abridged, the freedom of all others is diminished (Emerson, 1970).

LEGAL RIGHTS OF WOMEN

The Constitution, which protects the mass media as institutions and freedom of expression as an abstraction, does not yet contain a provision protecting any fundamental rights of women other than the right to vote.[3] To the extent that specific rights of women have been recognized and protected under law, they have been developed by the courts' interpretation of the equal protection clause of the Fourteenth Amendment, which was adopted in 1869 to bar the states from denying the newly freed slaves the rights provided white men in the Constitution (U.S. Constitution, Amendment XIV, section 1)[4]. The rights of women are not a given; they must be interpreted, one by one, by the judicial lawmaking process or outlined in laws adopted by Congress and state legislatures. Not until 1971 did the Supreme Court first rule that discrimination on the basis of sex was a violation of the equal protection clause (*Reed v. Reed*, 1971).[5] The Supreme Court balanced freedom of the press against prohibitions on sex discrimination when it ruled in *Pittsburgh Press v. Pittsburgh Commission on Human Relations* (1973) that a newspaper could not publish sex-segregated want ads.[6]

WOMEN AND THE MEDIA

As other parts of this book demonstrate, women own and manage relatively few mass media institutions and generally lack the economic resources to establish their own in significant numbers. Even where women fill many lower-ranking positions in which they create the messages that are printed or broadcast, the media remain male institutions, with male definitions of what news is and what is entertaining. Women also fill substantially fewer news-making roles in society than men, making it more difficult to get their messages into the media from the outside, which often causes the activities and interests of women to be segregated out of the mainstream of the news and entertainment into women's ghettos (Tuchman, 1978; "Women Writing More," 1988). Lacking substantive social, political, and economic equality with men in the media and society, then, women have less access to means of telling the truths of their experiences in effective and meaningful ways through the mass media.

FEMINIST JURISPRUDENCE

Feminist jurisprudence, or the study of the relationship between law and society from the point of view of women, takes several forms. It rests on the premise that law and the legal system are male institutions that see and treat women as men see and treat women (MacKinnon, 1983, p. 644). The law, feminist theory argues, embodies male standards, rules, and principles as universal and preserves and protects the needs and interests of men (Polan, 1982; Williams, 1982).[7] While it claims to be neutral and to rely on objective judgment, the law, at best, is neutral and objective from the perspective of men's experience (MacKinnon, 1982, pp. 539; Scales, 1986, pp. 1376-1380).[8] Feminist jurisprudence seeks to address legal issues from a perspective that takes into account the experiences and realities of women's lives in this patriarchal system. It strives to listen to and believe what women say of their personal experiences and takes what women say seriously (MacKinnon, 1982, p. 535; 1987, pp. 110-113; West, 1987, pp. 81-89; 1988, p. 60).

Perspectives on the meaning and importance of difference and equality tend to distinguish the various strains of feminist jurisprudence, but there remains considerable overlap and fuzziness around the edges (Dalton, 1987-1988; Freedman, 1983; Littleton, 1987; Menkel-Meadow, 1985; Minow, 1987; Schneider, 1986). At issue are questions about whether women are the same as or different from men in legally relevant respects; whether differences, if they exist, should be recognized in law; and how equality should be defined in the existing or a substantially changed legal system. Some feminist legal analysts have focused on the difference between "formal" equality in the letter of the law and "substantive" equality, questioning whether changes in the law could result in meaningful equality because women have unequal power and status with men (Olsen, 1984, p. 397; Polan, 1982, p. 301).

Much of the feminist critique of existing law has focused on the harm women suffer and how that has been either inadequately addressed by or entirely ignored in the law (A. Dworkin, 1981, 1985; MacKinnon, 1979, 1983, 1984, 1985, 1987; West, 1987, 1988).[9] Women's experience has been disregarded, it is argued, because until recently women have been relegated to the separate sphere of home and family which has been regarded as private and essentially exempt from the influence of the law, while men conducted business in the public realm, which is regulated by law (Polan, 1982, pp. 298-299; Taub & Schneider, 1982, pp. 118-124; Williams, 1982, pp. 177-178). The law did not enter the private realm; man's home was his castle, and he was free to dominate and harm women in that sphere with legal impunity.[10] Among feminists' recent efforts has been the attempt to make known the harm women have suffered in the private—as well as public—spheres and to seek legal redress for these wrongs for both individual women and women as a group. A central problem for feminists has been communicating the concept of harm that is personally experienced and subjective, to a male legal system that demands objectivity and abstraction (West, 1987, p. 85; 1988, pp. 64-66). The task is difficult because, first, until recently women have told only each other about the pain they have suffered (MacKinnon, 1982, pp. 519-520, 535-536; West, 1987, p. 96),[11] and, second, "women often find painful the same objective event or condition that men find pleasurable" (West, 1987, p. 81).[12]

Liberal Feminist Jurisprudence

Feminists who take a liberal approach in their critiques of the law argue that, although the law and men as a group have not fully recognized the fact, women are rationally and politically the same as men and therefore are entitled to share equally in all the rights and privileges provided or protected by law (MacKinnon, 1983, p. 640; West, 1987, pp. 83, 91). They seek integration of women into a reformed legal system. The focus of liberal legal feminists, as it is for classical liberals, is individual autonomy, the opportunity for everyone to exercise free will and share in decision making. The failed Equal Rights Amendment to the Constitution was a liberal mechanism that would have established as fundamental law women's equal rights with men. Both legislation and litigation against sex discrimination in employment and education and for women's rights seek reforms based on liberal conceptions of women's legal status. This legal work has produced some important gains for women (Dalton, 1987-1988, p. 4; Segal, 1984; Williams, 1982, p. 178).

The strictest of liberal-legal feminists seek formal equality and have opposed any legal rule or practice that distinguishes between men and women, even when such opposition works to the disadvantage of women.[13] Most feminist legal theorists argue, however, that there are differences between men and women that should be recognized in strategies to reform the law and society and in differences in the law as well. However, the range of views on difference is considerable. At one end is the strictly biological argument that only women become pregnant and bear children, and that employment policies, practices, and benefits should recognize this fact with special treatment in the law if necessary (Williams, 1982). Others focus on social, cultural, and psychological differences resulting from different roles men and women have traditionally filled in society.

A considerable amount of feminist legal analysis rests on the arguments made in Carol Gilligan's book, *In a Different Voice* (1982). Gilligan claims that boys and girls make moral decisions in different ways. Males tend to make decisions in a generalized, legalistic way, depending on abstract rules and recognition of rights in the search for justice. Females tend to address the particular, with concern for maintaining relationships and fostering care for individuals.

Accepting Gilligan's view on differences, some argue that the law and legal system should be reformed to incorporate the female ethic of care (Karst, 1984; Sherry, 1986). For example, legal scholar Christine A. Littleton (1987) proposes an "equality of acceptance" that requires that "social institutions react to gender differences . . . in such a way as to create equality between complementary male and female persons, skills, attributes and life styles" (p. 193). The test of equality would be whether women and men are equally capable of exercising a right under the resulting law (Littleton, 1987, p. 198). Others argue that to adopt Gilligan's or any of a number of similar premises that men and women have different natural qualities, values, or characteristics, or even to recognize the biological fact of pregnancy, is to risk the perpetuation of the stereotypes that the law and society have traditionally used to the disadvantage of women (Dalton, 1987-1988, p. 5; Kerber et al., 1986; Menkel-Meadow, 1985, pp. 40, 41, note 8; Olsen, 1984, pp. 398-400; Scales, 1986, p. 1381; Williams, 1982, pp. 178, 187-188, 190).

Radical Feminist Jurisprudence

From the radical feminist perspective, the law and society are based on a patriarchal system of inequality characterized by male supremacy and dominance of women, and both are in need of re-vision, not mere reform.[14] Radical feminists view gender as a male construction of the inferior nature and subordinate place of women in society, a construct that is internalized by women (MacKinnon, 1982, pp. 529, 533; Scales, 1986, p. 1393). In the radical view, the legal method of objectivity does not accommodate women's experience because it separates observer from observed (MacKinnon, 1982, pp. 536-541; Scales, 1986, pp. 1376-1380). The law, radical feminists argue, must accept subjective accounts of women's personal experience as valid evidence of women's reality (MacKinnon, 1982, pp. 519-520, 533-537; Scales, 1986, p. 1399).

Radical feminists seek major social change resulting in women's having equal power with men. They believe that winning formal equality with men is inadequate so long as the system is a hierarchy in which men have power and women do not. Among the goals articulated by radical legal feminists are an equality that ends dominance and disadvantage altogether. They do not want to be equally powerful with powerful men and together dominate some other group. The legal system as envisioned by radical feminists would be fair with reference to "real human predicaments" (Scales, 1986, p. 1380) rather than to abstract principles. It would address the life experiences of women, and it would approach legal claims and claimants by seeking relationships among them rather than opposition or differences between them (Scales, 1986, pp. 1387, 1392).

FEMINIST PERSPECTIVES ON FREEDOM OF EXPRESSION

From the liberal feminist perspective, freedom of expression is one of the fundamental liberties that women have at least nominally enjoyed for a considerable period of time. It can be argued that the government has met its obligation with regard to women's negative freedom of expression; it has not generally prevented women, on the basis of their sex, from speaking and writing. Through exercise of this right women have carried out the debate about women's inferior role in society, and many feminists agree with legal scholar Robin West's (1987) conclusion that "First Amendment principles further more than they hinder feminist goals" (p. 138). A cursory review of the cases suggests that the courts have not used gender as an explicit criterion in determining whether First Amendment rights to speak or publish should be upheld or limited in particular cases. Indeed, some of the principals in landmark First Amendment cases have been women, including Elizabeth Baer, one of the defendants in *Schenck v. U.S.* (1919), the first such case decided by the Supreme Court.[15]

The presence of feminist content or content of particular importance to women, however, has been the basis for limiting distribution or circulation of books and magazines to library patrons and schoolchildren. A variety of women's publications have been among the materials removed from public and school libraries (Doyle, 1983; *Newsletter on Intellectual Freedom* [*NIF*], 1979-1988).[16] *Ms.*, the mainstream feminist magazine, has been targeted several times, although a federal court ordered a New Hampshire school board to return it to library shelves.[17] To the extent that their feminist content is the basis for the censorship of publications, the enforcement of the First Amendment is failing to meet the liberal notion of equal application of the law. It is likely that feminist work has been censored in administrative decisions that are not made public.[18]

Radical feminists ask more, if not more important, questions than simply whether or not freedom of expression has been enforced in a sex-neutral manner. Do women have substantive equality with men to exercise this freedom? Are women's needs and interests negatively affected by the system's preference for freedom of expression over other rights and values? Is freedom of expression as it has been defined of equal value to men and women? Is there need for an interpretation that acknowledges differences between men and women? Have women been equally able to use the courts to affirm these rights when they are abridged?

As do other fundamental liberal rights guaranteed by the Constitution, freedom of expression rests on the premise that all people are equal. In a system in which that is not true, the radical view is, women do not have equal access to the benefits of this right (MacKinnon, 1987, pp. 129, 208). Catharine MacKinnon, one of the authors of the feminist antipornography ordinance for Minneapolis, has been an outspoken critic of the liberal position that freedom of expression must be absolutely protected from government interference (see MacKinnon, 1985, 1987, pp. 206-213). She points out that the courts have never accepted an absolutist interpretation of the First Amendment, but those who have free speech present it as if it were legal fact and it has become "the implicit standard from which all deviations must be justified" (1987, p. 208).

Court decisions, MacKinnon (1985) argues, "have justified exceptions to First Amendment guarantees when something that matters is seen to be directly at stake. What unites [these cases] . . . is harm, harm that counts" (p. 28). The problem for women and other relatively powerless groups is that their harm has not mattered. For those whose gender, race, or class effectively precludes them from exercising free speech, MacKinnon argues, negative freedom from government restraint does not provide useful protection or an opportunity to speak. This freedom is more likely to be used by those who have it to harm women and others who do not (MacKinnon, 1987, pp. 208-209).[19] In her view, freedom of speech is the liberal flag in which those who have it wrap themselves while denying it to others (p. 208). The radical feminists' goal is to change the legal system so that women and their harm matters when balanced with freedom of expression.

To make the First Amendment meaningful to women, MacKinnon (1987) argues, the state must also take an affirmative approach, providing a right of access that would guarantee women the opportunity to speak (pp. 207-208).[20] She says that it would work like affirmative action in employment: "Some people's access has to be restricted in the interest of providing access to all" (p. 208).

FEMINIST PERSPECTIVES ON LIBEL AND PRIVACY

The torts of libel and invasion of privacy are intended to provide the legal means for people who have been harmed by the publication of statements about them to seek redress and damages from the publishers. The Supreme Court has ruled that the First Amendment limits the circumstances under which damages may be awarded so that the media are not unduly harmed by huge damage awards or frivolous suits that sap their time, energy, and resources.

To oversimplify a bit, a libelous statement or image is untrue, and it harms the subject's reputation. Whether the subject can find redress in the law, however, depends on how the publisher came to circulate the libel and whether the subject is a public or private person. To protect the system of freedom of expression, the Supreme Court bars plaintiffs from winning libel cases unless the publisher was at fault (*New York Times v. Sullivan*, 1964; *Gertz v. Welch*, 1974). As a consequence, the primary focus in most libel cases is not on the falsity of the statement or the harm the subject suffered, but on whether the publisher knowingly lied, was reckless in publishing potentially damaging information, or was negligent about the reliability of the information published (Bezanson, Cranberg, & Soloski, 1987, pp. 104-107).[21] This balance between harm to the system of freedom of expression and harm to a person as a consequence of libel was struck in favor of the First Amendment in the 1964 Supreme Court libel decision in *New York Times v. Sullivan* and modified in *Gertz v. Welch* in 1974.

Privacy law involves four different torts, or wrongs: (a) publication of information that puts the individual in a false light, (b) public disclosure of private information, (c) appropriation or use of a person's name or image for commercial purposes without consent, and (d) intrusion into an individual's personal space (Prosser & Keeton, 1984, p. 851). The legal possibility of recovery for damages in privacy cases varies with the nature of the wrong. In false light cases, the Supreme Court has ruled that the First Amendment is more important than factual errors that put a plaintiff in a false light. Recovery is limited to those false light cases in which the publisher is at fault (*Time v. Hill*, 1967; *Cantrell v. Forest City Publishing Co.*, 1974), just as in libel cases.

In private facts cases, the courts must determine whether disclosure is of public interest, or newsworthy, and whether disclosure would offend a reasonable person (Prosser & Keeton, 1984, pp. 856-857). If the case involves information disclosed in open court or court records, the Supreme Court has ruled under the First Amendment that the public interest in government affairs bars recovery (*Cox Broadcasting Corp. v. Cohn*, 1975).

Whether the subject gave explicit or implied consent is the central question the courts must answer before awarding damages in appropriation and intrusion privacy cases (Prosser & Keeton, 1984, p. 867). Consent may also be an issue in private facts cases.

Women have not played a substantial role in the development of the torts of libel and privacy. Relatively few plaintiffs in libel and privacy cases are women, and libel has not been a central focus of the feminist critique of the law.[22] Although feminist concern for reproductive rights has focused on the constitutional right of privacy, feminists have not devoted much attention to the privacy torts.[23] But, because libel and privacy are the torts intended to provide means of redress for individuals harmed by publications, there is reason to question how this area of the law relates to women's experience and how it has addressed injuries or harm claimed by women. Libel and false light privacy claims will be addressed together here because of their similarity; the private facts and appropriation torts will be addressed separately.

The promise of the law of libel and privacy to right wrongs committed by the media is rather empty. One study found that only 11% of libel plaintiffs and 17% of privacy plaintiffs won their suits against media defendants (Bezanson et al., 1987, p. 116).[24]

Whether the libel and privacy law works from the liberal feminist perspective depends on whether women have equal opportunity with men to use the law and whether women's cases are treated the same as similar cases involving men. The available data on libel and false light privacy litigation do not answer these questions directly. They do show that only 11% of libel plaintiffs in one study were women and that more than 60% of the libel cases involved plaintiffs who were considered public, as opposed to private, persons (Bezanson et al., 1987, pp. 7, 10).[25] The researchers argue that the small proportion of women among libel plaintiffs is explained by the fact that women are underrepresented among public figures and officials, who initiate most libel cases (Bezanson et al., 1987, p. 7).[26]

Despite women's relative absence from public positions that would make them the primary actors in hard news stories, women may be no less vulnerable to false reports and invasions of privacy in those contexts in which they are identified in the media—as minor actors, subjects, and victims in hard news stories; as subjects of feature stories and pictures; as participants in reported social and cultural events; and in various roles in ads, cartoons, and entertainment content and programming. Feminist legal critiques suggest that in libel and invasion of privacy women's injuries have been unspoken because of inferior social status and lack of experience in using the legal system to seek redress.[27]

To the degree that women suffer different kinds or different degrees of harm from the harm men experience as a consequence of false statements about them or invasions of their privacy, the law is likely to fail to serve women more than men. As sex objects in this society, women are especially vulnerable to reputational harm from portrayals of a sexual nature.[28] Some women have filed libel suits when falsely identified as participants in sexual activity or false light privacy cases when the publication of images created the false impression that they consented to being publicly portrayed in the nude or as participants in sexual activity. Other cases have been filed as appropriation, or private facts cases. A survey of a variety of such cases involving sexual portrayals found that the plaintiffs rarely won (Colker, 1986, p. 41).[29]

Seen in a feminist light, these cases often involve contradictions between conflicting social expectations of women: They are expected to be modest and virginal, but available for men to use at will; and once they have breached modesty or lost their virginity, they are less worthy of compassion and legal protection.

A Feminist Reading of Pring v. Penthouse

How sexual portrayal cases are handled in court demonstrates the point that when women suffer harm, the law ignores their injuries and society trivializes their claims. In *Pring v. Penthouse* (1982) an award-winning baton twirler and former Miss Wyoming sued *Penthouse* for libel and false light invasion of privacy because it published a fictional story about a baton-twirling Miss Wyoming who could cause men to levitate by performing fellatio on them, which she did during the Miss America pageant.[30] As a consequence of the story, Pring testified, she was subjected to street harassment, obscene phone calls, and lewd propositions so distressing that she left college. She also said that parents withdrew their daughters from her baton-twirling classes (Spence, 1986, pp. 305-308).[31]

In overturning the jury ruling in Pring's favor, the Court of Appeals relied on rationality, saying that the *Penthouse* story could not be "reasonably understood" as presenting facts about Pring (*Pring v. Penthouse*, 1982, p. 442).[32] By using the reasonableness standard the court denied the reality of the harassment and rejection Pring experienced, defining such reactions away as irrational. The contrast between the appellate court's decision and Pring's claims exemplifies the point that what women find painful, men may experience as pleasurable sexual fantasy.

Pring's male attorney questions a misogynist legal system that permits defendants to try women plaintiffs as witches and whores by probing into their private sexual lives when women challenge a male prerogative such as freedom of expression (Spence, 1986, pp. 17-23, 111-112, 132-133, 190). The Pring case is frequently trivialized. Pring is often represented as having filed the suit to gain publicity to advance her career.[33]

The Consent Defense

The concept of consent used in the law of privacy rests on the liberal presumption that free and equal people, acting in their own self-interest, voluntarily consent to diminish their liberty for other objectives, such as money. From the feminist perspective that women are not free and equal but rather are subordinate to men, we cannot assume that women give consent freely or that they act in their best interests if they do consent, nor can we reasonably assume that women who do grant consent are not harmed anyway (Colker, 1983, pp. 214-222; McKinnon, 1987, pp. 100, 180-183).

A substantial number of privacy cases involving sexual portrayals revolve around the question of whether or not the subject gave consent for publication.[34] A typical case involves pictures for which an aspiring model or entertainer agrees to pose. Often there is no payment; the woman and the photographer each get copies of the pictures for their portfolios. The subject may sign forms giving the photographer broad, unspecified authorization to use the pictures (*Douglas v. Hustler*, 1985). Sometimes pictures are taken for a specific purpose to which the woman agrees and they are used later for another purpose to which the subject has not consented (*Ann-Margaret v. High Society Magazine*, 1980; *Douglas v. Hustler*, 1985; *Martin v. Senators, Inc.*, 1967). After the pictures are published, causing the woman harm, she turns to the law to seek redress through an appropriation suit. If it can be demonstrated that the woman gave broad enough permission to cover publication of the pictures or gave implied consent by her actions or failure to withhold consent, she cannot win, regardless of the harm she suffers as a consequence of publication. At a minimum, the subject is likely to suffer harm because of the false impression created that she consented to public distribution of the sexual portrayal; she may also suffer additional harm, including embarrassment, loss of reputation, and economic losses (*Douglas v. Hustler*, 1985; *Martin v. Senators, Inc.*, 1967; *Russell v. Marlboro Books*, 1959).[35]

As the cases cited above and other women's experiences reveal, some women pose nude or engage in sexual acts for money—on camera or off—because they feel they have no economic alternatives. In some instances, women's consent has been coerced through sexist flattery, deception, threats of physical or psychological harm, or actual injury (MacKinnon, 1987, pp. 180-183).[36] Finally, as illustrated in some of the sexual portrayal cases, and more frequently noted with regard to other sexual abuses of women, when women say no or grant limited consent, they are often ignored or not taken seriously, and when they report the offenses or sue for damages, they are not believed (Chamallas, 1988; Colker, 1983, p. 216).[37]

Drawing on her feminist critique of how the Supreme Court has handled a variety of cases involving women and other relatively powerless individuals and groups, legal scholar Martha Minow (1987) argues that courts perpetuate systematic discrimination if they base decisions on "apparent choices made by plaintiffs, victims, or members of minority groups as a justification for holding against them. The Court may presume incorrectly that the choices are free and uncoerced, or the Court may wrongly attribute certain meanings to a choice" (p. 84). As a corrective to passive reliance on the liberal assumptions of the law, she suggests that judges consider the human consequences of their decisions rather than "insulating themselves in abstractions" (p. 89). Minow's critique also suggests that judges should actively question whether consent was voluntarily made by a person who understood the possible consequences and who was in a truly equal position to grant informed consent.

The Public Interest and Reasonable Person Standards

In privacy cases involving public disclosure of private facts, the primary defense is that the information was of legitimate public interest, or newsworthy, and that the disclosure would not offend a reasonable person (Prosser & Keeton, 1984, p. 851). The courts have, with a few exceptions, accepted a circular argument as a definition for "public interest" with regard to privacy law. The argument is as follows: The media are intended to appeal to the public; the public read, watch, and listen to the media; therefore, what is in the media is of public interest. In effect, then, the public interest is what the media say it is; indeed, from 1974 to 1984, the media lost less than 3% of the private facts cases that reached appeals courts (Bezanson et al., 1987, p. 116).

From a feminist perspective, the problem with the public interest standard for public disclosure of private facts cases is that the media are male institutions and conduct business with male definitions of news and entertainment. The "reasonable person" has not been specifically defined in privacy law, but in the feminist view he is male, because males dominate the legal system and the media.

Feminists argue that using these standards for privacy cases gives the courts license to discount women's experience of harm.[38] If a sexual portrayal published without consent is uniquely or particularly offensive to women or other relatively powerless people, the courts can say, in effect, that they are supersensitive, because reasonable people—white men—would not be offended.[39] If a woman is nude when she escapes from being held hostage, her photograph is news (*Cape Publishing v. Bridges*, 1982).[40] If a state hospital sterilizes a woman against her will because she is judged unstable by a doctor, her name is newsworthy in a story about abuses of public trust at the hospital (*Howard v. Des Moines Register*, 1979).[41]

From a radical feminist perspective, the private facts standards allow the media to exploit the sexuality of women so long as it is used to make news or to entertain and the public buys, watches, or tolerates it. Regardless of the theory of gender difference one considers, it seems likely that if women held equal power—not merely equal numbers—in the legal system and in the media, women's conception of harm would be incorporated into the definition of the offensive and harm would be balanced against the media's interests in publicizing private facts or appropriating women's images.

FEMINIST APPROACHES TO OBSCENITY AND PORNOGRAPHY

To date, the only area of media law to receive a considerable amount of attention from those engaging in the feminist analysis of the law is obscenity. The attention grew out of women's recognition that although women and children are usually the subjects of the depictions in pornography, the law of obscenity had never considered pornography a women's issue. Under existing law, material that meets the Supreme Court's definition of obscenity is not protected by the First Amendment and may be regulated. The Supreme Court's definition of obscenity is that which

> the average person, applying contemporary community standards, would find that, taken as a whole, appeals to the prurient interest; that which depicts and describes in a patently offensive way sexual conduct as described by state law; and that which, taken as a whole, lacks serious literary, artistic, political or scientific value. (*Miller v. California*, 1973)

The definition of obscenity addresses sexually explicit material as a gender-neutral offense against community morality and sensibilities (Henkin, 1963), but it contains the "average person" standard, which represents the male view (MacKinnon, 1985, p. 21).[42] Many feminists regard pornography as harmful to women, not simply offensive to them. According to MacKinnon and Andrea Dworkin, the best known of the advocates of this position, pornography that shows women in positions of subordination says, in effect, that the social role of woman is to be violated and dominated and, further, that women want to be treated that way (A. Dworkin, 1981, 1985; MacKinnon, 1984, 1985, pp. 206-213). In this view, pornography eroticizes the subordination of women to men. Because of the threat that pornography poses to women of being abused, MacKinnon and Dworkin also argue, pornography has the effect of silencing many women's speech against it or making their speech wholly ineffectual (A. Dworkin, 1985, pp. 17-20; MacKinnon, 1985, pp. 56-68). Their intent was to treat these experiences seriously and to develop a legal remedy. From this perspective, pornography, like sexual harassment in employment and education, discriminates against women on the basis of sex and should be treated as such in the law.[43]

Drawing on the testimony of women who described experiencing a wide range of harms—including physical abuse—suffered because of pornography, MacKinnon and Dworkin drafted an ordinance for Minneapolis that treated pornography as sex discrimination in violation of women's civil rights. They defined pornography as "the graphic sexually explicit subordination of women through pictures or words that also includes" (MacKinnon, 1985, p. 22) one or more of nine specific characteristics, such as "women are presented as sexual objects who enjoy pain or humiliation" (A. Dworkin, 1985, p. 25).[44] If material meets the definition, the ordinance empowered women to file complaints with the civil rights commission or civil suits in court to seek redress from those who created or used pornography. Women would have had a legitimate claim when they were coerced into participating in the production of pornography, when pornography was forced on them, when they were assaulted on account of specific pornography, or when they were subordinated because of the trafficking in, or availability of, pornography.

MacKinnon and Dworkin hoped the ordinance would avoid conflict with the First Amendment, but the courts found that conflict did exist (A. Dworkin, 1985, pp. 22-23; MacKinnon, 1985, pp. 26-32, 1987, pp. 207-208). MacKinnon continues to argue that the courts can balance the First Amendment rights of pornographers against the right of women to be free from harm, and they can uphold similar legislation if they would only decide that harm to women matters (1987, chap. 16).[45]

Although the civil rights ordinance is the most familiar feminist approach to pornography, it is not universally supported by feminists (Burstyn, 1985; Snitow, Stansell, & Thompson, 1983). Perhaps the most common reaction among feminists is to agree with the Dworkin-MacKinnon critique of pornography, but to question the wisdom of their reliance on the patriarchal state, through civil rights commissions and the courts, for enforcement.[46] This reaction rests on the liberal belief that freedom of expression has done feminists more good than harm. Some fear that passage of such an ordinance will trigger a backlash against women that will result in suppression of sexually explicit feminist material, such as feminist exposés of violence against women and feminist works on women's health and sexuality, particularly lesbian sex (Colker, 1985, pp. 698-699, notes 70-74).[47] Some argue that the MacKinnon-Dworkin ordinance reflects only one view of sexually explicit material, which disregards the fact that some women, even feminists, regard images of sexual domination and submission as erotic (Snitow et al., 1983; West, 1987, pp. 116-117).

The fact that antipornography civil rights ordinances have been adopted with the enthusiastic support of politically conservative, fundamentalist religious groups—which are antifeminist on most women's issues—is of particular concern to some critics of the Dworkin-MacKinnon approach. Because of the nature of the coalition, these critics argue, feminist issues are vulnerable to being overshadowed, co-opted, or ignored in the enforcement of the law (Burstyn, 1985).

MEDIA LAW AS IF WOMEN MATTERED

Media law, it turns out on examination, is not much different from other law from the perspective of women. The First Amendment, for the most part, does protect women's voice from legal constraints. As a result, women can advocate reform necessary to create a society that may better value women's contributions. Individual women with the necessary resources have at least some access to an audience for their messages as a consequence of the First Amendment; for these women the barriers are social, political, and economic rather than legal. The First Amendment, which has so far never been interpreted authoritatively to deny protection for feminist speech, does provide a solid base from which to launch legal challenges to censorship and to punishment of sexually explicit or politically radical feminist expression. To the extent that existing First Amendment law is applied in a gender-neutral manner, it nearly meets liberal feminist visions of law in an egalitarian future.

But is that enough? Like most liberal components of the law, the First Amendment does nothing to ensure that those who lack social and political power and economic resources can actually exercise the liberty it promises or be free of harm from its exercise by the powerful causes. In short, the First Amendment provides formal equality rather than substantive equality for the exercise of free expression. It does more to protect the abstract idea of freedom of expression than it does to see that people can actually speak.

The analysis of the law of libel, privacy, and obscenity reveals that the First Amendment has also served as a barrier to the relatively powerless who seek redress for injuries suffered as a consequence of other people's exercise of freedom of expression. The tests the courts have adopted and the manner of their application to the facts of specific cases have militated against recognition of many injuries, particularly those to which women are most vulnerable; they perpetuate the harm of sexual objectification of women. Indeed, media law lags behind other areas of the law, such as sexual harassment and employment discrimination law, that have begun to recognize the fact that women's experience is different from men's in this patriarchal society and that the difference is often harmful to women.

The feminist challenge to media law is to find a means of protecting expression that treats women as if they matter as much as abstract principles do. Feminist legal analysis needs to re-vision the law to address the harm communication causes women and other relatively powerless people as individuals and as groups in society. Where the balance will be struck between freedom from harm and freedom of expression is a question that remains to be answered.

NOTES

1. About 93% of state and federal judges are men.

2. The First Amendment also provides for freedom of assembly or association, freedom to petition government for redress of grievances, and freedom of religion.

3. The Equal Rights Amendment (H.R.J. Res 208, 92nd Cong., 1st Sess., 1971), which failed to win ratification, provided: "Equality of rights under the law shall not be denied or abridged by the United States or by any state on account of sex."

4. It provides in relevant part: "No state shall . . . deny to any person within its jurisdiction the equal protection of the laws."

5. In the case, the Supreme Court ruled that an Idaho law that gave preference to men over women as administrators of the estates of the deceased violated the equal protection clause.

6. The more recent cases in which the Supreme Court ruled that some private clubs must admit women involved the balancing of the First Amendment freedom of association against the rights of women to be free from sex discrimination: for example, see *Roberts v. U.S. Jaycees* (1984).

7. "Courts will do no more than measure women's claim to equality against legal benefits and burdens that are an expression of white male middle-class interests and values" (Williams, 1982, p. 175).

8. "Feminist analysis begins with the principle that objective reality is a myth" (Scales, 1986, p. 1378).

9. The feminist analysis of rape, sexual harassment in employment and education, domestic violence, incest, and pornography focuses on harm women and children experience.

10. The Supreme Court has recognized a constitutional right of privacy as protection against government intrusion into personal zones of privacy, which include physical places such as one's home and psychic spaces in which one makes the personal judgments that represent a person's individuality and autonomy (*Griswold v. Connecticut*, 1965). Feminist critiques of this concept of privacy include Taub and Schneider (1982), MacKinnon (1987, pp. 100-102), and Allen (1988).

11. This has occurred in women's consciousness-raising discussions, which explore the personal and value subjective truth (MacKinnon, 1982, pp. 519-520, 535-536).

12. For example, the office pass is sex and pleasurable for men, harassment and painful for women.

13. Feminist debate over equal versus special treatment came to a head in regard to pregnancy benefits for working women (Krieger & Cooney, 1983).

14. MacKinnon (1987, p. 176) refers to this group as simply "feminists," unmodified by a traditional political label that detracts from the emphasis of feminism on women as a group.

15. Consider also Anita Whitney in *Whitney v. California* (1927), Alma Lovell in *Lovell v. Griffin*, 1938, and several of the defendants in *Yates v. U.S.* (1957). None of the cases involves expression of feminist views, however.

16. Among the most frequently removed or threatened books is *Our Bodies, Ourselves*, removed from one school library because it was "anti-Bible, antimale, and antisystem" (*NIF*, July 1977, p. 100). In another, it was challenged for its feminist point of view (*NIF*, July 1981, p. 92). (See also *NIF*, July 1975, p. 105; September 1975, p. 138; July 1981, p. 92; May 1982, p. 100, 101; March 1983, p. 29; May 1986, p. 78; November 1987, p. 223; January 1988, p. 3.) A minority of the Alabama schoolbook committee challenged books for "propagating feminist views" (*NIF*, March 1983, p. 39). Other feminist books that have been removed from libraries are *Fear of Flying* (*NIF*, May 1982, p. 87), and *The Women's Room* (Doyle, 1983, p. 3).

17. A federal district court issued the order to the Nashua, New Hampshire, school board in 1979. Not until 1982 did the district decide to comply (*NIF*, July 1979, p. 1; March 1982, p. 44; May 1982, p. 83). (See also *NIF*, November 1981, pp. 152, 182; January 1982, p. 9; March 1986, p. 38).

18. Suppression of women's speech is likely to be discussed among women and to be discoverable only by talking with them.

19. For example, MacKinnon argues, Blacks are harmed by the protected speech of the Ku Klux Klan; Jews are harmed when Nazis are protected in their hateful demonstrations through Jewish neighborhoods; women are harmed by the protected self-expression of pornographers.

20. MacKinnon's right of access is similar to Jerome Barron's (1967); his right of access, however, would occur primarily in response to expression already carried in the media.

21. The Iowa Libel Research Project found that 87% of media libel cases decided by appellate courts between 1974 and 1984 focused mainly on the issue of fault (Bezanson et al., 1987, p. 106).

22. Only 11% of the plaintiffs in libel cases covered in the Bezanson et al. (1987, p. 7) study were women. The only known feminist critiques of libel law are Colker's studies (1983, 1984-1985, 1986). Defense attorney Gerry Spence, a man, has published an essentially feminist critique of a libel case (1986).

23. The literature on the right of privacy and reproductive rights is voluminous. See Allen (1988, chapter 4) and Olsen (1984). Colker (1983, 1985, 1986) addresses the tort of privacy.

24. For cases that reached appellate courts between 1974 and 1984, the success rates varied widely among the privacy torts: false light, 11.5%; private facts, 2.8%; appropriation, 33.3%; intrusion, 37.5%.

25. Public persons in libel law are those who hold or run for public office or who thrust themselves into the public eye. They are people who have high visibility in the media, either locally or nationally.

26. Colker (1983) argues that when women file libel actions, they are frequently ruled to be public figures even though they do not seem to meet the legal definition of public figures (p. 213).

27. Women socialized in this society may regard their libel injuries as private and unimportant or believe that the legal system will regard them as trivial, especially if they observe how the legal system has treated other wrongs against women, such as rape and domestic violence.

28. Colker (1986) lists all such cases she could identify. Some of the plaintiffs were men (pp. 41-43, note 7). A considerable number of women's libel and privacy cases do involve their portrayal as sexual objects.

29. The success rate is not reported, but it does not seem to be worse than that found in Bezanson et al. (1987). Colker found plaintiffs won appropriation cases more often than others, a finding that corresponds to the Bezanson et al. data.

30. The story, "Miss Wyoming Saves the World," by Philip Cioffari, was published in the August 1979 issue of *Penthouse*. Kimerli Pring held the Miss Wyoming title in the summer of 1979. Cioffari attended the Miss America pageant in which Pring competed. A jury awarded Pring the largest amount of damages in a libel case up to that time, but the court of appeals overturned the verdict and the Supreme Court declined to hear the case.

31. She continued to be harassed and shunned after the case was completed (Spence, 1986, pp. 457-458).

32. See also Colker (1983, pp. 225-226).

33. The case is often cited in discussions of large jury awards of damages in libel cases and dismissed with a joke. See, for example, Smolla (1986), who says Pring was worried that readers would assume "where there's smoke there's fire" (p. 164). See also Spence (1986, pp. 307, 458). Many feminists would argue that Pring invited the *Penthouse* abuse by assuming a role as a sex object. Others would respond that Pring agreed only to participate in the pageants, and that to argue otherwise is to blame the victim for her injury.

34. Consent is the primary defense in appropriation cases, and it may be a relevant defense in some private facts cases. Colker (1986) also considers the implication of consent, when none was given for a sexual portrayal, as the injury in some false light cases.

35. Colker (1986) argues that the woman is harmed in part because her sex-based civil rights are violated; she is "only portrayed sexually because she is a woman" (p. 46, note 31). Vanessa Williams, Miss America 1984, was forced to resign after pictures taken in a scenario similar to that described were published in *Penthouse* (Colker, 1984-1985, p. 687; Smolla, 1986, pp. 160-162).

36. The most well-known presentation of this point involves Linda Marchiano, who was hypnotized, imprisoned, beaten, and threatened by her agent-husband to consent to partici-

pation as Linda Lovelace in the movie *Deep Throat* (Colker, 1983, p. 216; Lovelace, 1980; MacKinnon, 1985, pp. 32-38; Steinem, 1983, pp. 243-252).

37. "Having power means, among other things, that when someone says, 'this is how it is,' it is taken as being that way. When this happen in law, such person is accorded what is called credibility. When the person is believed over another speaker, what was said becomes proof" (MacKinnon, 1985, p. 4). On sexual harassment, see, for example, MacKinnon (1979, pp. 161-162; 1987, pp. 110-113; also see Chamallas, 1988, pp. 801-810). On rape, see Estrich (1987, pp. 42-56) and Chamallas (1988, pp. 797-800).

38. West (1987) argues that men's "conception of pain—of what it is—is derived from a set of experiences which *excludes* women's experience" (p. 144). Colker (1983) argues that the reasonableness standard harms women by defining sensitivity from a male point of view (p. 227).

39. The same critique applies to the "reasonably understood" standard used in the *Pring* case discussed above. Chamallas (1988) discusses the use of a "reasonable victim" standard as a means of seeing sexual harassment from the perspective of its usually female victims (pp. 806-809). This approach might be appropriate to private facts cases.

40. Also at issue in this case was the fact that Hilda Bridges was outdoors in a public place. Allen (1988) argues in a different, but relevant, context that people deserve some degree of privacy even in public places (pp. 123-152).

41. The court also argued that the subject's identity was public record because her name appeared in a letter written to the governor about abuses at the hospital; therefore publication was constitutionally protected under *Cox Broadcasting Corp. v. Cohn* (1975).

42. The "average person" standard is comparable to the "reasonable person" standard of private facts privacy law. The average person is not the most highly sensitive or the most vulnerable.

43. MacKinnon (1979) was prominent in the development of the legal argument that sexual harassment was sex discrimination, a view the Supreme Court accepted in *Meritor Savings Bank v. Vinson* (1986). MacKinnon (1987) says: "It became possible to do something legal about sexual harassment because some women took women's experience of violation seriously enough to design a law around it, *as if what happens to women matters*" (p. 103; emphasis added). MacKinnon and Dworkin took the same strategic approach to their design of an antipornography law: They listened to what women said and designed a law that addressed the harm they suffered (MacKinnon, 1985).

44. The Minneapolis ordinance was vetoed by the mayor in 1984. A slightly different version has been published as a model antipornography ordinance (A. Dworkin, 1985, pp. 24-29). A similar ordinance adopted in Indianapolis was found unconstitutional by a federal court of appeals, and the Supreme Court affirmed that decision without substantial review (*American Booksellers v. Hudnut*, 1985). Sandra Day O'Connor, the only woman on the Supreme Court, voted to give the case a full review.

45. The court has done this with regard to pornography featuring children (*New York v. Ferber*, 1982).

46. Several writers suggest that the courts do not have a good record with regard to female sexuality in general. They have trouble distinguishing among stranger, acquaintance, and marital rape, and consensual sex; they fail to see abortion as an issue about a woman's control over the use of her body; they have been unpredictable in deciding on pregnancy benefits and related reproductive issues. See Allen (1988), Chamallas (1988), Estrich (1987), MacKinnon (1987), and Tong (1984).

47. For example, see the discussion above about censorship, particularly about *Our Bodies, Ourselves.*

REFERENCES

Allen, Anita L. (1988). *Uneasy access.* Totawa, NJ: Rowman & Littlefield.

American Booksellers v. Hudnut, 771 F. 2d 323 (7th Cir. 1985), *affirmed* 475 U.S. 1001 (1986).

Ann-Margaret v. High Society Magazine, 498 F. Supp. 401 (S.D.N.Y. 1980).

Barron, Jerome A. (1967). Access to the press: A new First Amendment right. *Harvard Law Review, 80,* 1641-1678

Bezanson, Randall P., Cranberg, Gilbert, & Soloski, John. (1987). *Libel law and the press.* New York: Free Press.

Burstyn, Varda. (Ed.). (1985). *Women against censorship.* Vancouver: Douglas & McIntyre.

Cantrell v. Forest City Publishing Co., 419 U.S. 245 (1974).

Cape Publishing v. Bridges, 423 So. 2d 426 (Fla. App. 1982), *cert. denied,* 464 U.S. 893 (1983).

Chamallas, Martha. (1988). Consent, equality, and the legal control of sexual conduct. *Southern California Law Review, 61,* 777-862.

Colker, Ruth. (1983). Pornography and privacy: Towards the development of a group based theory for sex based intrusions of privacy. *Journal of Law and Inequality, 1,* 191-237.

Colker, Ruth. (1984-1985). Legislative remedies for unauthorized sexual portrayals: A proposal. *New England Law Review, 20,* 687-720.

Colker, Ruth. (1986). Published consentless sexual portrayals: A proposed framework for analysis. *Buffalo Law Review, 35,* 39-83.

Cox Broadcasting Corp. v. Cohn, 420 U.S. 469 (1975).

Dalton, Clare. (1987-1988). Where we stand: Observations on the situation of feminist legal thought. *Berkeley Women's Law Journal, 3,* 1-13.

Douglas v. Hustler, 769 F. 2d 1128 (7th Cir. 1985).

Doyle, Robert P. (1983). *List of books some people consider dangerous.* New York: American Library Association.

Dworkin, Andrea. (1981). *Pornography.* New York: G.P. Putnam's Sons.

Dworkin, Andrea. (1985). Against the male flood: Censorship, pornography and equality. *Harvard Women's Law Journal, 8,* 1-29.

Dworkin, Ronald. (1985). *A matter of principle.* Cambridge, MA: Harvard University Press.

Emerson, Thomas I. (1970). *The system of freedom of expression.* New York: Random House.

Estrich, Susan. (1987). *Real rape.* Cambridge, MA: Harvard University Press.

Freedman, Ann E. (1983). Sex equality, sex differences and the Supreme Court. *Yale Law Journal, 92,* 913-968.

Fund for Modern Courts. (1985). *The success of women and minorities in achieving judicial office: The selection process.* New York: Author.

Gertz v. Welch, 418 U.S. 323 (1974).

Gilligan, Carol. (1982). *In a different voice.* Cambridge, MA: Harvard University Press.

Griswold v. Connecticut, 381 U.S. 479 (1965).

Henkin, Louis. (1963). Morality and the Constitution: The sin of obscenity. *Columbia Law Review*, *63*, 391-414.

Howard v. Des Moines Register, 283 N.W. 2d 289 (Iowa 1979), *cert. denied*, 445 U.S. 904 (1980).

H.R.J. Res. 208, 92nd Cong., 1st Session, 1971. (Equal Rights Amendment.)

Karst, Kenneth L. (1984). Women's constitution. *Duke Law Journal*, pp. 447-508.

Kerber, Linda K., Greeno, Catherine G., Maccoby, Eleanor, Luria, Zellia, Stack, Carol B., & Gilligan, Carol. (1986). On *In a different voice*: An interdisciplinary forum. *Signs*, *11*, 304-333.

Krieger, Linda J., & Cooney, Patricia N. (1983). The Miller-Wohl controversy: Equal treatment, positive action and the meaning of women's equality. *Golden Gate University Law Review*, *13*, 513-572.

Levi, Edward H. (1949). *An introduction to legal reasoning*. Chicago: University of Chicago Press.

Littleton, Christine A. (1987). Equality across difference: A place for rights discourse. *Wisconsin Women's Law Journal*, *3*, 189-212.

Lovelace, Linda. (1980). *Ordeal*. New York: Bell.

Lovell v. Griffin, 303 U.S. 444 (1938).

MacKinnon, Catharine A. (1979). *Sexual harassment of working women*. New Haven, CT: Yale University Press.

MacKinnon, Catharine A. (1982). Feminism, Marxism, method and the state: An agenda for theory. *Signs*, *7*, 515-544.

MacKinnon, Catharine A. (1983). Feminism, Marxism, method and the state: Toward feminist jurisprudence. *Signs*, *8*, 635-658.

MacKinnon, Catharine A. (1984). Not a moral issue. *Yale Law and Policy Review*, *2*, 321-345.

MacKinnon, Catharine A. (1985). Pornography, civil rights, and speech. *Harvard Civil Rights/Civil Liberties Law Review*, *20*, 1-70.

MacKinnon, Catharine A. (1987). *Feminism unmodified*. Cambridge, MA: Harvard University Press.

Martin v. Senators, Inc., 220 Tenn. 465, 418 S.W. 2d 660 (1967).

McKay, Robert B. (1959). The preference for freedom. *New York University Law Review*, *34*, 1182-1222.

Menkel-Meadow, Carrie. (1985). Portia in a different voice: Speculating on a women's lawyering process. *Berkeley Women's Law Journal*, *1*, 39-63.

Meritor Savings Bank v. Vinson, 477 U.S. 57 (1986).

Miller v. California, 413 U.S. 15 (1973).

Minow, Martha. (1987). The Supreme Court 1986 term—Foreword: Justice engendered. *Harvard Law Review*, *101*, 10-95.

Near v. Minnesota, 283 U.S. 697 (1931).

New York v. Ferber, 458 U.S. 747 (1982).

New York Times v. Sullivan, 376 U.S. 254 (1964).

New York Times v. U.S., 713 U.S. 403 (1971).

Olsen, Frances. (1984). Statutory rape: A feminist critique of rights analysis. *Texas Law Review*, *63*, 387-432.

Pittsburgh Press v. Pittsburgh Commission on Human Relations, 413 U.S. 376 (1973).

Polan, Diane. (1982). Toward a theory of law and patriarchy. In David Kairys (Ed.), *The politics of law* (pp. 294-303). New York: Pantheon.

Pring v. Penthouse, 695 F. 2d 438 (10th Cir. 1982), *cert. denied*, 462 U.S. 1132 (1983).

Prosser, William, & Keeton, W. Page. (1984). *Prosser and Keeton on law of torts* (5th ed.). St. Paul, MN: West.

Reed v. Reed, 404 U.S. 71 (1971).

Roberts v. U.S. Jaycees, 468 U.S. 609 (1984).

Russell v. Marlboro Books, 18 Misc. 2d 166, 183 N.Y.S. 2d 8 (N.Y. Sup. Ct. 1959).

Scales, Ann C. (1986). The emergence of feminist jurisprudence: An essay. *Yale Law Journal, 95*, 1373-1403.

Schenck v. U.S., 249 U.S. 47 (1919).

Schneider, Elizabeth M. (1986). The dialectic of rights and politics: Perspectives from the women's movement. *New York University Law Review, 61*, 589-652.

Segal, Phyllis N. (1984). Sexual equality, the equal protection clause, and the ERA. *Buffalo Law Review, 33*, 85-147.

Sherry, Susanna. (1986). Civic virtue and feminine voice in constitutional adjudication. *Virginia Law Review, 72*, 543-616.

Smolla, Rodney A. (1986). *Suing the press.* New York: Oxford University Press.

Snitow, Ann, Stansell, Christine, & Thompson, Sharon. (Eds.). (1983). *Powers of desire.* New York: Monthly Review Press.

Spence, Gerry. (1986). *Trial by fire.* New York: William Morrow.

Steinem, Gloria. (1983). *Outrageous acts and everyday rebellions.* New York: New American Library.

Stewart, Potter. (1975). "Or of the press." *Hastings Law Journal, 26*, 631-637.

Taub, Nadine, & Schneider, Elizabeth M. (1982). Perspectives on women's subordination and the role of law. In David Kairys (Ed.), *The politics of law* (pp. 117-139). New York: Pantheon.

Time v. Hill, 385 U.S. 374 (1967).

Tong, Rosemarie. (1984). *Women, sex, and the law.* Totawa, NJ: Rowman & Allenheld.

Tuchman, Gaye. (1978). *Making news.* New York: Free Press.

Wechsler, Herbert. (1959). Toward neutral principles of constitutional law. *Harvard Law Review, 73*, 1-35.

West, Robin L. (1987). The difference in women's hedonic lives: A phenomenological critique of feminist legal theory. *Wisconsin Women's Law Journal, 3*, 81-145.

West, Robin L. (1988). Jurisprudence and gender. *University of Chicago Law Review, 55*, 1-72.

Whitney v. California, 274 U.S. 357 (1927).

Williams, Wendy W. (1982). The equality crisis: Some reflections on culture, courts and feminism. *Women's Rights Law Reporter, 7*, 175-200.

Women writing more front-page news, but not making it, study says. (1988, March/April). *Media Report to Women,* p. 7.

Yates v. U.S., 354 U.S. 298 (1957).

4

Gender and Mass Communication in a Global Context

H. LESLIE STEEVES

This book is about gender and mass communication in the United States.[1] Yet we live in an information age with almost unlimited possibilities for intercultural influence. American television programs such as *Dallas* are beamed into homes on every continent, and Western wire services such as AP and UPI dominate the world news. AT&T's term "global telecommunity" implies information transfer capabilities beyond imagination two decades ago. These and related developments are making it inappropriate to study mass communication—including gender inequities therein—without attention to the larger global context.

This chapter attempts to provide some of that context. However, it is not possible in limited space to describe the status of women in relation to mass communication in every other country in the world—even if detailed and up-to-date information were available from every country. In addition, it is inappropriate for me—as an American—to attempt to represent the rest of the world. Rather, I will discuss global issues that I believe have implications for all women and that make a sensitivity to the rest of the world crucial in U.S. studies of gender and media.

While I will present descriptive information as a part of this discussion, such information should *not* be assumed to provide an accurate picture of what is known about gender and media relations around the globe. Rather, it is intended only to illustrate commonalities or differences that should concern us, and also to provide interested readers with a starting point for further study. Throughout this discussion I will note sources for readers, and I will argue that research and action can be enhanced by drawing on

AUTHOR'S NOTE: I would like to thank Elli Lester-Massman, Rebecca Arbogast, Marilyn Chafton Smith, and Pam Creedon for their thoughtful suggestions. I am also indebted to Margaret Gallagher's extensive work, on which this chapter relies heavily.

the works of women in other countries as well as by using media and information technologies to network globally.

WESTERN INFLUENCES ON
GLOBAL GENDER AND MEDIA ISSUES

One important reason for Americans to study gender and media issues elsewhere is to develop a sense of responsibility for the influences of the United States and other industrialized nations on the rest of the world's media and information systems. These influences include both Western patriarchy and Western feminism.

Cees Hamelink (1983) points out that cultures evolve, in part, in response to the need to adapt to their unique environments (p. 1). Cultures have influenced each other throughout history, providing new options that have been selectively incorporated or rejected. In recent centuries, however, the autonomy of many cultures to define their own destinies has been sharply curtailed. For example, European colonial powers engaged in systematic efforts to transform their colonized territories: They introduced European languages, religion (primarily Christianity), styles of government, law, education, and mass media, and, of course, European assumptions regarding gender roles. While transformation by coercion certainly still occurs in many parts of the world, the mass export of information and information hardware has radically altered the nature and pace of cultural influence, affecting industrialized as well as less developed countries.

Never before has the synchronization with one particular cultural pattern been of such global dimensions and so comprehensive. Never before has the process of cultural influence proceeded so subtly, without any blood being shed and with the receiving culture thinking it had sought such cultural influence. It is remarkable that this process should happen exactly when technological development seems to facilitate optimal possibilities for mutual cultural exchange. (Hamelink, 1983, p. 4)

Cultural imperialism (or "synchronization"[2]) has been the subject of much debate in the past two decades. Opposing sides are often described as "free flow" advocates, who believe that the information market will regulate itself and that everyone should have access to existing information, versus advocates of a New World Information and Communication Order (NWICO), where Western imperialism is curbed. A major outcome of these debates was the publication of the 249-page "MacBride Report," *Many Voices, One World* (International Commission for the Study of Communication Problems, 1980).[3] The report paid only token attention to women's concerns. It is true (as UNESCO, 1985, points out) that many of the problematic issues discussed in the MacBride Report are also problematic for women. These issues include media access and control, training needs, underrepresentation, and distortion.

> A truly serious analysis of these might have led to some detailed discussion of women in the contexts of, for example, transnationalization, of advertising, of the formation of public opinion, of infrastructures, of professional communicators. Instead, the issue of women is collapsed into two pages on 'equal rights for women', which sit uneasily in a chapter entitled 'Images of the World.' (UNESCO, 1985, p. 4)

Given the importance of such issues for women, from which point(s) of view should they be critiqued? "Women" certainly are not one homogeneous group, as the authors of this volume's chapters point out. Power relations among men and women, racial and ethnic groups, various classes, and men and women living in rural and urban areas may vary considerably from culture to culture. Western feminisms—for example, liberal and radical forms of feminism—have often ignored this immense variation.

Because of this, Western feminists are sometimes accused of meddling inappropriately in other cultures, particularly Third World[4] cultures. As Nicole-Claude Mathieu (1988) notes, "They are charged with ethnocentrism, imperialism, and even racism" (p. 5). At the least, Third World women often complain that Western women do not understand their unique circumstances[5] and their need to align with oppressed men. Neera Desai and Maithreyi Krishnaraj (1987) note that issues such as sexual freedom and sexual preference may not be as relevant in developing countries as in the West, and that in conditions of general deprivation, behaviors of "aggressive individualism" may be dysfunctional (p. 18).

In contrast to liberal and radical feminists, socialist feminists (such as Michèle Barrett, 1980) draw on Marxism to challenge the dualisms of the Enlightenment, especially the public-private dichotomy, and to emphasize capitalist class inequities, which they assume contribute importantly to patriarchy. In addition, many socialist feminists are attempting to address inequities of race and ethnicity (for citations, see Connolly and Segal, 1986). Socialist feminism has a wide following in Great Britain and in the rest of Europe. However, its Marxist underpinnings have not been widely accepted in the United States. I have noted elsewhere that socialist feminist efforts to draw on structural Marxism (Althusser, 1971) as well as Stuart Hall's (e.g., 1980a, 1980b) and others' writings on ideology have been particularly useful in analyses of women and mass communication (Steeves, 1987). I believe that socialist feminism's use of these theories as well as recent efforts to address a variety of inequities make this framework most generally useful throughout the world. However, socialist feminism is also a product of Western theory and politics. It should therefore be applied only critically and with collaborative efforts by local feminists.

FIVE GLOBAL GENDER ISSUES

Given this introduction, I will next draw on literature associated with both the NWICO debates and feminist theory to discuss five interrelated global issues that I feel are relevant to Western scholars and to all women. First, I believe we need to recognize and critique a major factor in Western patriarchal influence on media: the transnational corporations that, many believe, make up the highest economic level of global decision making. Second, given this recognition, we need to understand how transnational goals are supported via advertising, which, in turn, influences editorial and entertainment content. Third, it is important to be aware of global commonalities in women's experiences in mass media, regardless of the ultimate causes of these experiences. Fourth, it is useful to know how other women are resisting both indigenous and Western patriarchal influences. These responses can help us understand our commonalities and may offer models for research and action in our own country. Finally, the global linkages made possible by new information technologies are creating opportunities for collaboration with women around the world—both to critique these technologies and to use them for our own purposes.

Gender and Transnational Corporations[6]

Probably the most profound contemporary Western influences on gender and media inequities around the world are imposed by transnational corporations, which make international research, production, and distribution decisions. The significance of the values underlying these decisions and their inevitable effects on national media decisions, on local media organizations, and on media content therefore cannot be overlooked. According to the MacBride Report:

The transnational corporations have created models of productive efficiency with high-capacity technologies. The high rate of their profits stimulates further investment in communication industries. . . . In the electronics production industry, particularly, most of the firms who manufacture equipment for the production, transmission and reception of radio and television are based in the industrialized countries, are typically transnational and characterized by vertical integration. (International Commission for the Study of Communication Problems, 1980, p. 108)

Thus, with regard to communication technology, the world is increasingly at the mercy of the largest corporations, which happen to be based in about five countries, the most in the United States.[7] The fact that few women advance to the top of these companies means that women's input into research and development decisions, let alone distribution decisions, is minuscule. Also, since women are particularly likely to be poor, the new products introduced by these corporations to the market may be less accessible to them. A good example is videotex in Brazil, which was supposed to help democratize communication (e.g., from the peasants to country leaders). However, a color television and a telephone are required to use it—equipment obviously not available to the poor (Mattelart, Delcourt, & Mattelart, 1984, p. 58).[8]

Put simply, the market system relies on divisions of labor, power, knowledge, and wealth. The world market system is therefore consistent with the many dualistic assumptions of the Enlightenment science—that hierarchical distinctions exist among people—certainly among the classes and between the genders and the First and Third Worlds. Two issues that further illustrate these values are, first, the role of these corporations in military information research and, second, their hiring practices in electronics factories based in Third World countries.

Much of the research carried out in the largest transnational corporations is funded by the U.S. Department of the Defense. Because communication and information technologies are crucial to weapons systems, many communications technologies are initially developed for military purposes (Schiller, 1981, p. xiii). Of course, military systems around the world are almost universally male; and their technologies, according to many feminists, are not gender-neutral. Elise Boulding (1981) for example, points out that a major goal of technological research and development has always been the ability to control by force, and that men have been the leaders in this project: Men have always operated the "palace-temple-army-technology complex" and women have operated the "kitchen-garden-homecraft-childbearing complex" (pp. 16-17). The increasing militarism in the world is therefore an ominous phenomenon likely to subvert women's efforts to obtain more economic power. Also, while there is a growing feminist/antimilitary movement in the First World, including Israel and South Africa, this movement has so far excluded the Third World (Leonardo, 1985).

The invention of communication technologies in transnational corporations also affects women directly through jobs in electronics factories based in Third World countries. Whereas women's participation in the labor force often declines with modern economic growth and the introduction of new technologies that are typically operated by men,[9] an exception is the expansion of labor-intensive, electronics manufacturing for export, which has created large numbers of factory jobs for women in the Third World (Lim, 1981; Srinivasan, 1981; Ward, 1986). In these plants, young women without children are the favored employees. Lim (1981) quotes an investment brochure published by the Malaysian government that gives some of the reasons:

> The manual dexterity of the oriental female is famous the world over. Her hands are small and she works fast with extreme care. Who, therefore, could be better qualified by nature and inheritance, to contribute to the efficiency of a bench-assembly production line than the oriental girl? (p. 184)

Lim notes that these jobs do free young women from some very conservative norms of patriarchal societies and provide some financial and social independence (p. 189); however, they subject the women to new forms of exploitation. The jobs are low paying, unstable, and dead-end. In addition, many of the jobs are highly stressful and involve health risks.[10]

Representations of Women in Global Mainstream Media[11]

Given the the exclusion and oppression of women by Western transnational corporations, the next area to examine is how this power is translated into media representations and employment. To address these issues, UNESCO commissioned two major reviews of the literature worldwide related to women and media (Gallagher, 1981; UNESCO, 1985). These two projects provide excellent sources of information on women's representations and roles in mainstream mass media outside of the United States.[12] Also, *Media Asia* recently devoted an entire issue to women and media in Asian countries, with data on representations, employment, and education.[13] Newsletters such as *Media Report to Women*,[14] *WIN News*,[15] *Sex Roles Within Mass Media*,[16] and *Echo*[17] provide more updated information. The International Women's Tribune Centre, located in New York City, is another good resource.[18] In addition, conferences of organizations such as the International Association for Mass Communication Research and the International Communication Association have sessions for feminist scholarship and often provide the most current information.

In general, UNESCO's orientation to the study of representations can be described as socialist feminist. Both UNESCO reports assume that mass media contribute to systems of representation that make up ideological processes in society (Gallagher, 1981; UNESCO, 1985). Both reports also emphasize links between representations and the international economy. Their primary object of critique is advertising, the main factor in profits of the communication industry, and the key to the survival of most mass media.

Advertising. Most advertising space is bought by transnational advertising firms based in industrialized countries (Murdock & Janus, 1985). Since women in most cultures make the majority of private consumption decisions, they are an important target for these advertisers. One aspect of advertising that has gender implications is its persuasive, unidirectional nature. Advertising research has become highly sophisticated and can identify techniques that are most likely to sell goods and encourage materialistic values. Since products advertised are often nonessential, luxury types of items, poor women's oppressed status is likely to be reinforced by advertising, as is their status as consumers. In fact, international studies of media advertising have consistently reported images of women that reflect the capitalist and consumerist orientation of the Western agencies that create most of the advertisments and of the transnational corporations that make the products (Gallagher, 1981; UNESCO, 1985). Typical results are indicated in a study of fifteen national and three transnational women's magazines in Brazil, Chile, Colombia, Mexico, and Venezuela:

> On average 30 per cent of the total space in the magazines examined was devoted to advertising. But an important finding was that in many cases, identical advertisements were placed in different magazines and in different countries: for example, one advertisement for perfume, appeared simultaneously in six of the magazines studied. Moreover, a striking 60 per cent of *all* advertisements were for the products of transnational corporations, the majority of the articles associated with beauty or fashion, followed by products for use in the home. (Gallagher, 1981, p. 46, describing Santa Cruz & Erazo, 1980)

An extreme example of this partnership between transnationals and advertising is the transnational magazine, which is edited and produced in the

West but is superficially adapted to the language and culture of the countries in which it is distributed. For example, Gallagher (1981) describes *Amina*, which is produced in France and distributed in Francophone Africa. The magazine reinforces traditional gender relations, while at the same time describing the life-styles of "modern" women. These life-styles, however, are far beyond the reach of most of its readers. In addition, *Amina*'s advertising is primarily for the beauty and fashion products of transnational or French mail-order companies (pp. 25-26).

A second advertising issue is its impact on entertainment and editorial content. If accepted, advertising may have a profound effect on the content of locally produced media; new developments in cable broadcasting do not appear to be reversing this phenomenon (Gallagher, 1987b, pp. 30-31). Advertising likewise exerts influence on Western media content, which is then exported to other parts of the First and Third Worlds. Armand Mattelart and his coauthors (1984) point out that popular U.S. television series, like the advertisements embedded in them, negate inequities and contradictions in society (p. 100). Many European and other countries have recently acquired more channels (via satellites) but do not have the resources to produce their own programming. It is far cheaper for these countries to buy U.S. series than to attempt to produce their own. These sophisticated series utilize numerous technical devices (e.g., image and camera angle changes) that are known to appeal to viewers. As they become more popular, they tend to suppress or marginalize other forms of demand. Thus international-level competition tends toward uniformity. Mattelart et al. ask to what extent the United States has the power to say to the world, "I am your imaginary" (p. 89).

Entertainment and editorial content. The UNESCO literature reviews summarize what was known up to 1985 about representations of women in print and broadcast media in Latin America and the Caribbean, Western Europe, Central and Eastern Europe, the Middle East, Africa, Asia, Australia, and Canada, we well as the United States. In general, many of the same observations are made internationally that are made in the United States. Gallagher (1981) notes that her review "presents a picture remarkable only for its overall consistency when compared from one country to another" (p. 70). UNESCO (1985) does not note much change in this general picture, nor do more recent studies such as those in *Media Asia* (1987). These reports offer considerable evidence in support of their conclusions.

Media treatment of women can best be described as narrow. On film, in the press and the broadcast media, women's activities and interests typically go no further than the confines of home and family. Characterized as essentially dependent and romantic, women are rarely portrayed as rational, active or decisive. Both as characters in fictional media material and as newsmakers in the press and broadcasting, women are numerically underrepresented—an absence which underlines their marginal and inferior status in many spheres of social, economic and cultural life. Prevalent news values define most women, and most women's problems as unnewsworthy, admitting women to coverage primarily as wives, mothers or daughters of men in the news: in their own right, they make the headlines usually only as fashionable or entertainment figures. . . . Underlying practically all media images of women—though characterized somewhat differently from one country to another—is a dichotomous motif which defines women as either perfectly good or wholly evil, mother or whore, virgin or call-girl, even traditional or modern. (Gallagher, 1981, p. 71)

In media entertainment (whether film, print, radio, or television), Gallagher (1981) reports that women are grossly underrepresented—by about five to one in popular radio and television in much of Europe (p. 76). Also, much magazine content for women—including the popular *fotonovelas* of Latin America[19]—as well as broadcast content (e.g., soap operas), reinforces traditional ideologies of oppression and encourages escapism. Of course, much media entertainment throughout the world consists of exports from the United States, some of which are critiqued in other chapters in this volume. There is some evidence of contradictions between imported representations of women and indigenous values (Gallagher, 1981, p. 37). However, almost nothing is known about how these Western products are interpreted by women in other cultures. While it is likely that in most cases audiences "read" representations as they are intended, there are indications that—at least under certain conditions—Third World women may actively resist dominant messages (e.g., Mattelart, 1986, pp. 14-15).[20]

In media news, research indicates that women are mostly absent. In fact, according to Gallagher (1981) no country with available data reported that more than 20% of the news was about women, and in most cases the figure was much lower (p. 77). Most existing news about women is trivial—related to family status or appearance. Where important women's activities are covered, they are often simultaneously undermined or demeaned. U.S. news, of course, shows a similar pattern, including its coverage of international women's activities. This coverage is important because of its impact on foreign news, which often relies on Western releases. It is worth noting that even U.S. coverage of the three U.N. Decade for Women Conferences—1975 (Mexico City), 1980 (Copenhagen), and 1985 (Nairobi)—was often marginalized (placed in life-style sections) and sensation-alized (emphasizing conflict) (Cooper & Davenport, 1987).

Gallagher (1981) notes a possible exception to this grim summary. She suggests that in countries with commitments to social change—such as the People's Republic of China and socialist states of Eastern Europe—images of women were "exceptionally positive" (pp. 70-71). However, UNESCO (1985) expressed much more pessimism that economic philosophies could, in the end, control the combined forces of traditional and transnational ideologies. This report cites more recent research in Cuba, the Soviet Union, Vietnam, and the People's Republic of China that indicates a tendency to incorporate patriarchal assumptions within revolutionary themes as well as increasing uses of advertising that reflects commercial interests of the West (pp. 86-89).

In addition, it is possible that media content may improve for women as a consequence of efforts to use the media for development, though very little research has addressed this question. Gallagher (1981) speculated that although little evidence was available, images of women in some African countries might be benefiting from development projects (p. 71). A few other scholars have made similar suggestions. For example, Armand Mattelart and MichèleMattelart (1982) describe Mozambique's emphasis on small-scale media at the community level. While women may still be at a disadvantage, they are more likely to participate in media decision making at that level than where media are centralized in cities. This optimism is tempered by research on extension information programs in developing countries—programs often modeled after extension services in the United States. Louise Fortmann (1981) and Kathleen Staudt (1985) found that even though poor women grow 80% of the family food in East Africa, pertinent information on agricultural practices and technologies did not reach these women. Such information was much more likely to reach only the better-off women farmers and men. Likewise, Desai and Krishnaraj (1987) report that educational television and radio programs for women reinforce stereotypes and do not address women's real needs. Instead, women's issues are limited to "sewing, cooking, knitting, . . . how to become a good wife, good mother and improve one's looks." Although women make up 36% of agricultural workers in India, rural development programs are directed at men. At best, women might appear "as folk dancers or as health advisers for pregnant mothers" (p. 284).

Clearly this is a gloomy picture. However, it is important to point out that mass media are not just creators and reinforcers of patriarchal ideologies around the world; they also offer women and other disadvantaged groups a means of placing their issues on the international agenda. How might this be done? There are many possibilities. These include publishing research, such as studies cited in previous paragraphs, and carrying out and publicizing conferences and events. The most common strategy is to increase women working in mainstream media organizations.

Women's Roles in Mainstream Media Organizations

The UNESCO literature reviews indicate that throughout the world much more is known about images of women than about women's participation in media industries. There are many levels for discussion of women's participation. Certainly it is useful to know about women's success in obtaining media jobs, but it is also important to ask whether this will make a difference. In other words, will increased numbers of women change media content and policy? Or will women conform to the practices of existing structures?

Women's jobs in media. In general, employment data on women and media around the world are incomplete and unrealiable (Gallagher, 1981; *Media Asia*, 1987, Seager & Olson, 1986; UNESCO, 1985). Joni Seager and Ann Olson (1986) were able to report simple data on proportions of women in the media work force from only 46 countries, and on both print and broadcast media from only 25 (Chart 34). Their data indicate that women constitute more than 30% of the total media work force in Costa Rica, Chile, Taiwan, and Venezuela (35%), and in Cuba, Thailand, and the Unites States (40%). Women constitute 5% or less of the media work force in Bangladesh (1%), Peru and Japan (2%), and Haiti and Honduras (5%). Countries that reported only broadcast media data reported 30% or more women in the work force in Sweden (30%), Singapore (38%), and Jamaica (50%), and less than 5% in Australia (0%), Austria (2%), Ghana (3%), and Norway (4%).

Perhaps more revealing than numbers of women in media is specific information about their jobs. Gallagher (1981) found that detailed data from Latin America, Africa, and Eastern Europe were practically nonexistent, and data from Asia and Western Europe were incomplete (p. 86). The available data indicate serious problems of vertical and horizontal segregation, as is also the case in the United States.[21] These similarities are not accidental and may be significantly attributable to the impact of, first, colonial powers and, later, Western development agencies and multinational corporations. As previously noted, these various forces introduced not only media but Western assumptions about their operation.[22]

Gallagher (1981) found that throughout the world women are virtually absent from top executive positions, and at the lower levels, women are segregated into lower-paying clerical occupations. The few women in news positions typically handle traditional "women's" features and less important assignments. Other problems discussed by Gallagher include job conditions assuming male roles (e.g., the expectation of high performance in youth with no consideration for childbearing and child care), women's poor record of active union membership, protective legislation for media women (e.g., laws in some countries restricting overtime and night work for women), and inadequate training and education for women in media (pp. 94-99).

UNESCO's (1985) updated review notes a few new studies from several countries. However, none of this more recent information changes the general patterns reported earlier by Gallagher. UNESCO also cites research by Gallagher (1984) on the progress of men and women television employees over a ten-year period (from the early 1970s to 1983) in Belgium, Denmark, France, the Federal Republic of Germany, Ireland, Italy, the Netherlands, and the United Kingdom (pp. 80-81).

> In absolute terms and across all of the organizations studied, the average woman was at a disadvantage compared to the average man right from the date of recruitment. She was appointed to a lower-level job, in a lower salary band. Over time, this difference was actually increased (in organizations in Belgium, Denmark, France, Germany and Italy). (UNESCO, 1985, p. 81)

More recently, UNESCO (1987) published five case studies on professional women in broadcasting in five countries: Canada, Egypt, Ecuador, India, and Nigeria. Again, the similarities were more striking than the differences. In her introduction, Margaret Gallagher (1987a) notes women's minority presence, women's absence from technical jobs and senior management, and women's segregation into certain program-making areas such as educational and children's programs (p. 13).

Despite these pessimistic results, Anne Cooper (1988) reports recent findings that, at least in some ways, women may be making more progress in some Third World media than in the West. Her study of one week's television newscasts in Japan, the United States, Colombia, Jamaica, and Sri Lanka indicates that women have a more prominent role as reporters and anchors in the last three countries. She did, however, observe a bias against women as foreign correspondents in all five countries, as well as an apparently universal tendency to assign women to cover health stories. It is important to note that this type of research is rare. Gertrude Robinson (e.g.,

1981) is among the few other scholars who has conducted comparative research on women in media professions. There is great need for more such comparative research to document and analyze women's roles in mainstream media.

Relationships between media jobs and content. On the surface, it appears that research and political efforts to increase numbers of women employed in mass media, particularly at the higher levels, indicates a liberal feminist orientation. Many radical and socialist feminists would argue that such efforts ignore patriarchal structures that are unlikely to change with the simple addition of women. However, Zillah Eisenstein (1981), a socialist feminist, has argued persuasively that patriarchal structures and products cannot help but change as increasing numbers of women participate in them and appeal to them for support. Empirically, very little media research has addressed the issue.[23]

In their reviews of the minuscule amount of international research on connections between media portrayals and the gender of employees, Gallagher (1981, pp. 108-112) and UNESCO (1985, pp. 64-67) found little evidence that images of women in media are improved when women are producing the images. Although there is some evidence that women approach their work differently from men (e.g., Jensen, 1984),[24] it appears that traditional values usually prevail. For example, Cornelia Butler Flora (1980) found that a sexually explicit series of Venezuelan *fotonovelas* were written primarily by women. Gallagher (1981) cites a British drama producer to point out another problem: Women who do make it to the top may dissociate themselves from younger women, believing that others should have to sacrifice as much as they did (pp. 109-110). Yet another constraint involves traditional professional attitudes, which contribute to the devaluing of women's concerns.

UNESCO (1985) cites Angela Spindler-Brown (1984) to illustrate the extent of the problem via the experiences of an all-women collective working within the mainstream media. The collective, called Broadside, was hired by Channel 4 in the United Kingdom to produce a series of programs for airing in 1983. The group began with the intention of working in a nonhierarchical fashion, but was eventually forced into a traditional style by industrial and trade union pressures.

Even so, the relative lack of structure led to clashes with the Channel 4 management, whose administrative routines demanded individual leadership. Although the programmes—which applied a distinct women's perspective to current affairs issues—were a critical and popular success, *Broadside* was not

commissioned to produce another current affairs series for Channel 4.
(UNESCO, 1985, pp. 66-67)

Recently, Liesbet Van Zoonen (1988) has examined this issue in detail,
pointing out its complexity and the variety of assumptions involved. She
notes that those who assume women will produce different content sometimes make mutually exclusive assumptions: Some assume that there will
be less sex-stereotyped material as women share more equally in producing hard news, while others assume that a higher value will be associated
with "soft," "feminine" news (pp. 42-43). Both points of view may result
in the recruitment of more privileged women, who often have little sensitivity for lower-class and minority women.

In addition, it is important to examine the multifaceted environmental
constraints on the female or male gatekeeper (Gallagher, 1981; Spindler-
Brown, 1984). Of course, substantial environmental constraints are imposed by the transnational corporations that control the production and distribution of media and information equipment and software. Local roles
for women in media are important, but they can never compensate for
women's absence at the highest levels of corporate power. Patriarchal influences from other external sources (e.g., aid agencies) and indigenous
sources (e.g., government structures) pose other obstacles. Two overt
means of resisting patriarchy in mass communication are to develop national media policies that support women's concerns and create alternative
women's media.

Women's Resistance to the Global Media Oppression

National media policies. Feminist theory (e.g., Eisenstein, 1984) supports the value of efforts to change policy and law in order to thwart patriarchal influences—both from external and internal sources.[25] One way of reducing the spread of Western patriarchy and other undesirable Western
influences is to develop national information policies of *dissociation*,
which would allow for drawing selectively on the world's information resources. Hamelink (1983) argues that this is the only way in which developing countries, in particular, can autonomously define their own cultural
values. Unfortunately, most Third World countries have not yet attempted
to develop a real national information policy, though many have taken
some specific actions to limit the activities of transnational corporations
(Mattelart et al., 1984, p. 65). These actions include requiring the use of
the national language in advertising, requiring advertising to be created
within the country, limiting advertising activities in certain sectors such as

pharmaceuticals and food, and fixing quotas on the importation of foreign films and publications. Mattelart et al. note that such policies contain many inconsistencies (p. 66). For example, in Brazil, while there is tight control over the cinema industry, almost none of the restrictions apply to television. Marjorie Ferguson (1986) points out that Britain has imposed a 14% limit on foreign television programming; however, by far most feature films shown and videos rented in Britain originate from other countries, the largest proportion from the United States (pp. 65-66).

Mattelart et al. (1984) suggest that most countries underestimate the power of the transnational market to thwart national efforts to develop autonomous policies (p. 107). They also note that the New World Information and Communication Order's emphasis on quantitative information transfer has allowed many Third World governments to pass over embarrassing questions of power within their own societies and has therefore in fact limited the construction of a new order (p. 11). The same is true of some policies indicating an overemphasis on "cultural identity" or a denunciation of "evil others." For example, efforts to put quotas on imported films may serve merely as a mask for greater profits to sectional local interests, no doubt controlled by upper-class males.[26]

All of these complications suggest that even if national information policies can provide some cultural protection from the transnational market, it is important to ask: *Whose culture* is being protected? (See also Mathieu, 1988, p. 8.) To what degree are women, lower-class women, and minorities forgotten? Therefore, in addition to a policy of external dissociation, each country must develop media policies to protect these groups explicitly from indigenous forms of patriarchy as well—for example, policies on acceptable media representations of women and on women's employment in media industries. In preparation for the 1985 U.N. Decade for Women Conference in Nairobi, Kenya, a questionnaire was distributed to all U.N. member states by the U.N. Centre for Social Development and Humanitarian Affairs (UNESCO, 1985, p. 30). The questionnaire included a section on media policies, including "policies and guidelines requiring media to promote the advancement of women" (p. 33). A total of 95 governments responded to the questionnaire, though the completeness of their responses and interpretations of particular questions varied widely. Responses to this policy question addressed representations of women, women's employment, or both.

With regard to representations, only a few countries indicated they had policies on sex-role portrayals of women in media (e.g., Sweden and Denmark, p. 34), and it was generally unclear to what extent these policies were enforced. Several countries, however, indicated plans to develop regulatory codes on images of women or on antisexist language (pp. 34-36). Since these data were collected, the Canadian Radio-Television and Telecommunications Commission has adopted a detailed set of regulatory codes on representations of women.[27] The adoption of these codes in 1986 followed extensive research to evaluate a two-year trial period (1982-84) of self-regulation.[28] The research indicated that self-regulation was only partially successful. Therefore, the Commission decided that it would make broadcasters' license renewal contingent on following the guidelines developed in 1982, and it also set deadlines for clarifying and strengthening the guidelines. However, this is clearly the exception to the rule, and the possible complications of monitoring the enforcement of these widely publicized regulatory guidelines are as yet unknown.

In addition to information on policies addressing representations of women, the U.N. questionnaire obtained some information on policies related to women's employment in media. While many countries appear to have laws or policies against unequal pay and sex discrimination, many of these laws are vaguely worded and, in most cases, it appears that their effectiveness has not been evaluated. Such policies appear to have little impact on deeply entrenched patterns of inequality, and numerous obstacles to the successful enforcement of policy were reported in the questionnaires:

> Patriarchal or paternalistic attitudes are frequently quoted (Dominican Republic, Greece, Tanzania, Venezuela), and Italy cites loss of interest in the feminist movement. El Salvador lists "*el machismo y el hombrismo*"....Zimbabwe (along with Australia and Niger) mentions lack of funds; it also lists low awareness of the need to increase women's participation in the communication sector, and a lack of a clearly articulated government or private sector policy. Colombia notes "lack of political will". Australia mentions the "implicit feeling" in many organizations "that there exists no problem in this area". The United States notes resistance to change in a traditionally male field of employment. Other commonly cited obstacles are female illiteracy (e.g. Afghanistan), low out-reach of existing media (e.g. the Gambia), and male resistance to competition for jobs (e.g. the Philippines). (UNESCO, 1985, pp. 35-36)

The UNESCO report concluded that laws *against* discrimination were unlikely to be effective without strong accompanying policies of affirmative action. Only eight countries said they practiced affirmative action (Australia, Denmark, Norway, the United States, Sweden, Czechoslovakia, Indonesia, and Mexico). However, only the first five understood the question to refer to efforts to recruit women deliberately for particular posts or grades. The last three gave no indication that they understood the meaning of the term (UNESCO, 1985, pp. 42-43).[29]

Alternative media. Another important means through which women can resist patriarchal and Western hegemonic influences is by establishing their own media organizations. One such organization is the Isis collective (Women's International Information and Communication Service), based in Santiago and Rome, which uses multiple formats to publish audiovisual material and other information for women around the world. A recent publication, *Powerful Images: A Women's Guide to Audiovisual Resources* (Isis International, 1986) is a particularly good source for information on specific films and slide-tape programs dealing with women's concerns around the world. This publication also lists feminist distributors, filmmakers, and grass-roots organizations.

An excellent source of information on international media and media organizations for women is the *Directory of Women's Media*, published annually by the Women's Institute for the Freedom of the Press, based in Washington, D.C.[30] This publication lists women's periodicals, publishing houses, news services, radio and TV groups, regular radio and TV programs, video and cable groups, film and multimedia groups, music groups, art and theater groups, writers' groups, public relations and advertising groups, editorial services, authors' agents, speakers' bureaus, media distributors, media professional and change organizations, bookstores, and mail-order services.

The 1988 edition of this publication clearly reflects the degree to which North American and European women have organized to publicize women's points of view. For example, Table 4.1 summarizes information from the volume on women's periodicals.[31] Alternative media are often considered to be one step in the process of moving a marginal issue into the mainstream (Kessler, 1984). No Third World country lists more than two women's periodicals, while the United States lists well over 300. It is important to note that some of the publications based in the United States and other First World countries appear to have international circulations, and some deal specifically with Third World women's issues.[32] However, their actual diversity of circulation and availability to Third World women is questionable without further research. It should also be noted that not all of the Third World women's publications deal with women's issues in their own countries. For example, Zambia's two periodicals are both produced by the

Table 4.1. Periodicals for Women

Number of Periodicals	Countries
>50	United States (373)
40-49	Canada (46)
30–39	Britain (32)
20-29	—
10-19	Australia (15); West Germany, Netherlands (10)
5-9	France (9); Switzerland (8); Belgium, Italy, Sweden (6); Japan, New Zealand (5)
2-4	Mexico, Peru, Philippines (4); Austria, Brazil, India, Israel, Norway, Senegal, Sri Lanka (3); Chile, Fiji, Greece, Hong Kong, Pakistan, South Korea, Spain, Sudan, Zambia (2)
1	Barbados, Belize, Bolivia, China, Columbia, Denmark, Dominican Republic, Ecuador, Ethiopia, Finland, Ghana, Ireland, Jamaica, Kenya, Lebanon, Singapore, South Africa, Tanzania, Venezuela, Zimbabwe

SOURCE: Data are from Allen (1988).

African National Congress Women's Section and aim to publicize the plight of women living under apartheid.

Data on other women's media and publication activities indicate a similar trend. The United States predominates by far, Canada, Australia, and Europe follow, and a few Third World countries show some limited activity. However, again, some of the First World activity is international in nature. For example, the United States has six women's news services, three of which are international. The most well-known of these is WINGS (Women's International Newsgathering Services), which distributes its radio program via tape and satellite around the world.

It is important to point out that without detailed examinations of each of the various periodicals, wire services, media productions, or media organizations listed in the *Directory of Women's Media*, it is impossible to know to what extent they were or are independent of Western-influenced advertising or of national, patriarchal structures and ideologies. For example, the *Manushi* collective in New Delhi, India, has published a highly successful magazine that offers features and fiction confronting the oppression of women in Indian society. Through hard work and with the help of subscriptions and donations, *Manushi* has not accepted advertising depicting women in oppressive roles—which rules out most advertising

(Kishwar & Vanita, 1984, p. 304). However, the collective's publication has faced much local resistance. On March 11, 1986, *Manushi* workers went so far as to stage a hunger strike at the New Delhi post office to protest "years of harassment by postal department staff" (Sorting out the mail, 1986). The publication has managed to survive such resistance and retain its editorial policy. In contrast, Gallagher (1981) describes efforts by the editorial staff of *Viva* magazine in Nairobi to print stories on issues such as "prostitution, birth control, female circumcision, polygamy and sex education" (p. 138). In 1980 the editor was told to drop such issues because of threats to withdraw advertisements.

> In Kenya, as in most other countries, whether industrialized or developing, there is little choice when advertisers' support is necessary to survival, since about 90 per cent of all advertisements are channelled through a handful of advertising agencies. (Gallagher, 1981, p. 138)

In general, much more descriptive and comparative research is needed on the histories, publication processes, and content of alternative women's periodicals throughout the world, including the impact of advertising on content and on audience interpretations. As advertising becomes necessary, the line between "alternative" and "mainstream" often becomes difficult to distinguish, and the outcome may not be positive for women.

The Future: New Technologies and Global Networking[33]

It is evident from the above discussion that most of the research on women and media can still be described within the traditional categories of broadcast and print media. However, as Margaret Gallagher (1987b) points out, to think globally means to think in terms of an "information economy" where boundaries between traditional categories are likely to become more blurred:

> In the new broadband telecommunications systems, the same "wire" can deliver via our television screens not just traditional television programming, but individualised subscriber programming (pay-TV), videotex news, consumer catalogue and reference information, as well as specialised services such as electronic mailing, electronic shopping, home banking, security alarm systems, and so on. In other words, the television screen is becoming the common delivery station around which a wide range of formerly separate business, information and communications enterprises are converging. (p. 22)[34]

It is crucial that feminists critique the economic and political processes that produce these new information technologies as well as their consequences for women. Evidence from Europe and the United States so far indicates that new satellite, cable, and VCR technologies are not democratizing women's and minorities' access to media. Rather, they are opening up new opportunities for the exploitation of women via advertising and pornography (Gallagher, 1987b). Also, these new media technologies, like housework technologies, are likely to increase women's isolation in their homes.

In addition to critiquing new technologies, women can certainly invent their own technologies, as they have done throughout history (Stanley, 1983). Women also need to find ways to adapt new technologies to their own purposes. For example, both international networking and agenda-setting goals can be served via the creative use of computer technologies. Such networking may include women only or it may involve both men and women with common interests. Of course, computers can facilitate networking via newsletters such as those noted earlier.[35] But computers also make possible direct, inexpensive, two-way information transfers. Roberta Ritson (1988) describes a computer networking project for Health Learning Materials (HLM) coordinated by the World Health Organization in Geneva. Training materials are written in four languages and at least 20 participating countries are now being equipped with compatible microcomputers. Also, Norene Janus is directing CARINET, an international computer communications network that aims to provide low-cost information on a variety of development subjects.[36] Judy Smith and Ellen Balka (1988) argue that computer literacy is necessary for women's empowerment in a technological world. Of course, such empowerment means overcoming the computer "reticence" (Turkle, 1988) that afflicts many women.

There are many other obstacles women face in efforts to participate in and perhaps redirect the communications revolution (Gallagher, 1987b). The economic power of advertising and other transnational corporations are among the most serious of these obstacles. An important way to fight economic power is through political organization, and, at least in some countries, it appears that political organization is paying off in new policies on sex-role portrayals in the media and in affirmative action hiring policies.

In most instances, however, women have played little or no role in media policymaking. Achieving such participatory status will require a combination of strategies, including information sharing and support through networking. Such networking could be enhanced and supported via collaborative, *feminist* research among women—or perhaps between women and men—of different cultures. Feminist research does not imply Western forms of feminsm. It implies a common theoretical and political concern with women's oppression, and an understanding that women of each culture have the right and deserve the support to seek means of addressing their own problems of oppression.

SHARED, GLOBAL GENDER CONCERNS

In sum, there are many reasons to consider international perspectives in studies of gender and media inequities in the United States. First, we need to understand the power of the transnational economy and its often-blatant support for women's oppression in relation to media. Second, our efforts to study representations at home and their links to economic motives should take on added importance as we understand the extent to which these representations are exported abroad and also copied in local, foreign productions. Third, research on women's employment becomes more important as we see Western organizational values transferred via communication support strategies in development programs. (Of course, much development aid merely strengthens media organizations that were first set in place by colonial powers.) Fourth, we can all learn much by studying activities of resistance carried out by women in other countries—resistance via research, policymaking, and alternative feminist media. Finally, recent advances in telecommunication and information technologies make it imperative that women learn to use these technologies and collaborate internationally to use them for feminist purposes.

NOTES

1. A note on terminology: I sometimes have difficulty deciding whether to use the term *woman/women*, *gender* (the social construction of sexual difference), or *feminism* (the theoretical and political stance that women—as a gender—are oppressed and should seek change). However, this book and chapter are about *women, as a gender, from feminist perspectives*. I use all three terms frequently, but always with this underlying assumption. Therefore, while I have tried to make

contextually appropriate selections, the reader will notice instances where alternative terminology might also be appropriate.

2. Cees Hamelink prefers the term cultural *synchronization* over *imperialism*. *Imperialism* implies direct, aggressive acts by one culture to influence another. But world trends toward the desire for and adoption of Western ways are much more subtle than that. Hamelink points out many instances where cultural autonomy is being lost, but where acts of imperialism are not obvious.

3. A 16-member commission (headed by Sean MacBride of Ireland and including communication scholars and journalists from all major regions of the world) was established by UNESCO in December 1977 to carry out a comprehensive analysis of communication problems in society and make recommendations. The commission's report, popularly called the MacBride Report, was submitted to the director-general in February 1980 (International Commission for the Study of Communication Problems, 1980, pp. 295-297). I should note that the term *New World Information and Communication Order*, first used at the 1978 UNESCO General Conference, was also used in the MacBride Report, and appears to be the most popular current descriptor for the desired new order. However, other terms such as *New International Information Order* were used prior to 1978 and continue to be preferred by some (Hamelink, 1983, pp. 69-72).

4. The term *Third World* is used in the conventional sense to refer to countries that are characterized by less industrialization, less urbanization, greater poverty, and generally less economic development than First World countries. Of course, an emphasis on such economic distinctions appears to equate countries as diverse as Thailand, Kenya, the Philippines, and Ecuador, ignoring immense variation among them on other dimensions. I should also note that I use the terms *Third World*, *less developed countries*, and *developing countries* interchangeably in this chapter, though the latter two terms are also problematic: *less developed* because it also prioritizes economic development, and *developing* because it implies that First World countries are fully developed. See Pletsch (1981) for an excellent discussion of the "three worlds" concept.

5. Such circumstances include "caste in India, predominance of export-oriented industries in South-East Asia, significance of multinationals in Singapore, Malaysia and South Korea, sex tourism in Thailand and migration pattern in Philippines" (Desai & Krishnaraj, 1987, p. 3).

6. According to Thomas Guback and Tapio Varis (1982), a *transnational corporation*, or TNC, "is a corporation that owns or controls production or service facilities outside the country in which it is based" (p. 6). They further note that "instead of TNCs, one could also speak of multinational, international, or global corporations, firms, entreprises, or companies" (p. 6, summarizing United Nations, 1974, p. 25). Therefore, in this chapter the terms *transnational* and *multinational* will be used interchangeably to refer to large corporations with multiple branches in countries other than their home countries.

7. See the MacBride Report for a listing of the 15 transnational corporations that had the most control over communications operations at that time (International Commission for the Study of Communication Problems, 1980, p. 109). Of the 15, 11 were based in the United States. Since then foreign, particularly Japanese, corporations have gained a much larger share of the transnational market, including the communications market. (For current data on the largest U.S. and foreign transnationals, see "Special Report," 1988.)

8. Also, in general, videotex has developed into a male-controlled, male-oriented system with little information of interest to women (Gallagher, 1987b, pp. 25-26).

9. There has been much research on the gender impact of new industries that has indicated that important market activities by women were often displaced by factories staffed by men (e.g., Cain, 1981; Desai & Krishnaraj, 1987). Gallagher (1987b) cites evidence that women have lost out similarly in the production of new information technologies (p. 23).

10. These health risks are portrayed strikingly in *The Global Assembly Line*, a film coproduced by Maria Patricia Fernandez Kelly and Loraine Gray and distributed by New Day Films.

11. Steeves and Arbogast (in press) provide a more theoretical discussion of issues related to media representations of women, particularly in the Third World.

12. UNESCO is currently editing *World Communication Report*, a detailed volume on the status of mass media in most countries of the world. Each country has also been asked to supply information on women and media, including representations, employment, alternative media, networking, and legislation. Unfortunately, this volume was not available at the time of this writing.

13. *Media Asia* (1987) contains articles on women and media in the Philippines, Malaysia, Japan, Bangladesh, Nepal, Pakistan, India, Sri Lanka, and South Korea.

14. *Media Report to Women* is a bimonthly newsletter with reports of research, conferences, and political and legal activity related to women and media around the world. For information, write to Communication Research Associates, Inc., 10606 Mantz Rd., Silver Spring, MD 20903-1228.

15. *WIN News* is published quarterly and includes information on women's activities worldwide, with considerable emphasis on the Third World. Most issues have a section on "Women and Media," with information on recent publications and events. For information, write to Fran P. Hosken, 107 Grant St., Lexington, MA 02173.

16. *Sex-Roles Within Mass Media* is published once or twice a year in Stockholm, Sweden, and is financed by the Equality Group of the Swedish Television Company. Its purposes include maintaining an international mailing list of persons interested in gender and media, exchanging up-to-date information related to gender and media, and informing about upcoming meetings and

seminars. For information, write to Madeleine Kleberg, School of Journalism, University of Stockholm, Gjorwellsgatan 26, S-112 60, Stockholm, Sweden.

17. *Echo* is published quarterly by the Association of African Women for Research and Development (AAWORD), a pan-African nongovernmental association based in Dakar, Senegal. AAWORD has organized various research working groups, including a working group on Women and the Mass Media in Africa, which is currently in the process of organizing a bibliography that will include English, French, and Arabic literature (see *Echo*, Vol. 1, Nos. 2-3, 1986, pp. 7-8). For information, write to AAWORD, B.P. 3304, Dakar, Senegal.

18. The International Women's Tribune Centre (IWTC) was founded following the 1975 U.N. Decade for Women conference in Mexico City. The Centre's resources include newsletters in English, Spanish, and French related to women in development issues, regional resource manuals with information and citations on women's organizations and projects, development training manuals, information bulletins, annotated bibliographies, and contact lists (IWTC, 1984, p. iii). For information, write to IWTC, 777 United Nations Plaza, New York, NY 10017.

19. A *fotonovela* is a romance story in a comic book format, with pictures and captions. *Fotonovelas* are popular throughout much of the world, including Latin America, Spain, Italy, and parts of Africa. However, the only studies of this genre have referred to Latin America.

20. Hall's (1980b) suggestion that media messages may be read in a "dominant," "negotiated," or "resistant" fashion has been applied in efforts to identify circumstances under which dominant-hegemonic codes may be less effective for some women (e.g., Steiner, 1988). Also useful is Gramsci's theory of hegemony, which posits ideological institutions as a site for hegemonic cultural definition (e.g., Fiske, 1987, pp. 259-260).

21. The term *vertical segregation* refers to a concentration of women at lower organizational levels; *horizontal segregation* refers to their concentration in specific types of jobs. Both types of segregation characterize women's roles in U.S. media, despite the "feminization" phenomenon, discussed in other chapters in this volume.

22. Many studies of women in development have domonstrated that when cash economies were introduced, control of cash (via jobs) was primarily given to men. As in the West, women were assigned to the lower-paying, lower-prestige positions or to unpaid labor at home—or both (see, for example, Robertson & Berger, 1986).

23. There has been little such research in the United States either, as indicated by Muriel Cantor's (1987) recent report to the Benton Foundation.

24. Else Jensen (1984) found, in a study of women reporters and producers in Danish television, that women tend more often than men to make use of techniques that indicate authenticity, such as on-the-spot reporting, the use of documentary

material and interviews, and efforts to make connections to everyday life (cited by UNESCO, 1985, p. 65).

25. Steeves and Arbogast (in press) discuss the literature of development communication and feminist theory in relation to media law and policy in Third World contexts.

26. Ferguson (1986) points out another complication in devising national media policy in the face of transnational expansion: "Consumers buying their own dish aerials are beyond the reach of the receiving countries' regulations dealing with objective news reporting, advertising standards, questions of taste and decency or material suitable for children" (p. 62).

27. A copy of this policy statement, "Sex-Role Stereotyping in the Broadcast Media: Policy Statement" (CTRC Public Notice 1986-351) can be obtained by writing to the Canadian Radio-Television and Telecommunications Commission, Ottawa, Ontario K1A 0N2, Canada.

28. This research—on the portrayal of sex roles in Canadian television programming and advertising and radio programming and advertising—is presented in four volumes, all published in 1985 by the Canadian Radio-Television and Telcommunications Commission (CRTC). The reports indicate just how far behind the United States is in documenting the content of mass media. For example, Judith Cramer's chapter in this volume on radio indicates little recent U.S. research, while the CRTC has recently published two detailed volumes.

29. A related quesion asked whether specific recruitment policies are applied to the promotion of women. Only six countries (Australia, Denmark, New Zealand, Norway, the United States, Venezuela) gave a "yes" response, and the explanations and indications of supporting legal instruments varied considerably (UNESCO, 1985, pp. 41-42).

30. Information on this and related publications can be obtained by writing to Martha Leslie Allen, Editor, *Directory of Women's Media*, Women's Institute for Freedom of the Press, 3306 Ross Place, N.W., Washington, DC 20008.

31. These periodicals vary considerably, as indicated in Marilyn Crafton Smith's chapter in this volume on alternative feminist media. Themes include feminist legal issues, feminist political concerns, women's health, lesbian concerns, minority women, women's arts and literature, women and religion, women's sports, and feminist academic scholarship. Publications *not* listed are traditional, commercial women's magazines such as *McCall's*, *Ladies' Home Journal*, and *Family Circle*. Outside of the United States, the most successful alternative feminist periodicals and their respective circulations are *Emma* in West Germany (300,000), *Courage* in West Germany (70,000), *Spare Rib* in the United Kingdom (30,000), *Manushi* in India (10,000), *ISIS Women's World* in Italy (5,000), and *Broadsheet* in New Zealand (4,000). In contrast, *Ms*. has a circulation of 463,000 (Seager & Olson, 1986, Chart 34).

32. According to the *1988 Directory of Women's Media*, U.S. publications with international content and circulations outside of the U.S. include *Media Report to Women* (previously noted), *Connexions*, *Feminist Futures International Network*, and *International League of Women Composers Newsletter*. U.S. publications that emphasize Third World women's concerns include *Women's International Network (WIN) News* (previously noted), *The Tribune*, publication of the previously noted International Women's Tribune Centre, *Seeds*, *African Women Rising*, *Third Woman*, *The Voice of Guatemalan Women*, *Committee on South Asian Women Bulletin*, and *Asian Women United* (see Allen, 1988).

33. See also Ramona Rush and Donna Allen (in press).

34. Further, Rolf Wigand (1988) describes Intergrated Services Digital Networks (ISDN), "a public end-to-end, digital telecommunications network providing the capability to transmit voice, data, facsimile, telemetry, signaling (or dialing), and slow-motion video, either simultaneously or separately, on a single telephone line" (p. 30). According to Wigand, France and Germany already have advanced planning for ISDN.

35. These were *Media Report to Women*, *WIN News*, *Sex Roles Within Mass Media*, and *Echo*. In addition, Elli Lester-Massman has compiled a list of resources—primarily periodicals and newsletters—for information on women and communication in development. This list is available through the Women's Studies Program at the University of Wisconsin-Madison. It is published, in part, in *Feminist Collections*, Vol. 10, No. 1.

36. CARINET is described in *Development Communication Report* (1988, Vol. 60, p. 6).

REFERENCES

Allen, Martha Leslie. (Ed.). (1988). *1988 directory of women's media*. Washington, DC: Women's Institute for Freedom of the Press.

Althusser, Louis. (1971). *Lenin and philosophy and other essays* (B. Brewster, Trans.). London: New Left.

Barrett, Michèle. (1980). *Women's oppression today*. London: Verso.

Boulding, Elise. (1981). Integration into what? Reflections on development planning for women. In Roslyn Dauber & Melinda Cain (Eds.), *Women and technological change in developing countries* (pp. 9-32). Boulder, CO: Westview.

Cain, Melinda. (1981). Java, Indonesia: The introduction of rice processing technology. In Roslyn Dauber & Melinda Cain (Eds.), *Women and technological change in developing countries* (pp. 193-204). Boulder, CO: Westview.

Cantor, Muriel G. (1987). *Women and diversity*. Unpublished report to the Benton Foundation.

Connolly, Clara, & Segal, Lynne. (1986). Feminism and class politics: A round-table discussion. *Feminist Review, 23*, 13-20.

Cooper, Anne M. (1988, July). *Television's invisible women: A five-nation study of anchors, reporters and correspondents.* Paper presented at the annual convention of the Association for Education in Journalism and Mass Communication, Portland, OR.

Cooper, Anne M., & Davenport, Lucinda D. (1987) Newspaper coverage of international women's decade: Feminism and conflict. *Journal of Communication Inquiry, 11*(1), 108-113.

Desai, Neera, & Krishnaraj, Maithreyi. (1987). *Women and society in India.* New Delhi: S. Narain & Sons.

Eisenstein, Zillah. (1981). *The radical future of liberal feminism.* New York: Longman.

Eisenstein, Zillah. (1984). *Feminism and sexual inequality: Crisis in liberal America.* New York: Monthly Review Press.

Ferguson, Margorie. (1986). The challenge of neo-technological determinism for communication systems, industry and culture. In M. Ferguson (Ed.), *New communication technologies and the public interest* (pp. 52-71). London: Sage.

Fiske, John. (1987). British cultural studies and television. In Robert C. Allen (Ed.), *Channels of discourse* (pp. 254-289). Chapel Hill: University of North Carolina Press.

Flora, Cornelia Butler. (1980). Women in Latin American fotonovelas: From Cinderella to Mata Hari. *Women's Studies International Quarterly, 3*(1), 95-104.

Fortmann, Louise. (1981). The plight of the invisible farmer: The effect of national agricultural policy on women in Africa. In Roslyn Dauber & Melinda Cain (Eds.), *Women and technological change in developing countries* (pp. 205-214). Boulder, CO: Westview.

Gallagher, Margaret. (1981). *Unequal opportunities: The case of women and the media.* Paris: UNESCO.

Gallagher, Margaret. (1984). *Employment and positive action for women in the television organizations of the EEC member states.* Brussels: Commission of the European Communities.

Gallagher, Margaret. (1987a). Introduction. In UNESCO (Ed.), *Women and media-decision-making* (pp. 11-16). Paris: UNESCO.

Gallagher, Margaret. (1987b). Redefining the communications revolution. In Helen Baehr & Gillian Dyer (Eds.), *Boxed in: Women and television* (pp. 19-37). New York: Pandora.

Guback, Thomas, & Varis, Tapio. (1982). *Transnational communication and cultural industries* (Reports and Papers on Mass Communication, No. 92). Paris: UNESCO.

Hall, Stuart. (1980a). Cultural studies and the centre: Some problematics and problems. In Stuart Hall, Dorothy Hobson, Andrew Lowe, & Paul Willis (Eds.), *Culture, media and language: Working papers in cultural studies, 1972-79* (pp. 15-47). London: Hutchinson.

Hall, Stuart. (1980b). Encoding/decoding. In Stuart Hall, Dorothy Hobson, Andrew Lowe, & Paul Willis (Eds.), *Culture, media and language: Working papers in cultural studies, 1972-79* (pp. 128-138). London: Hutchinson.

Hamelink, Cees. (1983). *Cultural autonomy in global communications.* New York: Longman.

International Commission for the Study of Communication Problems. (1980). *Many voices, one world* (MacBride report). Paris: UNESCO.

International Women's Tribune Centre. (1984). *Women using media for social change.* New York: Author.

Isis International. (1986). *Powerful images: A women's guide to audiovisual resources.* Rome: Author.

Jensen, Else. (1984). *Video and sex-specific socialization.* Paper presented at the Fourteenth Conference of the International Association for Mass Communication Research, Prague.

Kessler, Lauren. (1984). *The dissident press.* Beverly Hills, CA: Sage.

Kishwar, Madhu, & Vanita, Ruth. (Eds.). (1984). *In search of answers: Indian women's voices from Manushi*. London: Zed.

Leonardo, Micaela Di. (1985). Morals, mothers, and militarism: Anti-militarism and feminist theory. *Feminist Studies, 11*(3), 600-617.

Lester-Massman, Elli. (1988). Recent periodicals on women in development: Challenging the paradigm? *Feminist Collections, 10*(1), 8-11.

Lim, Linda Y. C. (1981). Women's work in multinational electronics factories. In Roslyn Dauber & Melinda Cain (Eds.), *Women and technological change in developing countries* (pp. 181-191). Boulder, CO: Westview.

Mathieu, Nichole-Claude. (1988). "Woman" in ethnology: The other of the other, and the other of the self. *Feminist Studies, 14*(1), 3-14.

Mattelart, Armand, Delcourt, Xavier, & Mattelart, Michèle. (1984). *International image markets* (David Buxton, Trans.). London: Comedia.

Mattelart, Michèle. (1986). *Women, media and crisis: Femininity and disorder*. London: Comedia.

Mattelart, Michèle, & Mattelart, Armand (1982). "Small" technologies: The case of Mozambique. *Journal of Communication, 32*(2), 75-79.

Media Asia. (1987). *14*(4), 181-242.

Murdock, Graham, & Janus, Noreene. (1985). *Mass communications and the advertising industry* (Reports and Papers on Mass Communication, No. 97). Paris: UNESCO.

Pletsch, Carl E. (1981). The three worlds, or the division of social science labor, circa 1950-1975. *Comparative Studies in Society and History, 23*, 565-590.

Ritson, Roberta. (1988). Sharing health materials and information in developing countries. *Development Communication Report, 60*, 1 & 5.

Robertson, Claire, & Berger, Iris. (Eds.). (1986). *Women and class in Africa*. New York: Africana.

Robinson, Gertude J. (1981). *Female print journalists in Canada and the United States: A professional profile and comparison* (Working Papers in Communications). Montreal: McGill University.

Rush, Ramona, & Allen, Donna. (Eds.). (in press). *Communication at the crossroads: The gender gap connection*. Norwood, NJ: Ablex.

Santa Cruz, Adriana, & Erazo, Viviana. (1980). *Compropolitan: el orden transnacional y su modelo femino*. Mexico City: Editorial Nueva Imagen.

Schiller, Herbert I. (1981). *Who knows: Information in the age of the Fortune 500*. Norwood, NJ: Ablex.

Seager, Joni, & Olson, Ann. (1986). *Women in the world: An international atlas*. New York: Simon & Schuster.

Smith, Judy, & Balka, Ellen. (1988). Chatting on a feminist computer network. In Cheris Kramarae (Ed.), *Technology and women's voices* (pp. 82-97). New York: Routledge & Kegan Paul.

Sorting out the mail sorting division. (1986, March 11). *Manushi*, p. 40.

Special report on international business. (1988). *Forbes, 142*(2), 203-254.

Spindler-Brown, Angela. (1984). *Transforming television: Feminist experience in the U.K.* Paper presented at the Fourteenth Conference of the International Association for Mass Communication Research, Prague.

Srinivasan, Mangalam. (1981). Impact of selected industrial technologies on women in Mexico. In Roslyn Dauber & Melinda Cain (Eds.), *Women and technological change in developing countries* (pp. 89-108). Boulder, CO: Westview.

Stanley, Autumn. (1983). Women hold up two-thirds of the sky: Notes for a revised history of technology. In Joan Rothschild (Ed.), *Machina ex dea: Feminist perspectives on technology* (pp. 5-22). New York: Pergamon.

Staudt, Kathleen. (1985). *Agricultural policy implementation: A case study from Western Kenya.* West Hartford, CT: Kumarian.

Steeves, H. Leslie. (1987). Feminist and communication in development: Ideology, law, ethics, practice. *Critical Studies in Mass Communication, 4,* 95-135.

Steeves, H. Leslie, & Arbogast, Rebecca A. (in press). Feminist and communication in development: Ideology, law, ethics. *Progress in Communication Sciences, 11.*

Steiner, Linda. (1988). Oppositional decoding as an act of resistance. *Critical Studies in Mass Communication, 5,* 1-15.

Turkle, Sherry. (1988). Computational reticence: Why women fear the intimate machine. In Cheris Kramarae (Ed.), *Technology and women's voices* (pp. 41-61). New York: Routledge & Kegan Paul.

UNESCO. (1985). *Communication in the service of women: A report on action and research programmes, 1980-1985.* Paris: Author.

UNESCO. (Ed.). (1987). *Women and media-decision-making.* Paris: Author.

United Nations. (1974). *The impact of multinational corporations on development and international relations.* New York: Author.

Van Zoonen, Liesbet. (1988). Rethinking women and the news. *European Journal of Communication, 3,* 35-53.

Ward, Kathryn B. (1986, July). *Women and transnational corporation employment: A world-system and feminist analysis* (Working Paper 120). East Lansing: Michigan State University.

Wigand, Rolf T. (1988). Integrated services digital networks: Concepts, policies, and emerging issues. *Journal of Communication, 38*(1), 29-49.

5

Strategies on Studying Women of Color in Mass Communication

a. Overview and Theoretical Framework

JANE RHODES

When studying the literature on women and mass media, it is becoming increasingly important to ask, What women are represented by these data? Invariably, the research either has failed to distinguish among women's ethnic and racial identities or has examined only white women. Although the second and third waves of feminism have directed increasing attention to the concerns of women of color, this trend has failed to extend into mass communication research.

In the last decade, there has emerged a growing body of writing about Black women in history, literature, sociology, and psychology. (This discussion will review research by and about Black women, but it is important to note that it also reflects similar trends in the state of scholarship regarding all underrepresented groups of women—Hispanic, Asian American, Native American, Jewish, lesbian, disabled, and so on.) For example, one Black feminist literary scholar has traced the stereotyped roles of Black women in Anglo and Afro-American literature, such as the mammy, the concubine, the tragic mullato, and the matriarch, and suggests that Black women writers such as Paule Marshall, Toni Morrison, Gwendolyn Brooks, and Zora Neale Hurston have been instrumental in transforming these images (Christian, 1985).

Historical studies in the past 15 years have gathered the writings and documents of Black women since colonial times (Lerner, 1973), studied the emotional, physical, and sexual subjugation of female slaves (D. G. White, 1985), uncovered stories of Black women as leaders in the antislavery, women's suffrage, and civil rights movements (Giddings, 1984), and analyzed the Black woman's resistance to slavery and sexual oppression (Davis, 1981), as well as numerous other accomplishments.

Social scientists, beginning with Ladner in 1971, have acknowledged the Black woman's experience as a legitimate area of study, and numerous articles and books have been generated in the past 15 years that critique and analyze existing scholarship and create new theoretical perspectives.

But in the field of mass communication research, such progress is virtually nonexistent. A search of the literature in broadcasting, print media, advertising, or public relations is likely to come up blank when Black women are identified as the central focus for study. For example, a study I undertook in the spring of 1988 to explore dramatic representations of Black women on prime-time television uncovered one article about Black women (Dates, 1987), among dozens of publications about the portrayal of women and sexual stereotypes. When Black women were mentioned it was because, when faced with the data, researchers were shocked by the blatant stereotyping of Black women, or the fact that they were "largely ignored and excluded from significant TV roles" (Hinton, Seggar, et al., 1974, p. 423).

To date, research in all the areas of mass communication that have explored gender have focused on white women, and research exploring race has looked at Black men or Black people as a composite group. The intersection of race and gender, as it is manifest in the experiences of all women of color, has not been integrated into the research agenda. These trends are equally evident in quantitative and qualitative research. Recent discussions of gender, race, and class rooted in critical theory have sought a framework for discussing women of color and low-income women in communication studies. But little original research has been published to put this developing analysis into practice.

One exception has been in media history, particularly in studies of women's roles in the press. Work in the last decade has revealed that there were several dozen Black women journalists working for the Black press at the end of the nineteenth century, the most famous being Ida Wells-Barnett (Beasley & Gibbons, 1981, pp. 38-46); and women of color have gained an increasing (but still grossly underrepresented) presence in the nation's newsrooms in the past 15 years (Mills, 1988, pp. 174-195). But gaps in the history of Black women in the media continue to override what we know.

This exclusion of women of color in the research literature parallels their marginal status in society. Several factors are especially relevant:

(1) Economic status. Minority women have been and continue to be on the lowest rungs of the nation's economic ladder; they earn less money and own less property than white women or men in their racial group and are perceived to have limited economic power. Thus they have historically not been considered a lucrative target for advertisers, which would generate market research. Such proprietary research is frequently the launching point for scholarly examination in mass communication, but as long as women of color are ignored by advertisers there is less incentive for academics to engage in such inquiry.

(2) Political power. Just as they are perceived to lack economic clout, women of color are not viewed as having a significant voice in our system of governance. There are no women of color at the gubernatorial level, and their presence in Congress has been scanty since Shirley Chisholm's election; they are scattered in very small numbers through the courts and local governments, and their role in the political process is frequently behind the scenes. Thus they are less likely to be the focus of public opinion polling and other measurements of political trends, and they are even less likely to be included in media content regarding politics, except as token representatives.

(3) Body of knowledge. Because the overall state of scholarship on Black women is relatively new, many researchers are handicapped by their lack of knowledge. In general, white scholars, unless trained in some area of minority studies, have little familiarity with minority culture and history. This dilemma is even more acute when considering the experiences of minority women. The integration of women of color's experiences into academic curricula is crucial to developing scholarly interest in the subject.

(4) The women's movement. Bell Hooks (1984) suggests that poor and nonwhite women were alienated from the early white feminist movement because it was frequently antimale, it only "provided bourgeois white women with a public forum for expressing their anger," and it did not offer potential solutions to minority women's problems (pp. 68, 70, 75). Black women activists and scholars frequently shunned issues about gender, which they perceived to be irrelevant to their lives. Feminism was seen as a threat to the stability of the Black community, and black women were, and still are, often faced with demands from white feminists and Black men to choose which form of oppression is most important.

Black feminism emerged from the juncture between antiracist and antisexist struggles and has been most visibly manifest in the works of Black women writers (E. F. White, 1985, p. 7). In the 1980s a small group of

Black women have begun to construct a theoretical base that focuses on their status in society, and that theory has influenced much of the scholarly progress in other disciplines cited above. Beginning with the publication of the Combahee River Collective statement in 1977 (see Hull, Scott, & Smith, 1982), Black feminists have articulated a commitment to focus attention on the distinct needs and experiences of Black women and a critique of sexism in the Black community, while at the same time acknowledging a deep connection to and solidarity with Black men. Black feminism has distinguished itself from mainstream white feminism by insisting that the simultaneity of oppression based on race, gender, and class be the focus of inquiry.

Now that Black feminist theory has found a voice, it is time to apply it to the broad range of communication research questions that are being pursued today. If mass media are a prime force in the transmission of culture and societal values and norms, why have Black women been systematically excluded from this process? What is the interplay among advertising, marketing, public relations, and media content that enables the communications industries to pay scant attention to Black women as a group? Have the mass media deliberately or unintentionally contributed to the political and economic forces in America that have perpetuated Black women's low status?

At this stage, there are few data or analyses available to begin answering these questions. As other contributors to this book have discovered, we frequently do not know how many Black women are in the media work force, or in the audience. We do not know what their reactions to media content are, or how other consumers interpret media representations of Black women. We do not know the stories of many Black women's "firsts" in journalism and the entertainment media. We know little about their education, training, and job preferences as mass communicators.

The first step toward filling these gaps is to create a baseline of data; studies investigating women or minorities must separate women of color and evaluate their responses as those of a distinct population. Research projects must be developed to produce detailed audience profiles of Black women and other women of color at all economic levels. Communication researchers must familiarize themselves with the information accumulated in the social sciences and humanities, which have begun to address these and related questions. This research agenda must also be undertaken by researchers employing all methodologies; it is not enough for historians to study famous Black women, or for empirical analysts to count the numbers of Black women in a media market. Scholars in critical and cultural studies must begin to move beyond the analysis of class and gender and recognize that they too have ignored large segments of society.

It is not just a cliché to conclude that research on Black women in mass communication has barely exposed the tip of the iceberg. It will be generations before there is a body of knowledge sufficient to establish a broad picture of Black women's experience. And it will be a long time before there are enough scholars interested in this area to produce the flood of literature that can now be found on women and gender issues. An important key to these developments will be the cultivation and training of Black women scholars, who number only a handful in communication studies today. We can be optimistic in believing that the more we know about Black women and mass media, the better equipped we will be to press for changes in their representation as communicators, as the audience, and in media images.

REFERENCES

Beasley, Maurine, & Gibbons, Sheila. (1981). *Women in media: A documentary source book.* Washington, DC: Women's Institute for Freedom of the Press.

Christian, Barbara. (1985). *Black feminist criticism: Perspectives on Black women writers.* New York: Pergamon.

Dates, Jannette L. (1987). Gimme a break: African-American women on prime time television. In Alan Wells (Ed.), *Mass media and society.* Lexington, MA: D. C. Heath.

David, Angela. (1981). *Women, race and class.* New York: Random House.

Giddings, Paula. (1984). *When and where I enter: The impact of Black women on race and class in America.* New York: William Morrow.

Hinton, James L., Seggar, John L., et al. (1974). Tokenism and improving imagery of Blacks in TV drama and Comedy: 1973. *Journal of Broadcasting, 18*(4).

Hooks, Bell. (1984). *Feminist theory: From margin to center.* Boston: South End.

Hull, Gloria T., Scott, Patricia Bell, & Smith, Barbara. (Eds.). (1982). *But some of us are brave.* Old Westbury, NY: Feminist Press.

Ladner, Joyce. (1971). *Tomorrow's tomorrow: The Black woman.* Garden City, NY: Anchor.

Lerner, Gerda. (Ed.). (1973). *Black women in white America.* New York: Vintage.

Mills, Kay. (1988). *From the women's pages to the front pages.* New York: Dodd, Mead.

White, Deborah Gray. (1985). *Ar'n't I a woman? Female slaves in the plantation South.* New York: W. W. Norton.

White, E. Frances. (1985). Listening to the voices of Black feminism. *Radical America, 18*(2-3), 7-25.

b. Strategies for Research on Black Women and Mass Communication

PAULA MATABANE

During Spring 1988, I naively sought out some of my fellow Black women colleagues to participate in a panel discussion of prospects for mass communication research on Black women from a feminist or nonfeminist perspective. I thought that would be an easy enough task, but much to my surprise I met a wall of disinterest and in some cases hostility. Most were not interested in discussing anything related to feminism. I remembered the doubting looks some colleagues had given me eight years ago when I attended a National Women's Studies Association convention, but I really had not anticipated that in 1988 those same negative attitudes would prevail. Many Black women academics still feel alienated from feminism and are not enthused about pursuing the study of women. This lessens the prospects for developing a theoretically advanced body of mass communication research on Black women.

To promote this kind of research, we need a clearly articulated understanding of why we deem its pursuit important. The research has to have credibility for the researcher and for the environment in which he or she is working. For the Black woman in academia this is doubly important. Let me give you an example. I attended a local PTA equity conference during which the group leaders asked the participants to indicate in what work environments they had experienced they had felt strongly a part of the work group and an equal among their peers. The white men, the white women, and the Black men were able to identify settings where they had felt accepted. Without exception, the Black women said they had never been in work situations where they felt fully accepted. They were isolated either as women or as Blacks. No other group faced that dual rejection. The Black women present were able to identify only social settings—their clubs, churches, and other subcultural group—where they felt fully comfortable.

These responses drove home to me how much Black women are the outsiders in most social situations. I think some of the hostility that Black women feel toward feminism may stem partly from their perpetual "outsider" designation. They may distrust another label that may further that position. To be a feminist and a Black woman in academe may often be seen as courting rejection, especially on a Black campus where the women's movement is distrusted as an unwanted divisive force in the quest to achieve Black unity. One's credibility and avenues for promotion and tenure may be severely curtailed as a result.

It is also possible that many Black women may not feel any urgency to pursue women's studies because their social identification has usually revolved around being Black. One experiences so many negatives as a Black person, the experience of being discriminated against as a woman is often blurred.

Race is the major marked category in the United States. The work done by anthropologist Leath Mullings (1980) suggests that at the end of slavery, a number of Black women refused to go to work. This was not in emulation of white women, but rather a silent protest for higher wages for Black men. Black men could be paid substantially less if they were perceived as having only to earn enough to feed themselves and not also their families. Black women saw their fate as tied up with that of Black men, not with that of white women. In spite of the political alliances that have been forged around different civil rights and workplace issues between Black and white women, Black women have been very consistent in their primary identification with race and not gender.

The way in which the struggle for sex equality has been played out in the larger white society has also influenced Black women's attitudes toward the feminist movement. The media's emphasis on bra burning, battles of the sexes and lesbianism has alienated many Black women. Black women have long considered themselves in the forefront of the struggle for women's rights, by virtue of their working woman/mother roles, most often in hard, low-paying jobs. Issues of pay equity, child care, maternity leave, and health care are much more important to them than whether or not a white suburban housewife will wear a bra.

Then there's the *Color Purple* and *Women of Brewster Street* syndrome, reflecting a bias in the book publishing industry, which has a monopoly control over the marketplace for popular literature. Commercial publishers seem to prefer the work of the more radical Black women feminist writers, who tend to be very critical of Black men. The problem that many Black women have with this is not necessarily that the writers are not telling the truth; rather, Blacks grew up with the feeling that as a race we should not air our dirty laundry in front of the white world. Further, there is little balance in the perspective on Black life presented by the major publishing houses. The seeming predominance or preeminence of Black feminist writers appears as a conscious decision on the part of the white publishing world to present a distorted image of Afro-American life. The feminist or womanist perspective from which these Black women write begins to represent something that other Black women want to avoid. As a result, a lot of Black women do not want to be identified expressly with feminism or even generally with women's issues.

We also should consider that women in academe are not necessarily touched by the same problems that haunt the lives of nonprofessional, working-class women. Our lives are not typical, so we must consciously seek to develop a theoretical as well as a practical understanding of the intersection of race, gender, and class. We must define these issues in a manner that does not make other Black women feel threatened, but enhances our mutual understanding of the critical importance of women's studies to the well-being of Black people in general.

I think we must begin examining specific theoretical issues of Black women and mass communication if we are to contribute to a positive resolution of some of the problems facing us. Black women face triple oppression or jeopardy by virtue of their race, gender, and social class (which, for most Black women, is the lower-paid sector of the working class). In addition, there are special issues that face Black women in the United States as a result of racism. One outstanding issue is that of standards of beauty. This problem does not affect white women or Black men with the same impact as it does Black women. Black women are the only group in this society declared "ugly" and "unfeminine" a priori. Without a doubt, the mass media have played a highly significant role in the promotion and selling of this concept. We can ask numerous research questions regarding the relationship of beauty standards to Black women's media use patterns and spending patterns.

I have yet to see any scientific research on this issue, yet we know it is of paramount significance to Black people in general and Black women in particular. A sector of the cosmetic industry is dependent upon the pursuit of European beauty by Black women. Certain Black entrepreneurs in cosmetics have become millionaires as a result. I do not think that white feminists are conscious of this dual consciousness that many Black women have regarding beauty standards. White researchers need to understand this and other Black subcultural issues if they are to pursue research about Black women fruitfully.

Margaret Just Butcher (1957) argues that the best way to test the functioning of democracy in a society is to observe the impact of its institutions on minorities. In the case of the United States that means Blacks generally, and Black women in particular. But the pull of racism suggests that white researchers will not examine issues regarding Black women, because what they might consider a fringe group is of little consequence to them to study. Their social and cultural isolation from Blacks may leave white academics unprepared to develop a theoretically appropriate study of Black women. Thus it comes down to Blacks and Black women, specifically, needing to spearhead this research. This problem is aggravated by the sparse numbers of Black women researchers in mass communication. Of this group, only a tiny fraction has an interest in feminist theory or women's issues more broadly. Understandably, these Black women researchers would like to maintain their academic freedom to pursue a variety of research issues, not just issues about Black women. Those with the fewest resources must carry the burden. This situation points to the overall problem of who gets educated, goes on to graduate school, and obtains a Ph.D. The importance of getting this kind of research done and the dearth of Black women to actually do it suggests we need other strategies of approach.

Black women who are interested in research on women need to draw a circle to include other sensitive researchers, including Black men, white women, and white men in cooperative research projects. We need to promote coresearch as a way of getting other people involved in working with Black women, as equals, developing theoretical positions and interpreting data. This is a very important type of interaction, where we can begin to know each other and influence the "mainstream" research that our new research partners may be pursuing. Mainstream research needs to be designed to include research questions about Black women from a theoretical position that goes beyond simple statistical controls for gender and race.

If there is be to any state-of-the-art knowledge about Black women, their media use, and the influence of power relations in media on Black people we must begin to think about cooperation and not create ghettos of exclusiveness in our research. We need a substantial body of research that can influence other research activities. There are simply too few Black women researchers in mass communication to carry the ball alone. Further, we will most likely pursue these relationships among colleagues whom we know. Coresearch projects will not happen in the abstract. Meanwhile, we must seriously ask ourselves, can we allow this issue to lay fallow until Black women can take on the work?

White researchers, especially feminists, must begin to come to Black forums to present their research and generate discussion about their issues among Blacks and to obtain feedback. Too often, it is Blacks who are always reaching out to whites, at white-sponsored conferences, through white-edited journals, and so on. Too often, when Blacks do present their research, whites fail to make substantive comments or ask questions. The Black researcher's work goes unchallenged and perhaps unattended to. This problem obviously goes beyond the issue of women in research. Rather, it questions whether or not mass communication research in the United States will develop beyond ethnocentrism and narrow definitions of "mainstream." Perhaps feminist scholars will be in the forefront of expanding those boundaries.

The outcome of all of this will largely depend upon the significance one attaches to the research itself. As the media marketplace changes along with the demographics of the nation, it is logical to speculate that Black women will play a more important role indirectly and directly in the shaping of audience tastes and uses in the major electronic media markets. Women are often the primary socializers in a household, and this factor is amplified among Blacks, given the prevalence of female heads of households. Women influence the media tastes and use patterns of their families. The importance of the concentration of Blacks in the top ten media markets is increasing, given the growing trend among white viewers to use cable television channels and videocassette recorders while Black viewers maintain high viewing of the over-the-air television channels. Obtaining syndication in the top media markets suggests paying strong attention to the Black audience and its tastes and viewing habits.

There are no easy answers or conclusions to the problem of developing a substantive body of research on Black women in mass communication. Research requires dedicated and experienced researchers, support services, money, and outlets for publication. In this case the elements exist, but not in abundance. As a start we can at least begin to develop a theoretical base. It need not be rooted in feminist theory as now constructed, but Black women should establish the theoretical agenda and actively encourage its pursuit.

REFERENCES

Butcher, Margaret Just. (1957). *The Negro in American culture*. New York: Mentor.

Giddings, Paula. (1984). *When and where I enter: The impact of Black women on race and class in America*. New York: William Morrow.

Matabane, Paula. Black women on American television. *Western Journal of Black Studies, 6*(1), 22-25.

Mullings, Leath. (1980). Notes on women, work and society. In Ethel Tobach & Betty Rosoff (Eds.), *Genes and gender* (Vol. 3, pp. 15-27). New York: Gordian.

Seiter, Ellen. (1986). Stereotypes and the media: A re-evaluation. *Journal of Communication, 36*(2), 14-27.

Section B. Perspectives on the
Mass Communication Classroom

6

The "Glass Ceiling" Effect on Mass Communication Students

More than a century ago, the revered Cuban poet Jose Martí made an impassioned plea for educational opportunities for women, "something which will secure their happiness, because enhancing their minds through solid studies, they will live on a par with men as comrades, not at their feet like beautiful toys, and because of her self-sufficiency, a woman will not feel hurried to attach herself—as a reed to a wall—to the first passerby, but instead, she will ponder and decide, leaving aside the rogues and liars and choosing the industrious and sincere."[1]

Women faculty members, too, deserve to live "on a par" with their male colleagues. However, women who teach journalism often encounter a "glass ceiling" that limits the likelihood of their advancement. That is, they can envision a career track that would lead to the prestige and job security inherent in becoming tenured, but their chances of actual promotion are smaller than those of their male counterparts. This disparate treatment in tenure and promotion because of gender has been documented in several recent studies (see, for example, Adams, 1983; Bourguignon et al., 1987; Gillespie, 1987; Grunig, 1987; Sharp, Turk, Einsiedel, Schamber, & Hollenback, 1985).

What has been largely missing from discussions of the glass ceiling for faculty women is the impact this barrier may have on their students. As one expert on the campus climate for women—faculty and students alike—explained, federal policies such as Title IX have gone a long way toward abolishing the rules that once allowed male and female students (and their professors) to be treated differently (Sandler, 1984). However, increasing awareness of sex discrimination has not solved all problems of unequal treatment and opportunity.

Today's undergraduate is tomorrow's practitioner; today's graduate student is tomorrow's professor.[2] Thus focusing attention on the ramifications of sex discrimination in academia seems doubly appropriate: If the glass ceiling can be shattered, then both the communication professions and future generations of students stand to benefit.

This chapter begins with a brief examination of the discriminatory patterns and practices many academic women face. It goes on to explore the effects such discrimination may have on students. It concludes with strategies for change, with the hope of enhancing both women's chances to be promoted and the future success of their graduates.

These recommendations have special significance for three groups of students: minorities, women, and returning students. The typical university today enrolls fewer Black undergraduates than it did seven years ago (in terms of both numbers and percentages). So, too, is the number of Black graduate students declining.[3] And with women undergraduates outnumbering men, as Gillespie (1987) said, "One might wonder why a faculty member would persist in the use of the pronoun 'he' when over 50% of the students are now likely to be women." The growing percentage of female students is especially evident in programs of journalism and mass communication. Undergraduate enrollments, in particular, are polarized by gender. At the University of Maryland, for instance, women constitute 16% of all physics majors—compared with 73% of all journalism majors.[4]

Further, more than 40% of today's students are over age 25. Two out of every three over age 34 are women ("Small but Active Feminist Groups," 1986). Like minorities and all female undergraduates, these older, nontraditional students—overwhelmingly female—need new ideas and programs to meet their special situation.

A feminist perspective will be brought to bear on the problems facing these three types of students. That is, the chapter is written from a woman's perspective, and it is transformative in nature—seeking to empower students (and faculty) regardless of their age, race, or gender. It emphasizes an inclusive feminist consciousness rather than the exclusivity that characterized feminism earlier in this century, when the women's movement was marked by class, race, and political orientation (Schneir, 1972).

Just as feminist literature is not uniform in its analysis of inequality or in its recommendations for overcoming sexual oppression (Currie & Kazi, 1987), the recommendations that make up the final section of this chapter vary widely. These strategies should not be perceived as a monolithic solution for the barriers facing any single group of afflicted students. In fact, the relevant issues for any one group may be quite different from—if not in actual conflict with—the issues of another group. In the same way, what stands to benefit faculty women may not always be in the best interests of all of their students at all times. The challenge of this chapter lies in finding the junctures wherein injustices can be fought and equality won for significant numbers of women and people of color without sacrificing respect for the individualism that has characterized women's progress in academia to date.

Developing a lengthy list of alternative recommendations seems the best way to accommodate the differing work patterns between women and men and even among women (Bernard, 1964). As the director of women's studies at Duke University put it:

> We've got to remember that there's no homogeneity among women. We can't discuss "what women want" as if biology predetermines needs. As we focus more on women's issues, we are coming to grips with the fact that there are many different types of women. There is no one thing women, as a group, want; there are many things. (O'Barr, cited in O'Shea, 1988, p. 41)

PROBLEMS FACULTY WOMEN FACE

Findings of an extensive case study of women on a journalism faculty of a large eastern university show little direct evidence of sex discrimination on promotion and tenure (Grunig, 1987). However, in this case—substantiated by the experiences of women on a dozen other campuses—all women interviewed spoke of the subtle pattern of bias, misunderstanding, and insensitivity they believe contributes directly and indirectly to limiting their chances for success in higher education.

The main sources of inequality seem to be the small numbers and powerlessness of women on the typical faculty. In the department studied, for instance, women constituted less than one-fourth of the 21-person faculty (contrasted with a student body that was about two-thirds female). Only one of the department's 13 tenured professors was a woman. Related problems included tokenism, a heavier advising load for women, lack of role models in academia, and few opportunities for sharing resources and information, mentoring, networking, and coalition-building.

Causes of these problems included men's perceptions that women "didn't fit in" and women's own feeling that they lack power, their ineptness in negotiation, their real lack of influence and support (from home as well as from the university), the realization on the part of decision makers that women are almost "captives" of a geographical region, the burden of home responsibility that women continue to accept, the "imposter syndrome" that causes women to downplay or dismiss their accomplishments, and women's insistence on working independently. Other traditional causes of discrimination against women include sex-role stereotyping, male-female interaction, and social norms.

The study concludes with recommendations for enhancing the promotion and tenure picture for women. Crashing the "glass ceiling" that keeps faculty women from being advanced or receiving tenure depends on hiring more women to teach, sensitizing their male colleagues about difficulties peculiar to women, fostering women's risk-taking behavior, building supportive structures for women on campus and across campuses, and team-building between genders within departments of journalism.

Although each of these factors—problems, causes, and solutions—warrants an extensive examination in itself, the more pressing concern of this chapter is to look at the impact upon students, male and female alike. How does having few faculty women affect undergraduates, for example? And what is the consequence for graduate students who are advised by women faculty in junior roles? The next section of this chapter extrapolates from extensive literature to explore the effects of problems such as the small number of faculty women and their relative lack of power on their classes.

PROBLEMS STUDENTS FACE

The relatively small number of women who teach in the typical journalism or mass communication department represents an imbalance between female faculty and female students. Sharp et al. (1985) found that both male and female students are attracted to female teachers for advising, because they

> automatically think that the women are going to be more sympathetic and more understanding of them and should spend more time with them than male faculty members. They are more willing to presume upon a woman's time and take up more of a woman's energy with problems than they might with a male. (p. 51)

Advising is one of three kinds of university work considered "feminine" and thus frequently devalued. In fact, according to Knefelkamp (1987), advising—along with teaching and involvement with student activities (such as health services, resident life, and student organizations)—may be denigrated by male professors. In her view, these aspects of faculty work, often considered "hand-holding" for students, spark the need for a revolution to reassess promotion criteria. She argued that although the denigration or devaluation of advising is most often the case at large universities, the evaluation of such caretaking work tends to be a result more of socialization than of situation. In other words, men in all types of universities value research, for example, more than they do the relational work involved in student advising. With the growing majority of women undergraduates in journalism, and the preference of both male and female students for seeking female advisers, demands for such advising on female faculty without hope of reward or recognition for that work represents a double burden.

Although this imbalance in numbers can be counterproductive for women professors, their students suffer as well. Women students encounter too few same-sex role models and find few mentors—especially female senior professors who are powerful and well connected.

Thus the question of power, more than numbers alone, informs this discussion of women in academia. For faculty women to gain voice, they need to ascend to positions of power.[5] However, 9 out of 10 students attend institutions where men hold the top three administrative posts (president, chief academic officer, and dean). Although the proportion of women who are assistant professors is increasing steadily, only about 10% of all full professors are women (Sandler, 1984).

Only when women are promoted to top administrative positions or tenured faculty slots can they be truly effective as advisers, as mentors, as role models, as determinants of the classroom climate, and as shapers of the curriculum studied by male and female students alike. The following sections of this chapter deal with each of these five problem areas: advising, mentoring, role modeling, affecting the classroom climate, and transforming the curriculum.

Advising

As mentioned above, women faculty members are perceived to be more accessible than men to students in need of advice (Sharp et al., 1985). Additional literature dealing with female role behavior also suggests that women are expected to be more humanitarian and compassionate than men (White & Crino, 1981). One noted scientist argued, also, that faculty women—whom she considered more intuitive than men—make superior advisers because "they answer students' questions even before they know what to ask" (Wise, 1988). These perceptions may lead to demands that diminish the time remaining for research activities that ultimately lead to promotion and tenure (Grunig, 1988). Along the way, of course, the overburdened female adviser may not be able to devote the appropriate energy or time to all of the students requesting her help.[6]

Male professors cannot be expected to "take up the slack," especially with female students. Despite the fact that women in graduate school consistently make better grades than do men,[7] male faculty members tend to encourage same-sex students and to consider female students as less capable and less professionally committed than their male colleagues.[8] This, of course, is a serious perceptual problem for women in professional programs such as journalism. When male professors perceive their female students (especially those who are older and who have children)[9] to have less potential and less commitment to the field, they hesitate to invest time and energy in advising them.[10] Finally, graduate students whose dissertations are advised by someone of the same sex show greater productivity (Menges & Exum, 1983).

Women and minority faculty members at Ohio State University recently recalled their own experiences as students—commenting that their most valued advisers were those who counteracted the prevailing message that discouraged other women and minorities from pursuing professional goals. Students fortunate enough to have such advisers considered themselves better prepared for their role as professors. Others, however, complained of graduate advisers who did not respect them because of their gender or race and still others who did not consider female students as valuable future colleagues (Bourguignon et al., 1987, p. 29).

Mentoring

Closely related to the issue of advising—whether it be curricular, dissertation/thesis, or professional—is mentoring. The trusted counselor or guide, from the beginning of our understanding of the term, was an advantage for male students. (The original Mentor, friend of Odysseus, was entrusted with the education of Odysseus' son, Telemachus.) Just as the study of the journalism department described above shows that faculty women find too few mentors, so the literature suggests that their students find too few academicians willing or able to serve as special tutors in the ways of academia or the professions for which they prepare (for example, see Bourguignon et al., 1987). As Lewis (1975) explained "The vast majority of academics who survive graduate school, credentialing and publishing are either men or women who have been and continue to be selected and trained by men." Wise (1988) agreed, urging female students to be especially clear on what they want to achieve "because men won't help you; they're too busy grooming other men."

Because advancement in academia is a more current concern than is initial access (whether *access* means being hired for an entry-level teaching position or admitted to an undergraduate or graduate program),[11] mentoring has become central to the discussion of equality for women students and professors alike. However, without enough faculty women—and especially powerful female professors—the need for academic mentors is likely to go unmet. But why is this special attention so important for students in particular?

Direct benefits for the protege include recognition and encouragement, honest criticism and feedback, advice on balancing responsibilities and priorities, knowledge of the informal rules for success, information on how to act in a variety of settings (both academic and professional), training in how to make contact with authorities in a discipline or leaders in a field, skills for showcasing one's work, and a perspective on long-range academic or career planning (Hall & Sandler, 1983). Graduate students, in particular, consider close mentoring relationships with their advisers to be key determinants in feeling prepared for what they will encounter as faculty members themselves (Bourguignon et al., 1987, pp. 30-31; see also Adler, 1976).

Benefits accrue to the mentor as well.[12] In addition to the satisfaction inherent in helping develop a junior person's abilities, two major advantages for the sponsor include ideas for and feedback about his or her own projects and a network of former mentees at other universities or in the professions—people likely to increase the mentor's power and visibility (Hall & Sandler, 1983, p. 3). Thus developing the skills of female faculty members as mentors for female, minority, and older students also enhances the likelihood of advancement for the faculty. One noted feminist scientist recently argued for the creation of a formal reward system for faculty mentors (Colwell, 1988).

Unfortunately, the "who you know" being as important as the "what you know" creates problems for female champions and for their would-be proteges. Because introduction to the authorities within a department of the university or a corporation capable of hiring and promoting the graduate is one critical aspect of mentoring, the most powerful and well-connected people make the most effective mentors. Women, held to the lower ranks in academia, rarely have those connections.

Men, who tend to be more highly placed on the academic hierarchy, still may not serve female students well as advocates. Just as they tend to invest less time and energy in advising women than men, they are less willing to serve as mentors for female novices. The literature shows that men tend to affirm students of their own sex (Hochschild, 1975; Tidball, 1976) and to avoid mentoring relationships with women students in part because they fear the accusation of sexual harassment (Hall & Sandler, 1983, p. 4).

Minority students find even fewer mentors than do females. Duncan (1976) discovered that although 1 in 4 white students had mentors, only 1 in 20 minority students did. The irony is that minority students, who drop out at a higher rate than do majority students and more often for nonacademic reasons, have the greatest need for informal interaction with senior professors and are least likely to experience it (Duncan, 1976; also see Chitayat, cited in Hall & Sandler, 1983, p. 7).

Reasons for the difficulty minorities—especially minority women—have in securing mentors include the following (Hall & Sandler, 1983, p. 7):

> Senior professors, who tend to be white males, are uncomfortable working closely with students so unlike themselves.
> Senior professors who may be women or minorities are so overloaded with committee and other responsibilities they hesitate to take on proteges.
> These students have research interests that fall outside the mainstream of the discipline and thus are considered "risky" by senior faculty.

Finally, the many older women who enter or return to the campus have special needs for mentoring—needs that also often go unmet. They must learn of changes in the academic system since they left school, discover ways to balance family and scholarly demands, and be encouraged to venture into the new domain for which they are preparing. Barriers to these women's finding mentors include the faculty's doubt about their commitment to education (because of their tendency to enroll on a part-time basis), concern that their future accomplishments will be limited by age (thus making them poor candidates for an investment of time and energy), and the threatening aspect of their being of equal adult status (and perhaps greater life experience) (Hall & Sandler, 1983, p. 7).

Role Modeling

Advising involves the dedication of time and energy to one's students. Mentoring goes one step further, to encompass a personal relationship based on trust, encouragement, and the passing along of inside information to a favored novice. Both of these important avenues for academic and professional success involve one-on-one interaction between student and faculty member. As a result, the few women in the typical department of journalism or mass communication find themselves spread too thinly among the many female students, in particular, who stand to gain from this personal attention from another woman. Also, because powerful professors make the most effective advisers and mentors, the relative lack of influence most women enjoy in academia further limits their usefulness to students.

Thus we turn our attention to a more impersonal yet effective mechanism that can encourage female undergraduates and graduates to stay in school, to get their degrees, and to achieve professionally—role modeling. Role modeling depends less on power than do the previous two processes, so it shows great promise as a way to enhance students' scholarly and journalistic achievement. Still, role modeling for female, minority, and older students does require the visibility of professors like themselves in terms of sex, race, and age.

Role modeling can accomplish two main goals for students: showcasing a person worthy of imitation and dispelling any misperceptions a student may have about the determinants of his or her own success. Aspiring to accomplish what the role model has achieved can be a step forward in terms of goal-setting. Without taking classes from female professors who have managed to get hired in predominantly male university faculties, female graduate students may not believe that such entrée to what has been called a "bastion of male clubbiness" (Rohter, 1987) is possible—at least for the ordinary student. According to Bird (1968), without adequate numbers of role models,

> we are destroying talent. The price of occupational success is made so high for women that barring exceptional luck only the unusually talented or frankly neurotic can afford to succeed. Girls size up the bargain early and turn it down.

On the other hand, understanding the barriers that many entry-level women, Blacks, and older people in academia or the work force face adds a critical dose of reality. Otherwise, students may take for granted the achievements of faculty or professional women. A former vice president for academic affairs recently counseled female students to "be prepared for rebuffs, exclusion, criticism and rejection; it never lets up" (Colwell, 1988). Bernice Sandler, director of the Project on the Status and Education of Women sponsored by the Association of American Colleges, explained, "What I worry about is that many [students] think it will be easy to have a full-time career and a full-time family" (cited in Greene, 1986, p. 33).

Thus one key suggestion of the "velvet ghetto" study (Cline et al., 1986), a major research project funded by the International Association of Business Communicators to explore the influx of women into the study and practice of public relations, involved the development of career-path models. This would be accomplished largely through exposing students, men and women alike, to practitioners who had chosen different approaches to their personal and work lives.

Professors themselves, of course, can serve as role models—especially for graduate students intending to teach. Role modeling is most effective, according to the director of women's studies at the University of Maryland, when it is accomplished at least in part through self-disclosure. Beck (1983) argued: "It is vital to tell students who I am. Women need role models and visible support. The more students know about me, the more effective I can be as a feminist teacher" (p. 160). Thus she humanizes herself and personalizes the teaching process early on in her courses by sketching her intellectual history and the facts of her life that she considers relevant to the class.

Affecting the Classroom Climate

"Women Students Chilled Out on Campus" headlines a flyer on an informational packet designed by the Project on the Status and Education of Women (Sandler & Hall, 1986). Cornerstone of the packet is a paper assessing the climate for women faculty, administrators, and graduate students. The bottom line? "Chilly." Female students encounter faculty behaviors that discourage them in both subtle and overt ways. These barriers are considered so serious and so pervasive that authors of the report developed more than 100 recommendations to try to counteract them.

"Classroom climate" should be defined broadly enough to encompass the women students' situation throughout their collegiate experience—whether it be in class, in meetings with academic advisers, or socializing with peers. In these diverse settings, women on campuses throughout the country find themselves being treated differently from men (Sandler & Hall, 1986). Such discriminatory treatment may be unconscious. As the first female chemistry teacher at the University of Maryland explained, her colleagues need to be sensitized on the importance of providing an equitable setting for their female students. Greer explains: "We weren't educated this way. We didn't learn it because it wasn't there" (quoted in Greene, 1988, p. 10). Creating a fair classroom environment is important, in turn, Greer says, because "we know the way women are treated in the classroom has tremendous impact on their future career developments."

Even in the short run, however, students thrive in a climate that helps them move through a hierarchy of cognitive complexity. As undergraduates progress beyond the simple memorization that characterizes tasks during their first couple of years on campus, they need what Knefelkamp (1987) calls "an environment of psychological safety" in the classroom. She equates "classroom climate" with "classroom as a community," emphasizing several key variables that help make "climate" a viable concept:

- empathy
- support
- dialogue among peers and between students and professor
- mutual responsibilities
- self-discovery, only guided by the professor, who sets the tone for the overall classroom climate

Contrast these characteristics with what too many women encounter with their male professors. Devaluing women in the classroom ranges from the severity of sexual harassment to the seemingly trivial: frequent interruptions (including interruptions by male students), failure to be called on in the first place, lack of eye contact, forgetting women's names, using generic masculine language, and focus on appearance rather than accomplishments. The latter behaviors, often considered minor annoyances or called "micro-inequities," may be so commonplace and so subtle that the classroom situation is considered "normal." As Sandler and Hall (1986) put it, "Frequently, neither women nor those who treat them differently are aware of what has occurred; indeed, the possible lack of awareness by both parties is what make the behavior and its impact so insidious" (p. 2).

Hall and Sandler (1982) were careful to point out that women themselves may create a chilly climate for other women. They further noted that minorities and older students often experience a similar lack of attention and devaluation. Graduate students, in particular, suffer from what Hall and Sandler called the "male climate," where male professors are even more predominant and women students are fewer. An expert on the participation of women and minorities in science and engineering echoed this concern in her articulation of the suicide rates for graduate students: Nearly three times as many women as men try to kill themselves (Babco, 1988). Sandler and Hall (1986) termed minority women on campus "an endangered species," doubly likely to be neglected in the classroom (pp. 12-13).

The crux of the classroom climate problem, in Sandler and Hall's opinion, comes down to few women faculty and an abundance of insensitive men. As Atkins (1983) put it:

> The combination of invisibility symbolized by the "Faculty Locker Room" [male] and the high visibility of THE WOMAN adds up to an environment that makes growth slow and difficult. If women are set apart we are deprived of the warmth and acceptance that encourages full human growth. When we exist as outsiders and are forced to justify our existence or defend our presence in the University, we cannot perform to our fullest. (p. 9)

Transforming the Curriculum

Early in this country's most recent women's movement, Friedan (1963) lamented:

> That we have not made any respectable attempt to meet the special educational needs of women in the past is the clearest possible evidence of the fact that our educational objectives have been geared exclusively to the vocational patterns of men. (Chapter 13)

Now that women are the majority in journalism classes and in some aspects of the field itself, such as public relations, gearing the educational experience to their interests seems especially important. Appropriately, then, the newest standard of the Accrediting Council for Education in Journalism and Mass Communication calls for attention to the concerns of women and minorities—both students and faculty. However, more than 25 years later—Title IX, affirmative action, and the EEOC notwithstanding—Friedan's challenge had not been met.

Nothing short of a "transformation of the curriculum" seems adequate. This buzz phrase enjoys more lip service than realization at present, however.[13] Although the expression refers to integrating scholarship by and about women throughout the disciplines, few students actually are exposed. Schneir (1972) considered this situation a matter of "shocking ignorance" of the history of half the human race (p. xi). The president of Lincoln University expressed similar outrage: "In a world where demographic shifts have already stood the concepts of majority and minority on their heads, it is no longer intellectually defensible to presume to discuss human endeavor and human interaction from the perspective of only one group" (Sudarkasa, 1987, p. 42). An art historian recently called women in academia "the forgotten half" of the record (Ferris Olin, cited in McMillen, 1987).

Depriving women of their history, in Schneir's (1972) view, deprives them of their group identity. The president of Wellesley College has suggested courses informed by scholarship on women and minorities to help these previously excluded groups identify with their history and culture. Otherwise, she predicted they will come to see academia as "something entirely without reference to them and their own lives" (Keohane, 1986, p. 88). Another expert on college curricula agreed that equal representation of women in college texts and programs of research would increase educational excellence (Elizabeth Minnich, cited in Kaplan, 1987, p. 3).

Transforming the curriculum depends on changing the approach to courses as well as their content. However, the proliferation of departments of women's studies during this decade cannot be expected to counteract the patriarchal view that predominates on the typical campus. Women's studies has been considered a "continuing ghettoization of women's interests" (Kolodny, 1981; see also Dudovitz, Russo, Duvall, & Cramer, 1983).[14] The ghetto actually may be more like a posh suburb, however, for privileged, white, middle-class women. According to two teams of feminist scholars, women's studies is in danger of becoming an elitist enterprise (Bowles & Klein, 1983; Stanley & Wise, 1983). This hegemony of discourse does not allow for alternative models to meet the diverse needs of minority and older students, in particular.

A further problem inherent in relying on women's studies to eradicate the "blind spots" in students' education is that the courses reach too few students. Their audience tends to be small and homogeneous, rather than large and diverse. According to the director of women's studies at the University of Arizona: "We were reaching a fairly small portion of students. Unless you took a women's-studies course, you could graduate and never hear the words 'women' or 'gender' " (Myra Dinnerstein, quoted in McMillen, 1987, p. A15).

Instead of concentrating what knowledge exists about women and minorities into special, separate departments, then, this information should be an integral part of all fields. Challenging the monistic canon requires hiring more Blacks and women to teach. As Sudarkasa (1987) put it, "Their influence in fields in which they have been active shows why it is important to recruit such scholars in disciplines where they are few or nonexistent" (p. 42).

Revising the curriculum to reflect a more balanced view of minorities and women may require an all-out effort on a par with the ambitious New Jersey project. That state's Department of Higher Education recently allotted $362,500 to support a transformation of the curriculum at 56 public and private colleges there. In his speech to kick off the project, Governor Thomas J. Kean declared 1987 "the inaugural year of integrating the scholarship on women" (quoted in McMillen, 1987, p. A15). The project's director, Carol Smith, a professor of English at Rutgers University, described the program's implications as follows: "Not only has the State of New Jersey recognized the significance of scholarship on gender, but it also presented this as a model for other states" (quoted in McMillen, 1987, p. A15).

Although more than a hundred colleges are actively trying to integrate their curricula to reflect the concerns of women and minorities, a recent Ford Foundation study found that in nearly 40% of the cases, faculty members or administrators have resisted the changes (McMillen, 1987, p. A16).

CONCLUSIONS

Hoffman (1986) summarized the challenges facing educators when she described what she calls the difficulty of "applying theory to practice" in academia:

> The transformative potential in integrating the recent scholarship on women into the curriculum; of increasing the numbers, status, and authority of women staff and faculty on college campuses; and of challenging the bureaucratic forms of domination and subordination through organized resistance to centralized authority and depersonalized control remains a vision of what could be. (p. 118)

Looking at the case of the large eastern university and its discriminatory practices against the women who teach journalism there, and extrapolating from the literature to explore the effect of such discrimination on students, has yielded a similarly bleak picture. Too many students are victims of social, intellectual, and economic inequality. However, this study has produced little evidence that students, including women, are consciously trying to change their situation on campus—much less challenging such a powerful institution as the university.

Given the inferior position in which so many women, minorities, and returning students find themselves, the logical question is, Why do they acquiesce? Unlike some brave and independent faculty women, most students seem to subscribe to the myth of equality. Also, it seems likely that, course by course, semester by semester, many students are finding it all they can do simply to try to complete their degrees.

The educational process, though, happens in myriad circumstances—many of which happen to be stacked against women, Blacks, and older people. This chapter should establish that injustice strikes women who teach and women who study alike. If not actually mobilized by this discrimination, some may be gaining awareness of the problems they face. Gornick (1972) painted a picture that reflects this growing restiveness among many female faculty members and students:

> Behind the "passive" exterior of many women there lies a growing anger over lost energies and confused lives, an anger so sharp in its fury but so diffuse in its focus that one can only describe it as the price society must pay for creating a patriarchal system in the first place, and for now refusing to let it go. And make no mistake, it is not letting go.

Perhaps we have come to a point, then, when students are beginning to feel energized for the struggle. Women, minorities, and returning students, in particular, may be ready to work toward achieving equity on campus. This diversity of the student body adds richness to the faculty who teach, advise and encourage them—but it also creates the need for almost individual solutions that impedes progress on any large-scale, institutional basis. The following recommendations represent an effort to balance idiosyncratic situations with practical remedies affecting enough students to make real progress toward equality for all.

RECOMMENDATIONS

Putting these recommendations into practice will require the cooperation of men as well as the commitment of women. White men hold the doors of power; they may choose to open them or to keep them closed to women, minorities, and older students. Further, history has shown that no revolution succeeds if only a small group with special needs is emotionally involved. Instead, men in higher education must come to realize that what happens to their female colleagues in a sense happens to them. In other words, it is in the self-interest of men not to waste women's resources. And, as women's advocate Estelle Ramey (1988) said in a recent keynote address, "You can't ignore half the population—or you do so at your own peril."

Increased attention to the problems of female students and faculty members undoubtedly will cost men some comfort in the short run. However, the problems described above will not go away if we ignore them. Hoping this inequitable situation will evaporate on its own only leads to missed opportunities, thwarted ambitions, high levels of stress on the part of both men and women, and poor performance of the academic unit.

All of this is not to say that programs of journalism and mass communication are fundamentally flawed, or "rotten to the core"; rather, it is to suggest that academe must be altered fundamentally to become inclusive. The following map of the academic terrain shows the areas in which reform seems most possible. These places are situated along the same dimensions as the problem areas identified earlier: advising, mentoring, role modeling, affecting the classroom climate, and transforming the curriculum.

Advising

- Create a mechanism for rewarding advising and other, related responsibilities now considered "feminine."
- Develop counseling programs and referral services for nontraditional (older) students.
- Encourage female and minority graduate students to pursue areas of the discipline in which there are relatively few women and minorities now.

Mentoring

- Increase awareness among both faculty and students of the potential benefits of mentoring.
- Enhance the faculty's skill in mentoring, perhaps through publications that inform "how to" and "how not to." For examples, see the Association of American Colleges' pamphlet on academic mentoring (Hall & Sandler, 1983, p. 15).
- Create a mechanism for rewarding mentoring.
- Encourage communication professionals to become mentors—working through educators and advisers of student chapters of professional organiza-

tions who would, in turn, increase their base for networking among powerful professionals.

- Require students to seek mentors in their sequence areas, perhaps by making mentoring a component of every internship or volunteer work.
- Increase students' awareness of the discrimination they may face. As a male sociology professor has stated, "Much of the problem of inequality is rooted in perceptions that there is no problem" (Segal, 1988).[15] Educators cited in a recent magazine article emphasize the importance of young women considering the issue of discrimination while they are still in college and have "lifestyle choices" (O'Shea, 1988, p. 70).

Role Modeling

- Make the life stories of communication professionals available to students; stories should include the problems as well as the rewards inherent in their careers. This might be accomplished, as the "velvet ghetto" study (Cline et al., 1986) suggested, through student chapters of professional associations such as the IABC, the Public Relations Society of America, Women in Communication, or the Society of Professional Journalists. Look for women who preside over these professional organizations as well as city editors, news anchors, magazine publishers, heads of public relations or advertising firms, and corporate vice presidents in charge of communication.
- Include examples in textbooks of women and minorities in top managerial positions.
- Women and minority faculty members should "tell it like it is" when recounting their experiences. However, during self-disclosure they must take care not to pass along their own anger, suspicions, and fears (feeling victimized is disempowering). Students, as well, should feel free to self-disclose during class.

Affecting the Classroom Climate

- Adopt at least 14 of the 15 strategies proposed in the American Council on Education's "New Agenda of Women for Higher Education."[16] In addition to the explicit suggestion to provide a supportive climate in the classroom and elsewhere on campus, recommendations include seeking commitment from campus leadership to understand and address the concerns of women students, faculty, and administrators; considering how campus policies and planning affect men and women alike; establishing effective policies to contend with sexual harassment; auditing and reporting on the status of women on campus; developing policies that support children and families; appreciating diversity; creating a senior position of advocate for women; and fostering women's leadership, including minority women.

- Following general policy recommendations emanating from the "chilly climate" study (Sandler & Hall, 1986), develop a policy advocating nonsexist language; educate all members of the academic community about climate issues (primarily through workshops, informal discussions, and written materials); ensure that grievance procedures for students, faculty, and staff accommodate reporting of subtle as well as overt differential treatment; recognize women's[17] accomplishments; include women in informal professional and social activities; support formal and informal networks of women; avoid asking women to fulfill stereotypically "feminine" roles; provide women with ongoing feedback (both positive and negative) about their work; and make equitable treatment for all students and faculty part of the formal reward structure.

Transforming the Curriculum

- Following the recommendations in a recent paper arguing for a feminist research agenda in journalism and mass communication (Grunig, 1988), more research should be done about women—and women should be able to be promoted doing this kind of work.

- As advocated by the team assessing the status of junior faculty at Ohio State (Bourguignon et al., 1987, p. 63), consider reducing the teaching load for all untenured professors to help them get their research programs started. The team's report urges the enhancement of research support funds and opportunities specifically for women and minority junior faculty. Several respondents indicated that they "perceived a diminishment of the worth of their research if it was focused on either women or minorities" (Bourguignon et al., 1987, p. 64).

- Regularly gather demographic data by sex, race, and age. Information should be both statistical and anecdotal and should pertain both to students and to faculty, full- and part-time.

- Following the plan in operation at American University (Knefelkamp, 1987), approve no new courses in the general education curriculum without consideration of gender, race, class, and age.

- Develop courses especially for women who want to study the topic of women and journalism or mass communication. Provide male students the chance to study with and about females who are interested in this area.

Finally, an overriding concern that permeates all other considerations should be discussed: the need to recruit, hire, and promote more women and minorities. This understanding reinforces the importance of the recommendations listed in the initial case study of sex discrimination in promotion and tenure (Grunig, 1987). In addition, search committees should facilitate the hiring of more women and minorities mainly by (1) recognizing that these candidates may not have such detailed curriculum vitae as would men their age because they have faced different obstacles and enjoyed different opportunities; (2) becoming sensitive to the makeup of the committee, being careful at the same time not to overburden the small number of women constantly asked to serve on these draining groups; and (3) interviewing minority and female candidates who are not hired to find out whether they believe they have been treated equitably throughout the application process.

Other suggestions, borrowed from a treatise on recruiting minority professors, include (1) supporting aspiring professors who are ABD to finish their dissertations; and (2) becoming willing to hire one's own doctoral students. As one university official put it, "After all, if a student is good enough to get a Ph.D. at your school, why isn't she good enough to teach there?" (cited in Heller, 1988, p. A17).

Consider also the legal aspects of hiring women. What are the responsibilities of deans interviewing, hiring, evaluating, and firing women? What are the accompanying dictates of the human relations movement of the 1980s? Bring legal experts in personnel and civil liberties to campus to meet with those in a position to assess letters of application, to offer conditions of employment and promotion, and to dismiss faculty members. Cases of discrimination in hiring, promoting, or tenuring female employees or of sexual harassment (be it on the job, in an internship, or between professor and student) would be a logical starting point. Continue by developing a code of standard practice not so much legally as humanistically dictated.

In conclusion, recognize that the foregoing list of strategies, culled from extensive literature, personal experience, and anecdotal information, is deliberately incomplete. That is, it includes only recommendations that stand to enhance the development of both faculty women and their students.

NOTES

1. From the April 11, 1882, article, "Women's Education," *La opinion nacional* (Caracas, Venezuela newspaper).

2. One additional ramification: Because graduate assistants administer so many large, core courses, they have the potential to influence an immense undergraduate population. Thus the students already teach the students (Dudovitz et al., 1983).

3. Unlike other minorities, Blacks are showing a slight decline on the faculty as well—from 4.4% to 4% between 1981 and 1986 (American Council on Education, 1987).

4. These statistics are from the University of Maryland Office of Institutional Studies, as reported in Greene (1988).

5. For a counterargument, see Moglen (1983), who questions whether feminists should accept and use power within any "mainstream hierarchical structures that support relationships of domination and inequity" (p. 131).

6. Other impingements on faculty women's time include their assignment to a disproportionately large share of large, unprestigious undergraduate classes (Astin & Bayer, 1973) and governance activities (Turk, 1981). Service, in particular, presents a double whammy. According to junior faculty members at Ohio State University, service may not count at all (Bourguignon et al., 1987, p. 53). On the other hand, too much service may count against a faculty member—showing an inappropriate emphasis on this one of the three traditional criteria for promotion (at the expense of teaching and, particularly, research).

7. Gillespie (1987) explained that this phenomenon occurs despite the prediction that GRE scores consistently rank women lower as a group than men.

8. For enlightenment on the problem of these attitudinal barriers, see, for example, Tidball (1976) and Heyman (1977; cited in Speizer, 1981).

9. The pamphlet *Women Winners* (Hall & Sandler, 1982) argues that marriage and children tend to be advantages for male students, who are then perceived as mature and stable.

10. A related problem is the university's unwillingness to support married women students financially, assuming that their husbands will support them (Bourguignon et al., 1987, pp. 58-59).

11. As the director of women's studies at Duke University has observed: "Historically, the women's movement has been an attempt to change women's status, to gain access to male institutions. Now, we've moved beyond that. We've determined that the institutions themselves—the content, organization, and structure of law, business, academia—have to be changed. We're here, and we don't like what we see" (O'Barr, cited in O'Shea, 1988, p. 70).

12. Even the university benefits from mentoring, especially in terms of increased productivity of junior faculty and commitment of students, decreased attrition of graduate students and faculty (especially women and minorities), and increased likelihood that students or faculty who do leave will continue to support the institution rather than criticize it (Hall & Sandler, 1983, p. 3).

13. *Transforming* is the preferred term over other, seemingly synonymous, words. *Mainstreaming* or *integrating*, for example, are considered too narrow. As a member of Wellesley College's Center for Research on Women explained, the concept of a "transformed curriculum" prompts scholars to change how they approach their scholarly materials almost as second nature (Peggy McIntosh, cited in McMillen, 1987).

14. Volume 10, number 1, of *Women's Studies Quarterly* (1982) is devoted entirely to this concern.

15. This sentiment is echoed by Anne Summers, editor of *Ms.* magazine. In a recent interview, she recounted her findings from a series of focus groups with young women. She discovered not only a lack of awareness but actual resistance to the notion of feminism (cited in Williams, 1988).

16. For a synopsis of this report, see McMillen (1988). Copies are available for $2 from ACE's Publications Department, One Dupont Circle, Washington, DC 20036-1193.

17. The "chilly climate" report (Sandler & Hall, 1986, p. 18) emphasizes the need to recognize the special concerns of *minority* women.

REFERENCES

Adams, Harriet Farwell. (1983). Work in the interstices: Women in academe. In Resa L. Dudovitz (Ed.), Women in academe [Special issue]. *Women's Studies International Forum*, pp. 135-141.

Adler, Nancy E. (1976). Women students. In Joseph Katz & Rodney T. Hartnett (Eds.), *Scholars in the making: The development of graduate and professional schools* (pp. 202-203). Cambridge, MA: Ballinger.

American Council on Education. (1987). *ACE background paper I: A status report on minorities in higher education.* Washington, DC: Author.

Astin, H. S., & Bayer, E. (1973). Sex discrimination in academe. In Alice S. Rossi & Ann Calderwood (Eds.), *Academic women on the move.* New York: Russell Sage Foundation.

Atkins, Annette. (1983, Winter). The camels are coming, the camels are coming. *St. John's Magazine*, p. 9.

Babco, Eleanor L. (1988, April 13). Panel contribution at the minisymposium, "Women and the Sciences: Expectations, Reality, Hope," College Park, MD.

Beck, Evelyn Torton. (1983). Self-disclosure and the commitment to social change. In Resa L. Dudovitz (Ed.), Women in academe [Special issue]. *Women's Studies International Forum*, pp. 159-163.

Bernard, Jessie. (1964). *Academic women.* University Park: Pennsylvania Univesity Press.

Bird, Caroline. (1968). Foreword. In Caroline Bird, *Born female.* New York: D. McKay.

Bourguignon, Erika, Blanshan, Sue A., Chiteji, Liza, MacLean, Kathleen J., Meckling, Sally J., Sagaria, Mary Ann, Shuman, Amy E., & Taris, Marie T. (1987, November). *Junior faculty life at Ohio State: Insights on gender and race.* Columbus: Ohio State University Affirmative Action Grant Program, Office of Human Relations, and University Senate Committee on Women and Minorities.

Bowles, Gloria, & Klein, Renate Duelli. (Eds.). (1983). *Theories of women's studies.* London: Routledge & Kegan Paul.

Cline, Carolyn Garrett, Toth, Elizabeth Lance, Turk, Judy VanSlyke, Walters, Lynne Masel, Johnson, Nancy, & Smith, Hank. (1986). *The velvet ghetto: The impact of the increasing percentage of women in public relations and business communication.* San Francisco: International Association for Business Communicators Foundation.

Colwell, Rita R. (1988, April 13). Panel contribution at the minisymposium, "Women and the Sciences: Expectations, Reality, Hope," College Park, MD.

Currie, Dawn, & Kazi, Hamida. (1987, March). Academic feminism and the process of de-radicalization: Re-examining the issues. *Feminist Review, 25*, 77-98.

Dudovitz, Resa L., Russo, Ann, Duvall, John, & Cramer, Patricia. (1983). Survival in the "master's house": The role of graduate teaching assistants in effecting curriculum change. In Resa L. Dudovitz (Ed.), Women in academe [Special issue]. *Women's Studies International Forum*, pp. 149-157.

Duncan, Birt L. (1976). Minority students. In Joseph Katz & Rodney T. Hartnett (Eds.), *Scholars in the making: The development of graduate and professional schools* (pp. 233-241). Cambridge, MA: Ballinger.

Friedan, Betty. (1963). *The feminine mystique.* New York: Norton.

Gillespie, Patti P. (1987). *Campus stories, or the cat beyond the canvas.* Presidential address presented at the annual meeting of the Speech Communication Association, Boston.

Gornick, Vivian. (1972). Why women fear success. In Francine Klagsbrun (Ed.), *The first Ms. reader.* New York: Warner Paperback Library.

Greene, Elizabeth. (1986, April 23). Feminism on campuses draws support and scorn: Many students in the middle. *Chronicle of Higher Education*, pp. 31-33.

Greene, Jon. (1988, May 10). Report criticizes gender-bias here: Plan offers women opportunities. *Diamondback*, p. 1.

Grunig, Larissa A. (1987). *Shattering the "glass ceiling" in journalism education: Sex discrimination in promotion and tenure.* Paper presented to the Committee on the Status of Women, Association for Education in Journalism and Mass Communication, San Antonio, TX.

Grunig, Larissa A. (1988). *Legitimizing a feminist research agenda for journalism and mass communication.* Paper presented to the Joint Session on The Women's Situation: Progression or Retrogression? sponsored by the Public Relations Division and the Committee on the Status of Women, Association for Education in Journalism and Mass Communication, Portland, OR.

Hall, Roberta M., & Sandler, Bernice Resnick. (1982, August). *Women winners.* Washington, DC: Association of American Colleges, Project on the Status and Education of Women.

Hall, Roberta M., & Sandler, Bernice Resnick. (1983). *Academic mentoring for women students and faculty: A new look at an old way to get ahead.* Washington, DC: Association of American Colleges, Project on the Status and Education of Women.

Heller, Scott. (1988, February 10). Recruiting minority professors: Some techniques that work. *Chronicle of Higher Education*, p. A17.

Hochschild, Arlie Russell. (1975). Inside the clockwork of male careers. In Florence Howe (Ed.), *Women and the power to change* (pp. 47-80). New York: McGraw-Hill.

Hoffman, Frances L. (1986, May). Sexual harassment in academia: Feminist theory and institutional practice. *Harvard Educational Review, 56*, 105-121.

Kaplan, Peter. (1987, March 26). Female researchers face discrimination, visiting expert says. *Diamondback*, p. 3.

Keohane, Nannerl O. (1986, April 2). Our mission should not be merely to "reclaim" a legacy of scholarship—We must expand on it. *Chronicle of Higher Education*, p. 88.

Knefelkamp, Lee. (1987). *Women's moral development: On Carol Gilligan's work.* Presented at the graduate polyseminar, Feminism and Structures of Knowledge, University of Maryland, College Park.

Kolodny, Annette. (1981). Dancing through the minefield: Some observations on the theory, practice and politics of a feminist literary criticism. In Dale Spender (Ed.), *Men's studies modified: The impact of feminism on the academic disciplines.* Oxford: Pergamon.

Lewis, Lionel S. (1975). *Scaling the ivory tower: Merit and its limits in academic careers.* Baltimore: Johns Hopkins University Press.

McMillen, Liz. (1987, September 9). More colleges and more disciplines incorporating scholarship on women into the classroom. *Chronicle of Higher Education*, pp. A15-A17.

McMillen, Liz. (1988, January 27). Council asks colleges to adopt "new agenda" on women's issues. *Chronicle of Higher Education*, pp. A17-A18.

Menges, Robert J., & Exum, William H. (1983, March/April). Barriers to the progress of women and minority faculty. *Journal of Higher Education, 54*(2), 123-144.

Moglen, Helene. (1983). Power and empowerment. In Resa L. Dudovitz (Ed.), Women in academe [Special issue]. *Women's Studies International Forum*, pp. 131-134.

O'Shea, Catherine. (1988, August). Success and the southern belle. *Southern Magazine*, pp. 39-41, 43, 67-70.

Ramey, Estelle R. (1988, April 13). Panel contribution at the minisymposium, "Women and the Sciences: Expectations, Reality, Hope," College Park, MD.

Rohter, Larry. (1987, January 4). Women gain degrees, but not tenure. *New York Times*, p. E9.

Sandler, Bernice R. (1984, February 29). The quiet revolution on campus: How sex discrimination has changed. *Chronicle of Higher Education*, p. 72.

Sandler, Bernice R., & Hall, Roberta M. (1986). *The campus climate revisited: Chilly for women faculty, administrators, and graduate students.* Washington, DC: Association of American Colleges, Project on the Status and Education of Women.

Schneir, Miriam. (1972). Introduction. In Miriam Schneir (Ed.), *Feminism: The essential historical writings.* New York: Vintage.

Segal, David R. (1988, April 4). [Letter to the editor]. *Outlook* (University of Maryland faculty publication).

Sharp, Nancy W., Turk, Judy VanSlyke, Einsiedel, Edna F., Schamber, Linda, & Hollenback, Sharon. (1985). *Faculty women in journalism and mass communications: Problems and progress.* Syracuse, NY; report published with a grant from the Gannett Foundation. (Available from the Association for Education in Journalism and Mass Communication, College of Journalism, 1621 College St., University of South Carolina, Columbia, SC 29208-0251.)

Small but active feminist groups work to meet campus women's basic needs. (1986, April 23). *Chronicle of Higher Education*, pp. 31-32.

Speizer, Jeanne J. (1981). Role models, mentors and sponsors: The elusive concepts. *Signs, 6*(4), 698.

Stanley, Liz, & Wise, Sue. (1983). *Breaking out: Feminist consciousness and feminist research.* London: Routledge & Kegan Paul.

Sudarkasa, Niara. (1987, February 25). Radical and cultural diversity is a key part of the pursuit of excellence in the university. *Chronicle of Higher Education*, p. 42.

Tidball, M. Elizabeth. (1976). Of men and research: The dominant themes in American higher education include neither teaching nor women. *Journal of Higher Education, 47*(4), 373-389.

Turk, T. G. (1981). Women faculty in higher education: Academic administration and governance in a state university system. *Pacific Sociological Review, 24*, 212-236.

White, Michael C., & Crino, Michael D. (1981, Summer). A critical review of female performance, performance training and organizational initiatives designed to aid women in the work-role environment. *Personnel Psychology, 34*, 227-245.

Williams, Marjorie. (1988, February 17). The up-to-date Ms. *Washington Post*, pp. C1, C4.

Wise, Phyllis M. (1988, April 13). Panel contribution at the minisymposium, "Women and the Sciences: Expectations, Reality, Hope," College Park, MD.

7

Women in Mass Communication Education

Who Is Teaching Tomorrow's Communicators?

LINDA SCHAMBER

Who is teaching tomorrow's communicators? Some 76% are men. Who are tomorrow's communicators? About 60% are women.

These two facts alone raise many questions about women in mass communication education, questions that have been addressed by three studies that span the past 17 years. This chapter is an update of a 1985 study by Sharp, Turk, Einsiedel, Schamber, and Hollenback that was funded by the Gannett Foundation.[1] The purpose of the Gannett study was to determine the situations of female educators and to elicit their perceptions of their situations. It was designed to replicate and expand on a 1972 study of the status of women in journalism education by Rush, Oukrup, and Ernst.

Since the first study in 1972, the discipline called "journalism" has broadened to become "mass communication." Many more women have entered the field, both as faculty members and as students. Unfortunately, while it appeared that the teaching qualifications of women came close to equaling those of men in recent years, faculty women overall were still fewer in number at all academic ranks, occupied lower ranks, and were paid less than faculty men.

In 1988, women constituted about 24% of communication faculties. This was a larger proportion than the approximately 18% the Gannett study found in 1985, and a much larger proportion than the 7-8% found in 1972. In 1972, one woman administrator could be found in 172 journalism programs. In 1988, 62 women, or 17%, were identified as heads of 358 communication programs.[2]

Where did faculty women rank? Figure 7.1 compares numbers of male and female faculty members in 1988. The greatest difference was at the te-

Figure 7.1 Numbers of Male and Female Communication Faculty
Members by Rank in 1988

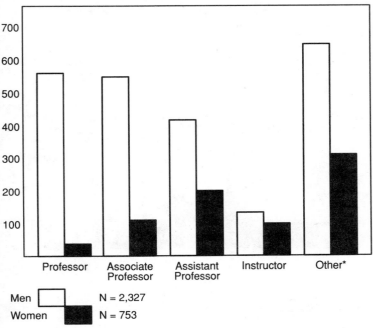

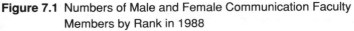

*"Other" includes part-time instructors, full- and part-time lecturers, adjuncts, and
visiting professors.

Based on counts of faculty members in the 1988 directory of the Association for Education in Journalism and Mass Communication. Included 179 programs that named
faculty. Excluded about 200 emeritus faculty, about 160 individuals whose gender
could not be determined by first name, and student instructors.

nured rank of full professor; the smallest difference was at the entry rank
of instructor. In 1988 women represented about 6% of all full professors,
17% of associate professors, 32% of assistant professors, 42% of instructors, and 32% of those with "other" (temporary, part-time) titles. Overall,
less than half (46%) the women were at the top three tenure-track ranks,
whereas two-thirds (67%) of men were at these ranks.

Figure 7.2 compares the distribution of female faculty members by rank
in 1972 and 1988. The proportion of women at each of the top three ranks
was nearly the same after 16 years, but the proportion of instructors
dropped 10 percentage points, while "others" rose 7 points. Obviously,

Figure 7.2 Distribution of Female Communication Faculty Members by Rank in 1972 and 1988

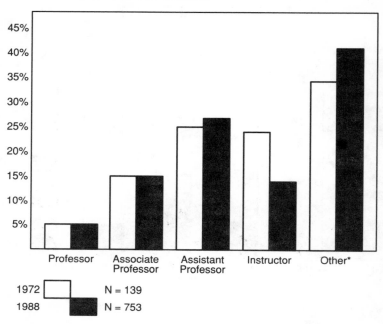

1972 □   N = 139
1988 ■   N = 753

*"Other" includes part-time instructors, full- and part-time lecturers, adjuncts, and visiting professors.

Based on counts of faculty members in the 1988 directory of the Association for Education in Journalism and Mass Communications, and the 1972 directory of the Association for Education in Journalism. Included 179 programs (1988) and 163 programs (1972) that named faculty. Excluded emeritus faculty, faculty whose gender could not be determined by first name, and student instructors.

women had entered teaching, but apparently not at full-time ranks, from which they could best be promoted.

What were academic women paid? According to the 1987-88 annual demographic survey by the Association of Schools of Journalism and Mass Communication (ASJMC), the average salary for all female faculty ($29,676) was $5,373 less than, or 85% of, the average salary for all male faculty ($35,049) (Stuart, 1988). Administrative salaries were much closer: The average salary for female administrators ($59,952) was $1,832 less than, or 97% of, that for male administrators ($61,784).

Table 7.1 Average Salaries of Male and Female Communication Faculty Members by Rank and Qualifications in 1987-88

	Male		*Female*		*Difference*	
Rank						
professor	43,577	(261) a	45,143	(17)	−1,566	(244) b
associate professor	34,662	(323)	33,618	(63)	1,044	(260)
assistant professor	29,076	(234)	28,369	(122)	707	(112)
instructor	25,907	(77)	23,906	(61)	2,001	(16)
Highest degree held						
doctorate	37,401	(463)	33,132	(109)	4,269	(354)
master's	31,877	(334)	27,069	(130)	4,808	(204)
bachelor's	33,208	(50)	27,027	(16)	6,181	(34)
Years of teaching experience						
21+	40,073	(176)	37,651	(19)	2,422	(157)
16-20	37,825	(140)	35,559	(17)	2,266	(123)
11-15	35,439	(152)	32,403	(45)	3,036	(107)
6–10	32,600	(154)	28,899	(57)	3,701	(97)
1–5	30,581	(171)	27,009	(84)	3,572	(87)
< 1	27,069	(11)	25,905	(16)	1,164	(−5) b
Years of industry experience						
21+	35,063	(109)	28,593	(10)	6,470	(99)
16–20	35,398	(86)	29,319	(22)	6,079	(64)
11–15	34,464	(127)	28,124	(39)	6,340	(88)
6–10	35,077	(175)	31,097	(66)	3,980	(109)
1–5	35,266	(231)	29,484	(77)	5,782	(154)
< 1	35,566	(57)	29,998	(16)	5,568	(41)

SOURCE: Adapted from Stuart (1988, Table 8). Based on survey data for 1,178 faculty and 72 administrators in 93 programs.
a. All salaries are weighted up or down to 9 months. Frequencies appear in parentheses.
b. Negative figures resulted when the figure for female was greater than the figure for male.

More detailed comparisons show a great deal of variation. Table 7.1 breaks out average salaries for male and female faculty according to rank, academic degree, years of teaching experience, and years of industry experience.[3] Women's salaries in 1987-88 were lower in all categories except one. For the first time, the average salary of female full professors was $1,566 more than, or 104% of, the average salary for men at the same rank. But these women represented a very small proportion of faculty.

In other categories, the smallest difference, as in previous years, was between assistant professors, where the average salary for women was 98% of that for men. The greatest difference was between those holding bachelor's degrees, where the average salary for women was 81% of that for men. Men's salaries were, in fact, higher than women's in all other categories in the ASJMC report: recency of hiring and major teaching field, and school's geographical region, degree programs, enrollment size, and accreditation status. The survey also found that women faculty on average received lower raises than men (Stuart, 1988).

What were women's qualifications for faculty positions? The 1985 Gannett study included a national survey of women in mass communication education and a content analysis of bylines in scholarly communication journals. The typical survey respondent had nine years of industry experience and either had or was working on her Ph.D. The content analysis found that women published as many articles as men, and some more than men, and that the proportion of female authors far exceeded their proportion on faculties. The 1987-88 ASJMC report showed 43% of female faculty holding doctorates (compared to 55% of men); 58% of women with six or more years of teaching experience (77% of men); and 60% of women with six or more years of industry experience (63% of men). In short, if women were less qualified in the past, they were fast catching up in earning their academic credentials.

How did student populations compare to faculties? According to Peterson's (1988) report on student enrollments, in 1986-87 about 60% of all communication students were female, a proportion that had held steady since 1980. The major area that continued to attract the most women was public relations, with 68% female students. And 40-45% of doctoral students and doctoral graduates—tomorrow's educators—were women. In view of 24% female faculties, and in view of the female-intensive careers for which students were being prepared, were female students being short-changed in terms of role models?

Minorities presented a somewhat different picture. While reliable data were difficult to obtain, recent reports showed that roughly 4% of all faculty and up to 10% of all students were minorities. It is also worth noting that the proportion of women among minority students—65%—was higher than the proportion of women among students of all races. In fact, the very highest proportion of women—72% or more—was found among minority students at the master's level.[4]

Mass communication education was not unique in its gender-related disparities. Similar gaps existed in most disciplines between small proportions of female faculty and large proportions of female students. Average salaries of female faculty members at all ranks across disciplines were lower. Furthermore, higher education in general was plagued by problems that included dropping enrollments and cutbacks on hiring and salaries. These problems affected both men and women—most often younger individuals—who wanted to enter teaching or who sought faculty promotion and tenure.[5]

So far a few situations have been presented that raise many questions. To address these questions, the 1985 Gannett study researchers attempted to probe perceptions of women's status in communication education. They first contacted female educators through a questionnaire survey, then both female and male educators through in-depth interviews. The survey, which was intended to replicate the 1972 survey, was an immediate eye-opener in terms of two trends. One was that the field had broadened so much that a true replication in terms of gathering demographic data was impossible. The other was that attitudes toward the status of women apparently had changed substantially over the more than a decade that had passed between surveys, a time that saw the rise and fall of the ERA ratification movement and changes in many other social and political issues concerning women. As an indication, perhaps, that interest in the topic had waned (or conditions had improved), the Gannett researchers noted that only a third of their addressees returned questionnaires, whereas nearly three-fourths had responded to the 1972 survey.

On the whole, the nearly 200 women who did respond to the Gannett survey had a much more optimistic outlook than did the 1972 respondents. Some 75% of respondents felt that sex discrimination was not a major problem, compared to only 23% in 1972. The Gannett study respondents perceived better treatment of women in academia, and saw female faculty as better educated and more assertive.

Still, a fourth of the respondents did perceive gender-related problems, and a fourth also said they were dissatisfied with their jobs. The three areas of greatest concern continued, as in 1972, to be salary, appointment to administrative positions, and promotion. More than ever, the question was why. The researchers decided to ask 26 leaders in the field — male and female administrators and faculty members—for their opinions and suggestions. This interview portion of the study yielded some refreshing insights.

The first of four main interview questions was, How do you account for the imbalance between the large proportion of women studying mass communication and the small proportion of women teaching mass communication?

Most interviewees felt that the imbalance was a reflection of the past, when men outnumbered women in both industry and academia. Some noted that, for potential faculty members, there is a time lag of at least a decade after earning the bachelor's degree during which they must get industry experience and earn graduate degrees. Others mentioned two more factors that might slow women's progress into teaching: family obligations, and the fact that the industry was drawing away many of the best women by offering high salaries.

There was quite a bit of comment—more than expected—on the importance of role modeling. A male administrator said there was a need for "some of the special characteristics women bring; a certain kind of sensitivity perhaps men don't have, certain kinds of interests that men perhaps do not have." He also said women "have an enormous extra workload that is not on anybody's books . . . of being role models for women students, and advisers on an incredible number of things that male faculty would never have—and that strains their energies tremendously. They need help. They need colleagues to help share the burden."

The second question: Why were the Gannett survey respondents far less likely to see sexual discrimination as a problem with their careers than were their 1972 counterparts?

The interviewees agreed that, as one male administrator put it, "Things are better and people realize they are. There are more women in higher positions. . . . Things are better throughout journalism faculties." But several female interviewees cautioned against being overly optimistic. A faculty member said, "I don't know how people could be in this field and not feel that discrimination is a problem. I think either they are ignorant and blissfully breezing along, thinking that nothing is going to happen to them, or else they think the people it has happened to brought it on themselves."

Another experienced female academic said that some women had not been in college teaching long enough to see exactly what was going on: "The longer you're on the job as a woman, the higher you get, the more you look around, the more you open your ears, the less satisfied you become." Many new female assistant professors, according to another faculty woman, were so delighted to have their jobs that they did not want to be critical.

One woman described the "queen bee syndrome," which she said explains the behavior of many female professors under the age of 35. The queen bee, she said, "is the only female around, and she honestly believes she made it on her own. She is surrounded by adoring males and doesn't care about other women. When she thinks about the other, less fortunate women, she rationalizes, 'If they were just as good as I am, they would have gotten where I've gotten and wouldn't be complaining.' "

But many female interviewees stressed that women in communication education in the 1980s had not gotten there on their own. One said that these younger women are the "beneficiaries of some people who fought very hard and went through a lot of pain. . . . They fought the fight and they fought it so effectively that it is no longer socially acceptable, or academically acceptable, or considered acceptable professional practice for discrimination to be visible."

Most women said the equal rights movement did have a positive effect, although very few of them were actively involved in it. With regard to affirmative action, several administrators complained that the procedures were burdensome, and some women said the policy could work against women in cases where, once hired, they were not taken seriously.

The third question: How valid were the concerns of the Gannett survey respondents regarding salaries, appointment to administrative positions, and promotion and tenure?

Most interviewees perceived that women faculty were paid less than men across the country, but—interestingly—that salaries and raises were awarded fairly at their own institutions. A common response was that current salary differences were a reflection of the past. A male administrator said, "There have been discrepancies, past disparities, past inequities, but I think these are changing." In his own program, he said the women hired in the past five or six years were "doing as well as, if not better than, men." Another male administrator explained that "the salary you eventually receive is based on your entry salary. We have people who, since we hired them, have raised their qualifications and deserve more money but they must go into a grievance situation [with the union] in order to raise their salaries."

A female faculty member wondered whether women might not be less active than men in seeking to improve their salaries—for example, by using outside offers as negotiating leverage. On the other hand, a male administrator said he had found that women understand the reward system. "They are much more systematic about it. A lot of men just bumble into the academy and shuffle from one rank to another or even down in the process. I have found that the women tend to want to know, 'What do I have to do?' or 'What is it going to take to get promoted?'"

On the matter of women being moved into administrative positions, many interviewees did perceive some discrimination. They also felt that women simply had not been on faculties long enough. A male administrator said "the most vigorous women these days in journalism education are perhaps in their early 30s to early 40s, and administrators for the most part tend to come from the age of 45 up." Still others said women may be more reluctant than men to leave teaching for the bureaucracy and conflicts of administration.

While the overwhelming majority of interviewees did not see sexual discrimination as a problem in promotion and tenure decisions, about half said it took women longer to be promoted than men. This lag was associated with women's heavy family commitments or with a lack of knowledge about how to build credentials that balance teaching and research activities. "Women continue to accept the burden of the nurturing role," said a female interviewee, "and because they do, they are more likely to see teaching as a more important activity than research."

On the other hand, a male administrator said, "Any woman who is relatively visible in the field and has good credentials and is productive can generate offers from other institutions. In so doing, she becomes a retention case at her own school and most universities have the capability to increase salary at that point and sometimes to offer early promotion and tenure."

Still others noted that it was difficult, in view of recent budget cuts, for any faculty member—man or woman—to be promoted or tenured. "The people who have come along lately have had a much harder time than people who came along 10 years ago," said a male administrator.

Virtually everyone who was surveyed or interviewed claimed that overt discrimination was no longer a problem. But the topic of subtle discriminatory attitudes turned up some interesting responses. Very few of the men interviewed were aware of any sort of problem at all. But well over half the female survey respondents said they thought women have to work harder than men to get ahead, and women interviewees readily named specific problems.

Several female interviewees said it was because the incidence of outright sexual discrimination had been reduced that subtle discriminatory practices have become more of an issue. One said that because men no longer dare to be blatantly discriminatory, "all the discrimination I'm talking about is subtle. . . . It's hard to prove, hard to put your finger on. If people are honest, they'll admit that it's going on. It happens when the review board and personnel committees look over a candidate's records in the department. If they don't understand the journals that women are publishing in or something, then, boy, they must not be reputable. . . . Women have two choices: either do the traditional stuff and don't make waves, or fight."

One woman complained of being addressed less deferentially by male colleagues, staffers, and students; of being called by her first name instead of addressed as "doctor" or "professor." A female administrator complained, "We have some [male] international students who don't like to be taught by a woman and they freely admit it. They don't like this program being run by a woman."

Two male interviewees concurred with the women interviewed. One said deans and graduate directors were sometimes guilty of acting paternalistically toward women. The other said he was "sure that dozens of slurs occur, some intended and some unintended." Their seriousness, he went on, depended "on the sensitivity of the female faculty."

The final interview question was, What kind of future do you see for women in communication education?

The responses were quite optimistic. Interviewees noted that many women were entering at the lower academic ranks and needed time to move up. They were less optimistic about women moving into administration. Many mentioned other problems that span all of college education, such as dropping enrollments and budget cutbacks.

In short, the optimism was tempered by many "buts." A statement made at the beginning of this chapter and supported by data bears repeating: Faculty women overall were still fewer in number at all academic ranks, occupied lower ranks, and were paid less than men. The "buts" were supported by the perceptions and concerns of survey respondents and interview subjects:

> . . . but women faculty's qualifications nearly equaled those of men.
> . . . but female students were not being provided with enough female role models.
> . . . but faculty women were still very concerned about salaries, administrative appointments, and promotion.

The "buts" were not resolved by the research, but the research clarified the issues and pointed out directions for future action. These suggestions, some of which are already being implemented, came out of the Gannett study:

- Recruit more female students into graduate programs as a step toward encouraging them to become professional academics and academic administrators. Portray teaching and administration as viable career opportunities. Offer personal support, and set up grants and other financial aid programs.

- Encourage junior faculty women to balance teaching and research activities so they can build better files for promotion and tenure. Encourage them to seek advice from colleagues on how to advance their careers, and to network with more experienced faculty women across the country.

- Continue the work of the Committee on the Status of Women of the Association for Education in Journalism and Mass Communication (AEJMC), formed in 1972, to track women and men at all levels of education; monitor affirmative action and accreditation practices concerning recruitment, hiring, promotion, tenure, and salary; and encourage workshops on administration.

Women in communication education have indeed made progress, but they have not achieved parity. It is apparent that no woman can afford to play the role of queen bee.

NOTES

1. The Gannett report was mailed to administrators of journalism and mass communication programs and to academic libraries across the country. It can also be obtained for $2 from the AEJMC, College of Journalism, 1621 College St., University of South Carolina, Columbia, SC 29208-0251.

2. Frequencies and percentages varied according to source. Current figures were based on head counts by first name (where gender was determinable) in the 1988 AEJMC directory (Coleman, McGill, & Williams, 1988) and on the 1987-88 ASJMC demographic survey (Stuart, 1988). Sources of earlier figures were similar and are cited in the report of the 1985 Gannett study.

3. Stuart (1988) notes in the introduction to the ASJMC report that "reported data on number of years professional and teaching experience are, in a number of cases, questionable." She explained that where the survey assumed that respondents would indicate years of full-time experience, many apparently included part-time experience, because the sum of both kinds of experience was impossibly high for their ages. The complete demographic report was sent to member schools. It is available to nonmembers for $10 from the ASJMC, University of South Carolina, College of Journalism, 1621 College St., Columbia, SC 29208-0251.

4. The 4% minority faculty was reported by Stuart (1988) in the ASJMC report. In a 1987 interview, Stuart said she did not analyze minorities (e.g., according to gender or salary) further because individuals would be identifiable. Some student enrollment totals in Peterson's (1988) report were inaccurate or did not jibe across tables for gender and level of study. Data on minority students depended on which schools reported, how they reported, and the fact that numbers of minorities in some categories were very small.

5. Sources on trends in higher education include annual reports of the National Center for Education Statistics (e.g., *Digest of Education Statistics* and *The Condition of Education*), reports of the American Association of University Professors, and articles in the *Chronicle of Higher Education* and popular sources such as the *New York Times* and weekly newsmagazines.

REFERENCES

Coleman, Lillian S., McGill, Jennifer H., & Williams, Fred L. (Eds.). (1988). *Journalism and mass communication directory*. Columbia, SC: Association for Education in Journalism and Mass Communication.

Peterson, Paul V. (1988). Journalism and mass comm enrollment leveled off in '87. *Journalism Educator*, *43*(1).

Rush, Ramona R., Oukrup, Carol E., & Ernst, Sandra W. (1972). *More than you ever wanted to know about women and journalism education*. Paper presented at the annual conference of the Association for Education in Journalism.

Sharp, Nancy W., Turk, Judy VanSlyke, Einsiedel, Edna F., Schamber, Linda, & Hollenback, Sharon. (1985). *Faculty women in journalism and mass communications: Problems and progress*. Syracuse, NY; report published with a grant from the Gannett Foundation. (Available from the Association for Education in Journalism and Mass Communication, College of Journalism, 1621 College St., University of South Carolina, Columbia, SC 29208-0251.)

Snyder, Thomas B. (1987). *Digest of education statistics 1987*. Washington, DC: U.S. Department of Education, Office of Educational Research and Improvement, National Center for Education Statistics.

Stuart, Elnora W. (1988). *1987-88 Association of Schools of Journalism and Mass Communication faculty/administrator demographic survey*. Columbia, SC: ASJMC.

PART II

The Profession

Section A. A Close-up of Women in, on, and Through Mass Communication

8

Economic Equity and the Journalistic Work Force

SUE LAFKY

A T-shirt recently sold by the American Association of University Women offered a humorous insight into one of the most serious concerns of the women's movement: "For a woman to make as much in a day as a man, she'd have to work till 10:30 at night . . . then who'd make dinner?"[1] The discrepancy in salaries between men and women workers, and the dual work roles that women have had—outside the home as part of the paid labor market and within the home as part of the unpaid labor market—have been major concerns and rallying points for the modern women's movement.

U.S. Bureau of the Census data have shown that the difference in the earnings ratio of women to men in the full-time U.S. labor force remained fairly stable between 1955 and 1983, with the annual earnings of women averaging between 57% and 64% of those of men during the two decades.[2] In 1986, however, there was a change in the ratio, and some cause for celebration among those concerned about economic equity for women and men workers, when Census Bureau statistics showed that the average wage for full-time female workers had jumped to 70% of the amount earned by men.[3]

WOMEN IN THE WORK FORCE

The decrease in the earnings gap was preceded by a number of changes in women's participation in the work force, including an increase in the percentage of women workers and a decrease in occupational segregation (see, for example, Beller, 1984; also see other chapters in Reskin, 1984). Bianchi and Spain (1986), in a study for the National Committee for Research on the 1980 Census, linked this increased participation to several factors: the decline in the average number of children per American woman from more than three to fewer than two; the doubling of the proportion of women with a college degree from 6% to 13% during the past two decades; and the increase in divorce, bringing about the necessity for women to earn a living outside the home.

Many of these changes have been reflected in the journalistic work force. This chapter deals with some of those changes, although the major focus is on comparing the income of men and women journalists. Many of the data for this study come from my own secondary analysis of a study of U.S. journalists conducted in 1982-83 by David H. Weaver and G. Cleveland Wilhoit (1986) of Indiana University. Data from the 1982-83 study are compared to data on women and men's income from the 1971 survey of U.S journalists by sociologists John W. C. Johnstone, Edward J. Slawski, and William W. Bowman (1976). Specifically, this chapter involves a demographic profile of men and women journalists; a comparison of the real earnings of women and men journalists in 1971 and 1982-83; an examination of the best predictors of income for men and women journalists in 1982-83, with a particular focus on gender-related interactions for the sample as a whole; and a comparison of women's income as a percentage of men's for some of the significant predictors of income for women and men journalists in 1982-83.

Weaver and Wilhoit found that the participation of women in the journalistic work force had increased between the time of their study and the study by Johnstone and his colleagues in 1971. When Johnstone et al. wrote their much-quoted portrait of American journalists, they made frequent mention of the news*men* who made up about 80% of their sample. A decade later, Weaver and Wilhoit found that it was more appropriate to use the non-gender-specific title "journalist" to describe those who worked in U.S. newsrooms. By 1982, nearly 34% of the journalists in the United States were women, and the proportion of women journalists under 25 years old did not lag much behind the proportion of women in the labor force as a whole (Weaver & Wilhoit, 1986, p. 21).

Women and men journalists, like their counterparts in other fields, were more likely to be college educated in 1982-83 than they were in 1971 (Weaver & Wilhoit, 1986, p. 41). However, while men in journalism were more likely than women to hold college degrees in 1971, the gap had closed by 1982-83.[4] And like their counterparts in society as a whole, women journalists were more likely to be unmarried than they were the decade before, and were less likely to be married than their male counterparts.[5]

INCOME FOR WOMEN IN JOURNALISM

A number of studies have documented that women in journalism, like their counterparts in other fields, have made less money than men in their chosen occupation. When Johnstone et al. conducted their study of U.S. journalists in 1971, they found that women in journalism made an average of 64 cents for each dollar earned by the average man in the field. One of the most significant findings of the Weaver and Wilhoit study was that the disparity had lessened considerably (Johnstone et al., 1976, p. 82-83), with women earning an average of 71% of what men in journalism made in 1981.[6]

Although Johnstone and his colleagues found in 1971 that the median annual income of men younger than 25 was 36% higher than that of women, Weaver and Wilhoit (1986, pp. 82-83) found essentially no disparity at that age level. In addition, Weaver and Wilhoit found that among journalists between the ages of 25 and 34, the disparity between men's and women's salaries had dropped from 17% to 13% in the decade between Johnstone et al.'s study and theirs. Overall, the median male-female salary disparity had dropped from 55% to 40% during the decade.

Researchers disagree as to why the wage gap appears to be narrowing between men and women workers. Gordon Greene, assistant division chief of the income branch of the U.S. Census Bureau, has argued that it is because "women are making progress in entering higher-paying occupations" (McClure, 1988, pp. 6, 8). For example, from 1979 to 1986, women's representation rose from 34% to 45% of accountants and auditors, from 28% to 40% of computer programmers, and from 10% to 15% of attorneys. The Census Bureau data show that both "men and women have lower wages in woman-dominated fields," he said, adding that he believes that if more women enter male-dominated fields, the market would guarantee increased wages for those women in more traditional jobs (McClure, 1988, pp. 6, 8).

However, the Women's Research and Education Institute (WREI), an independent agency that started as the research arm of the Congressional Caucus on Women's Issues, has countered that Greene, and others who share his viewpoint, focused on the good news at the expense of the impending bad news. Both the U.S. Bureau of Labor Statistics and the WREI have found that what others have hailed as "progress" in closing the gap in male-female earnings actually had to do with falling wages among men. An AFL-CIO report noted that real wages have been sliding since 1977, and that real hourly earnings dropped 6% between 1979 and 1985 (McClure, 1988, pp. 6, 8).

One area that has recently gained the attention of researchers is a trend that has been labeled "occupational resegregation." Some labor force analysts believe women are moving into male-dominated fields only to discover that their growing presence has led to lower wages. The WREI is currently undertaking a study of whether women are confronting economic inequalities regardless of the field they pursue (McClure, 1988).

Researchers do agree that the concentration of women into occupations different from those of men plays a crucial role in accounting for male-female earning differentials (for example, see Bayes, 1988). There are those who have voiced the fear that the increasing participation of women in the journalistic work force and in other areas of mass communication, such as public relations, could lead to lower earnings for everyone in those fields.

In fact, while Weaver and Wilhoit found that the gap between the incomes of men and women had narrowed, they also found that journalists as a whole had less earning power in the 1980s than they did in the 1970s. The median journalist in 1981 had about $7,000 less annual purchasing power than the median journalist in 1970 (Weaver & Wilhoit, 1986, p. 82).

In its twenty-fourth annual survey of the public relations field, *pr reporter* reported that for 1987, the U.S. median salary stood at $45,000, the same level as in 1986. The author of that study attributed this stagnation to "further restructuring of the work force toward lower-paid younger and female personnel" (Jackson, 1988). By 1987, according to the report, women accounted for 48.1% of all public relations practitioners—up 3.2 percentage points from the previous year and a higher climb than the 2.3 points from 1986 to 1987.

In a study for the International Association for Business Communicators discussed by Carolyn Garrett Cline in Chapter 14 of this volume, Cline et al. (1986) found evidence that the better-paying areas and departments within the public relations and business communication fields appeared to be those with the greatest salary gap, and those in which the predominantly male employees earned the largest mean salaries (pp. vi, 2-4). Limitations in their study kept the research team from finding solid evidence to support that finding, however, and they suggest that more research needs to be done on this question.

Weaver and Wilhoit found that the median journalist had about $7,000 less annual real purchasing power than the median journalist who was interviewed in 1971 by Johnstone et al. A comparison of the incomes of men and women in the 1971 and 1982-83 studies illustrates rather dramatically the decline in purchasing power (see Table 8.1). In 1981 dollars, more of both sexes were in the under-$9,359 category and fewer were in the over-$32,760 categories.

Table 8.1.   Income for Men and Women Journalists, 1970 and 1981, in 1981 Dollars (in percentages)

	1970		1981	
Income	*Men*	*Women*	*Men*	*Women*
Below $9,359	4.7	19.5	22.2	33.7
$9,360-$14,039	5.0	15.7	16.3	26.6
$14,040-$18,719	8.9	17.8	14.2	14.5
$18,720-$23,399	15.4	15.3	11.8	8.9
$23,400-$28,079	17.0	15.5	13.2	7.1
$28,080-$32,759	14.3	9.6	8.8	4.1
$32,760-$37,439	12.1	4.8	4.8	2.7
$37,440-$42,119	6.0	0.9	3.2	0.0
$42,120-$46,798	3.5	0.2	1.4	1.5
$46,800-$51,479	3.7	0.5	2.4	0.3
Above $51,480	9.3	0.2	1.7	0.6

NOTE: The Consumer Price Index was used to compare the 1970 and 1981 earnings.
SOURCE: Figures for 1970 were calculated from Bowman (1974, pg 149, Table 3.20); figures for 1981 were obtained from a secondary analysis of data from the Weaver and Wilhoit survey.

THE HUMAN CAPITAL MODEL

Scholars have also disagreed as to why the wage gap between men and women exists. One explanation involves applying the human capital model, which posits that since women do not anticipate working for as many years, they therefore invest less in acquiring labor market skills (Mincer & Polachek, 1974, pp. 76-108). Economists Jacob Mincer and Stanley Polachek have argued that when women leave the labor force to rear children, their job skills become stale and they suffer a wage penalty when they reenter. They have also argued that employers may invest less in women employees because they believe women may take time out of their careers to have children and that, as employers, they will not enjoy the same return on their investment that they will with male employees. In this sense the human capital explanation is a supply-side model focusing on variation in job preferences and qualifications that men and women bring to the job market.

Yet the human capital model also offers a potential demand-side explanation for the decrease in real earnings for workers during the past few years. Under this model, discrimination is a cost to the employer because it leads to a smaller pool of potential workers, and this smaller pool leads to higher wages. In contrast, if there is a lessening of discrimination, the larger size of the work force would allow employers to pay workers less money.[7]

An alternative explanation to the human capital model is a demand-side model that focuses on prelabor market or societal discrimination.[8] Francine Blau and and Marianne Ferber (1986) of the University of Illinois at Urbana-Champaign have described this as "the multitude of social influences that cause women to make decisions that adversely influence their status in the labor market" (p. 182). Societal discrimination differs from labor market discrimination, which occurs when two equally qualified persons are treated differently solely on the basis of sex, race, age, disability, or some other factor. Societal discrimination adversely affects the economic status of women by producing differences in economic outcomes between men and women that cannot be accounted for by differences in productivity-related characteristics or the qualifications of the individual (Blau & Ferber, 1986, p. 229).

In using multiple regression—a statistical technique for estimating the relationship between a continuous dependent variable and two or more continuous or discrete independent variables—both Johnstone and his colleagues and Weaver and Wilhoit found gender to be a statistically significant predictor of income.

In both studies, the strongest predictor of income was years of experience in the news media (Johnstone et al., 1976, p. 236; Weaver & Wilhoit, 1986, p. 86). The second strongest predictor for the study by Johnstone et al. was city size—a variable not included in the Weaver and Wilhoit study. Johnstone et al. found that although regional factors did have an effect on income, the size of the market seemed to explain away much of the impact of the organization size and media sector on income levels (p. 140). Other statistically significant predictors in the 1971 study included level of education, the selectivity of the college attended, the prominence of the news organization the journalist worked for, and the scope of the journalist's managerial duties.

Johnstone and his colleagues call their finding that being male was a positive predictor of income to be "the most startling finding" to emerge from their analysis (p. 140), and conclude that a systematic wage discrimination favoring men pervades the U.S. news media (p. 142). For the 1971 study of journalists, gender was the third strongest predictor of income among all of those surveyed and was the second strongest predictor among those who earned college degrees. They write:

> One is further ahead in predicting earnings by knowing simply that a journalist is a man than by knowing what his job functions are, what region of the country or sector of the industry he works in, how much formal school he has had, or the size or prominence of the news organization he works for. (p. 140)

Weaver and Wilhoit (1986, pp. 82-87) found that the size of an organization's editorial staff was the second strongest predictor of income, followed by whether the editorial staff of the organization was represented by a union—a predictor that was not addressed in the regression analysis conducted by Johnstone and his colleagues. Other positive predictors for the Weaver and Wilhoit study were working for a television station or newsmagazine, the respondent's level of education, and having managerial duties.

Variables in Weaver and Wilhoit's analysis that were not statistically significant were region of the country; whether the organization was group owned or independent; working for a radio station, daily newspaper, or weekly newspaper; whether the respondent had reporting or editing duties; age; whether the respondent worked for an organization of prominence; and whether the respondent had a journalism major or minor in college or had earned a graduate degree.[9]

In a national study of the earnings of local television news reporters discussed in Chapter 12 of this book, Conrad Smith, Eric S. Fredin, and Carroll Ann Ferguson (1988) found that market size was the strongest predictor of income—accounting for 51% of the variance. Smith et al. drew upon the work of sociologists Toby L. Parcel and Charles W. Mueller (1983) to ask whether women and men journalists had obtained equivalent returns for their investment in the labor market and for the resources they possess. The human capital perspective outlined by the sociologists led Smith et al. to hypothesize that interactions between gender and various market, organization, and individual characteristics might influence the returns that men and women receive on their investment in the labor force.

Smith et al.'s analysis showed that the older the reporter and the larger the market, the better the return on earnings for men. They also found that the women television reporters benefited financially more than men by moving relatively often, by moving to larger markets, or both. Women also were found to benefit more than men as the proportion of men within an individual news organization increased, and women also benefited more than men financially when they earned awards for their work (see Smith et al., 1988).

PREDICTORS OF INCOME IN 1981

In looking at the best predictors of income for the 1982-83 sample of journalists, the dependent variable, income, came in response to the question, "Would you please tell me what your total personal income was, before taxes, from your work in the communications field during 1981?"

Although income was measured by actual dollar amounts as well as in ordinal-level categories, the 15 ordinal-level categories were used here in order to maximize the number of cases used in the analysis. The lowest category for the dependent variable was below $10,000 and the highest category was over $75,000.

Whenever possible, variables that would provide tests of the human capital model or that had been statistically significant predictors of income in previous studies were chosen for inclusion as the independent variables in the regression equation.[10]

It was hypothesized that the relationship between earnings and various organizational and individual characteristics would not be the same for men and women, and that interactions between gender and these variables would be statistically significant. Although results of the study by Smith et al. (1988) suggest that a number of other interactions might be statistically significant,[11] I chose for the sake of simplification to focus on four gender-related interactions—gender and age, gender and years of experience, gender and organizational size, and gender and education. The most frequent approach to the possibility of interaction is the inclusion of multiplicative terms in the multiple regression equation. In this study, ordinary least squares regression was used.[12]

In the multiple regression analysis (Table 8.2), gender was a significant predictor of income. In a regression equation with gender as the sole independent variable, the b showed that there was a $6,556 difference between men's and women's incomes. When other variables were taken into account in the main effects model (Table 8.2), there was still a $2,700 overall income advantage for males.[13]

Table 8.2   Predictors of Income for U. S. Journalists, 1982-83
               (multiple regression, N = 927)

Variable	Main Effects Beta	b	Main Effects and Interactions Beta	b
Being female	−.10	−2701***	.14	3722
Years of experience	.40	480***	.45	536***
Year began work for current employer	.03	42	.03	40
Organization size	.30	49***	.30	49***
Medium				
newsmagazine	.21	10950***	.21	10506***
television	.09	3284**	.08	3073**
daily newspaper	−.12	−3059**	−.13	−3269**
weekly newspaper	−.10	−2701**	−.10	−3343**
wire service	−.02	−917	−.02	−1252
Managerial duties	.13	3158***	.12	3119***
Union shop	.13	3525***	.12	3419***
Level of education	.12	1449***	.14	1774***
Marital status:				
married	−.04	−926	−.05	−1428
single	−.16	−4240***	−.18	−4779***
widowed	−.04	−3809	−.03	−3189
Age	−.06	−62	−.07	−77
Being white	.03	1934	.03	1647
Constant		6708		9571
Adjusted R^2 = .52913				
Gender-related interactions				
gender/experience			−.11	−206*
gender/age			.00	−13
gender/education			−.18	−1146
gender/organization size			.02	5
Constant				6287
Adjusted R^2 = .53240				

*p < .05; **p < .01; ***p < .001.

Years of experience was the strongest positive predictor of income—a finding that was expected because of the previous analysis by Weaver and Wilhoit. Age was not a statistically significant predictor of income, and neither was the year the respondent began working for the organization for which she or he was employed at the time of the survey. However, it should be noted that the variables of age and the year that the respondent started working for his or her current organization were both highly correlated with years of experience. Age and years of experience with current organization were significant predictors of income when included in regression equations without years of experience as an independent variable.

Two other fairly strong positive predictors of income were the size of the news organization's editorial staff and working for a newsmagazine. Working for a weekly newspaper, a wire service, or a daily newspaper were not statistically significant predictors of income.

Other positive predictors of income for the sample as a whole included working for a television station, having managerial duties, and having more years of education. And, as also was expected from the Weaver and Wilhoit analysis, being a female was a negative predictor of income, as was being single. It is important to note, however, that being single was strongly correlated with being younger and less experienced. Therefore, that finding may be a statistical artifact. Being married or widowed was not a significant predictor of income for the sample.

The finding that race was not a statistically significant predictor of income should be interpreted cautiously, given that only about 5% of the 1,001 journalists interviewed were people of color.

In the second multiple regression analysis (Table 8.2), designed to look at the effect of the gender-related interactions on income, only one statistically significant interaction—between gender and years of experience—was found. This interaction favored men, with women earning about $206 less than men for each year of experience they had accumulated.

A further comparison of the predictors of income for men and women journalists was possible when separate regression runs were made for each group and the betas and b's were compared. Overall, the statistically significant predictors for women and men journalists were similar, with two notable exceptions: working for a television station and level of education (see Table 8.3). Working for a television station was a positive predictor of income for women but not for men. The level of education was a statistically significant positive predictor of income for men but not for women. An examination of the interaction effects showed that the direction of the

Table 8.3   Predictors of Income for Women and Men Journalists, 1982-83

Variable	Women (N = 307)			Men (N = 620)		
	Beta	b	T	Beta	b	T
Years of experience	.33	353	4.109***	.43	513	2.744***
Year began work for current employer	−.02	−20	−.205	.02	31	−.469
Organization size	.39	50	7.579***	.29	49	8.291***
Medium						
newsmagazine	.24	9266	4.389***	.21	11412	5.906***
television	.15	4207	2.521*	.07	2840	1.889
daily newspaper	−.10	−1868	−1.311	−.14	−3652	−2.856**
weekly newspaper	−.09	−1902	−1.262	−.11	−3987	−2.771**
wire service	.01	605	.219	.03	−1877	−.898
Managerial duties	.15	2831	3.460***	.13	3363	4.205***
Union shop	.14	3118	2.811**	.13	3792	3.691***
Level of education	.05	518	1.183	.13	1696	4.205***
Marital status:						
married	.03	559	.450	−.10	−2751	−1.799
single	−.11	−1984	−1.501	−.22	−6444	−3.851***
widowed	−.04	−1958	−.857	.01	2249	.315
Being white	.04	1518	1.038	.05	3947	1.897
Age	−.12	10928	3.195	−.08	−88	−1.156
Constant					9687	2.744
Adjusted R^2 = .48061				Adjusted R^2 = .50665		

*p < .05; **p < .01; ***p < .001.

effects for the interaction between gender and education favored men. It is possible that such an effect would have shown up if a larger sample had been available.

An examination of the median income for women and men in journalism showed that the gap between men's and women's income was quite small for journalists with less than 10 years of experience and those under

25 years of age (see Table 8.4). Women in each of these categories earned 95 cents for each dollar earned by their male counterparts. More research with these cohort groups will be needed to see whether the wage gap between men and women stays the same or widens over time.

Overall, the results shown in Table 8.4 should be interpreted cautiously, and in conjunction with the findings of the multiple regression analysis, because a journalist's income cannot be predicted by a single variable such as age. In fact, as dramatic as the differences between men's and women's income are by age, the regression analysis shows that age was not a significant predictor when other control variables—particularly years of experience—were included in the regression equation. However, seeing the differences between men's and women's wages broken down by age, experience, medium, managerial duties, and whether the respondent worked in a union shop do demonstrate salary inequities by gender.

Table 8.4   Median Income for Men and Women Journalists, 1981

	Men $	Women $	Difference $	Women's Income As a Percentage of Men's
Age				
under 25	10,571	10,017	554	95
25-34	17,975	15,600	2,375	87
35-44	26,000	15,100	10,900	58
45-54	29,960	17,000	12,960	57
55 and older	25,125	12,125	13,000	48
Education				
some high school	20,499	—	—	—
high school graduate	17,933	11,990	5,943	67
some college	19,500	12,000	7,500	61
college graduate	19,801	13,990	5,811	71
some graduate training	23,050	16,916	6,134	73
graduate degree	26,156	20,000	6,156	76
Years of experience				
under 5	11,525	11,000	525	95
5-9	17,500	16,820	680	96
10-14	24,999	20,050	4,949	80
15-19	29,050	17,500	11,550	60
20-24	25,900	15,500	10,400	60
over 25	29,833	24,000	5,833	80

Table 8.4   Median Income for Men and Women Journalists, 1981
(continued)

	Men $	Women $	Difference $	Women's Income As a Percentage of Men's
Size of editorial staff				
1-10	16,000	11,998	4,002	75
11-25	17,987	11,975	6,012	67
26-50	20,950	19,925	1,025	95
51-100	26,150	18,933	7,217	72
more than 100	31,875	26,025	5,850	81
Managerial duties				
yes	22,000	16,830	5,170	76
no	18,988	13,002	5,986	68
Union				
member	27,950	22,000	5,950	79
nonmember	16,400	12,802	3,598	78
Medium				
daily newspaper	22,000	15,037	6,963	68
weekly newspaper	15,020	10,992	4,028	73
news agency	25,050	11,500	13,550	46
newsmagazine	35,000	28,500	6,500	81
television	17,050	16,812	238	99
radio	16,000	11,960	4,040	75

NOTE: Data on 62 people were excluded from this table because they had worked less than one year.

DISCUSSION

The findings of this study support the findings of other statistical studies of the wage gap that have found that no more than 50% of the disparity in earnings between men and women can be attributed to free-market supply factors such as differences in skill, effort, responsibility, education, family investment, or the personal human capital resources that men and women bring to their jobs (Treiman & Hartmann, 1981, p. 22) The results of this study do not lend support to the explanations of the wage gap set forth by human capital theorists.

A complete explanation for the complex ways that sex discrimination works in the journalistic work force is beyond the scope of this study. The statistical analysis cannot explain, for example, how premarket discrimination (by families through the socialization process or by the actions of those in educational institutions) or the exclusionary practices of employers (because of their own tastes, statistical discriminations, and/or the tastes of employees or the market) might explain who gets hired or who seeks jobs in the journalistic work force (see Blau, 1984).

The fact that wages for journalists have declined in constant dollars as more women have entered the field is a finding that supports the occupational resegregation hypothesis as well a demand-side model. There are alternative explanations for this finding, however. In order to test further the hypothesis that the increased participation of women in an occupation leads to a decline in real wages, it would be necessary to compare the real earnings of men and women in a number of occupations over time.

It is clear, however, that women receive less of an economic return for their years of experience, and that this is an issue that needs continued attention by those in the field. This finding may support Mincer and Polachek's (1974) assertion that when women leave the labor force to bear and rear children, the skills they have become stale and they suffer a wage penalty when they reenter. However, there are other possible explanations for this finding, and the finding is countered in this study by the fact that being married was not a negative predictor of income for women.

Blau has pointed out that one potential problem with the human capital model is that wage discrimination may influence the amount of human capital (including experience) that women accumulate. Yet another possibility is that the lower returns of experience for women may reflect employer discrimination in permitting women access to on-the-job training opportunities needed for advancement (Blau, 1984).

Weaver and Wilhoit's finding that the income gap between women and men is narrowing for younger journalists who are in the beginning stages of their careers is encouraging. It will be important to continue to document the career paths and wage histories of these journalists over time, and to look at the real wages of women and men journalists in comparison to those of women and men in other occupational groups.

NOTES

1. From an advertisement by the American Association of University Women published in the June 1987 issue of *Ms.* (p. 26).

2. See Bianchi and Spain (1986, p. 172). The ratio has stayed near 60% in most years.

3. From U.S. Census Bureau statistics quoted by *Washington Post* reporter Rich Spencer (1986).

4. While 60% of the men and 50.8% of the women journalists had earned a college degree in 1971, the numbers increased to 74% of the men and 73.6% of the women in 1982-83.

5. The 1971 figures are taken from Bowman (1974). The figures for 1982-83 come from my own research for my doctoral dissertation at Indiana University.

6. While the median income for male journalists was $11,955 in 1970, the median income for women journalists was $7,702—a difference of $4,253. See Johnstone et al., (1976, Table 8.4, p. 237).

7. An explanation of this can be found in Smith, Fredin, and Ferguson (1988).

8. For a more in-depth explanation of these models, see Blau and Ferber (1986).

9. Results of Weaver and Wilhoit's multiple regression analysis are reported on page 86 of *The American Journalist*. The significance levels reported here were not published in the book and were obtained from a printout of the regression run used for that table. The published table mistakenly reports that the standardized regression coefficient for working at an organization in the North Central region was .41. However, that coefficient was actually -.04.

10. These variables were as follows: number of years that the respondent had worked in journalism; the year the respondent began working for her/his current employer; the number of editorial or news people employed in the respondent's organization; the highest grade the respondent completed in school, with choices ranging from grade school through graduate school; and age, with the answer recorded in number of years. Dummy variables were created for variables dealing with whether the respondent had any managerial responsibilities or supervised any editorial employees (1 = manager, 0 = nonmanager); whether editorial employees working for the respondent's news organization belonged to a union (1 = yes, 0 = no); and gender (1 = female, 0 = male). Also included were two variables found to be significant predictors of income in other studies—race and marital status. (It would have also been appropriate to test whether or not having children was a significant predictor of income. However, only journalists who had been married were asked this question, so I did not include it in the regression equation.) Because the number of journalists of color was so small—with about 95% of those interviewed being white—the racial categories were collapsed into white (1) or nonwhite (0). The dummy variables for marital status were married, single, and widowed (1), and divorced/separated (0).

11. Other interactions found to be predictors of earnings were market/news shop interactions (market/shop size/proportion male; market/unionization; market/news ratings); market/reporting interactions (market/news awards; market/education).

12. Missing cases were handled by pairwise deletion.

13. For an explanation of how to interpret multiple regression analysis, see Bohrnstedt and Knoke (1982).

REFERENCES

Bayes, Jane. (1988). Occupational sex segregation and comparable worth. In Rita Mae Kelly & Jane Bayes (Eds.), *Comparable worth, pay equity and public policy* (pp. 3-47). New York: Greenwood.

Beller, Andrea H. (1984). Trends in occupational segregation by sex and race, 1960-1981. In Barbara E. Reskin (Ed.), *Sex segregation in the workplace.* Washington, DC: National Academy Press.

Bianchi, Suzanne M., & Spain, Daphne. (1986). *American women in transition.* New York: Russell Sage Foundation.

Blau, Francine D. (1984). Occupational segregation and labor market discrimination. In Barbara E. Reskin (Ed.), *Sex segregation in the workplace.* Washington, DC: National Academy Press.

Blau, Francine D., & Ferber, Marianne A. (1986). *The economics of women, men, and work.* Englewood Cliffs, NJ: Prentice-Hall.

Bohrnstedt, George W., & Knoke, David. (1982). *Statistics for social data analysis.* Itasco, IL: Peacock.

Bowman, William. (1974). *Distaff journalists: Women as a minority group in the news media.* Unpublished doctoral dissertation, University of Illinois, Chicago Circle.

Cline, Carolyn Garrett, Toth, Elizabeth Lance, Turk, Judy VanSlyke, Walters, Lynne Masel, Johnson, Nancy, & Smith, Hank. (1986). *The velvet ghetto: The impact of the increasing percentage of women in public relations and business communication.* San Francisco: International Association of Business Communicators Foundation.

Jackson, Pat. (1988, September 12). 24th annual survey of the profession, part I: Salaries and demographics. *pr reporter,* p. 1.

Johnstone, John W. C., Slawski, Edward J., & Bowman, William W. (1976). *The news people: A sociological portrait of American journalists and their work.* Urbana: University of Illinois Press.

McClure, Laura. (1988, January/February). Wage gap between sexes is unchanged. *New Directions for Women,* pp. 6, 8.

Mincer, Jacob, & Polachek, S. (1974). Family investment in human capital: Earnings of women. In Theodore W. Schultz (Ed.), *Marriage, family, human capital, and fertility.* Chicago: University of Chicago Press.

Parcel, Toby L., & Mueller, Charles. (1983). *Ascription and labor markets: Race and sex differences in earnings.* New York: Academic Press.

Reskin, Barbara E. (Ed.). (1984). *Sex segregation in the workplace.* Washington, DC: National Academy Press.

Smith, Conrad, Fredin, Eric S., & Ferguson, Carol Ann. (1988, Spring). Sex discrimination in earnings and story assignments among local television news reporters. *Journalism Quarterly,* pp. 3-11.

Spencer, Rich. (1986, September 4). Female workers narrow "wage gap" with men, Census Bureau reports. (Louisville) *Courier-Journal,* p. 1. (Reprinted from *Washington Post.*)

Treiman, Donald J., & Hartmann, Heidi I. (Eds.). (1981) *Women, work, and wages: Equal pay for jobs of equal value.* Washington, DC: National Academy Press.

Weaver, David H., & Wilhoit, G. Cleveland. (1986). *The American journalist.* Bloomington: Indiana University Press.

9

Newspapers

Is There a New Majority Defining the News?

MAURINE BEASLEY

In 1985 the University of Maryland College of Journalism released preliminary findings of a study that called attention to the "new majority" in schools of journalism and mass communication. This referred to the growing influx of young women, who had tilted journalism school enrollment from predominantly male to predominantly female in less than a decade. At that time journalism enrollment was about 60% female. Today two-thirds of all graduates are women (Dow Jones Newspaper Fund, 1988).

The Maryland report was designed to call attention to discrimination faced by women as they moved from college into employment. It pointed out how the career paths of members of this "new majority" differed from those of the men who had preceded them, with women less drawn to newspaper work than to other forms of communications. It concluded that women were making an impact on the male-dominated field of journalism but that they encountered far more obstacles than men in advancing to the top. The entire study, titled *The New Majority: A Look at What the Preponderance of Women in Journalism Education Means to the Schools and to the Professions*, was published in 1988 (Beasley & Theus, 1988).

The Maryland research stopped short of answering the question of whether a new majority is defining the news. This chapter addresses that issue, reviewing the findings of the report and describing the remarkable uproar that it generated, chiefly from women newspaper editors. As director of the Maryland research, I contend that the report was misunderstood by journalists, who clung to outworn news concepts in covering the story.

First, a look at the research itself. Funded by a $34,000 grant from the Gannett Foundation, the study consists of four main segments: a summary of the historical discrimination faced by women journalism students attempting to break into the job market; a case study of the experiences of

Maryland graduates, both male and female; two roundtable discussions, one involving prominent women in the field and another involving recent graduates and students, focusing on problems confronting women; and four recommendations to journalism educators to assist women students in overcoming discrimination.

The historical overview traces the enrollment of women in journalism schools from the beginning of these institutions in pre-World War I days to the mid-1980s. By drawing on histories of journalism education, memoirs, biographies, and other data, the study traces how women were forced to settle for secondary status for decades within journalism schools as well as in the newspaper business to which journalism schools were oriented. Anecdotal evidence on women's status cited in the study highlights this finding, and includes the following examples.

- Carl W. Ackerman, a member of the first class at the Columbia University School of Journalism and later its dean, noted opposition to admitting women in 1912 by quoting a professor asked for advice on the subject: "His classic reply was that no teacher could teach mathematics to a boy if there was a girl in the room and that if a boy could learn mathematics with a girl in the room he would never grow up to be a man" (Ackerman, 1949). (Columbia allowed women to enroll only under a rigid quota system that remained in effect until the late 1960s).

- Florence R. Boys, woman's page editor of the *Plymouth* (Indiana) *Pilot*, who successfully syndicated her material, advised women students at the University of Missouri School of Journalism in 1924: "My woman's page was begun for my husband's paper. . . . It would probably be difficult, if not impossible, for a woman to make a good living on it alone. It is a good sideline for the wife or daughter of an editor" (*Women and the Newspaper*, 1924, p. 13).

- A woman journalism graduate who responded to a survey on women's status in journalism published in 1938 summed up the experiences of women attempting to obtain employment on daily newspapers: "With all the managing editors I have met, education and writing ability are not the essential they seek in a woman reporter. In the very few women they do take on (for flashy feature work), what they look for is the bold front and the 'gift of the gab' " (Logie, 1938, p. 27).

The Maryland study refers to articles in *The Matrix*, the magazine of Theta Sigma Phi, an honorary journalism sorority, that showed how World War II temporarily opened newspapers' doors to women, although they swung shut again after the war ended. The following are cited.

- A report in October 1940, on prewar prejudice against women expressed at a symposium for women journalism students at Ohio State University: "There seemed to be a general agreement among the members of the employers' symposium that women don't have any more chance for jobs on newspapers than Jews have of surviving in Germany" ("Employers' Symposium," 1940).

- A 1941 description by Abbie A. Amrine, a journalism graduate employed by a Kansas newspaper, on how the approach of war provided a long-sought opportunity to move from women's pages to general reporting: "Now taking the place of a man who has been drafted, I am working with the more drastic complications of deaths, accidents, rains, and community speakers. My conclusion is that the men have been impressing us with a false importance of their jobs."

- Exclamations by Betty Hinckle Dunn, national secretary of Theta Sigma Phi, in 1942: "Jobs, jobs, jobs! And no one to fill them. Odd, isn't it, how the job picture has changed in war months. Flippantly I tell my friends. 'The war means more opportunities for women and Negroes.' "

The Matrix was used as a barometer of attitudes toward women graduates because it circulated widely in schools of journalism, many of which had chapters of Theta Sigma Phi. Barred from joining Sigma Delta Chi, the male journalism fraternity, women, who constituted only a small fraction of journalism students, found professional support in their Theta Sigma Phi affiliation.

When women were urged to leave newspaper jobs at the end of World War II, *The Matrix* reported on the surge of domesticity that restricted women's roles. These examples were given in the Maryland study:

- A panel of established career women in Los Angeles told young journalism graduates to make marriage their primary aim, according to *The Matrix* of October 1951: "If you're playing with the idea of becoming a part-time mother—that is, combining your household with your premarital career—don't do it" (Sherwood, 1951).

- Betty Angelo, a reporter who resigned her job on the *Detroit News*, urged women journalism graduates in 1953 to seek jobs on metropolitan newspapers to hunt husbands: "I worked for a big city newspaper five years and met, among numerous other marriageable males, my husband—a newspaper editor on a rival paper. I could have saved myself a year and a half [spent working on a small-town newspaper] if I'd only come to the big city sooner."

Against this background of different expectations for men and women, journalism education remained almost totally male-dominated in the 1960s and early 1970s, although the proportion of women students increased. Women faculty, however, were grossly underrepresented in the teaching ranks, making up only 8% of the total in 1971-72. The Maryland research quotes from a survey of the status of women journalism educators at 60 colleges and universities presented at the Association for Education in Journalism convention in 1973. It concludes: "If you teach journalism in a college or university which has a sequence accredited by the American Council on Education in Journalism and you are a woman, you tend to be ranked lower, promoted more slowly and paid less than your colleagues who are male" (Marzolf, 1977, pp. 261-262).

In 1977, when journalism enrollment nationally reached a record 64,000, the proportion of women students reached more than 50%, but little notice was taken of this development. Since then the percentage has continued to climb. The Maryland study was the first to draw national attention to the influx of women into journalism schools and to point out the impact of this development on the employment market.

The study drew on figures gathered by Paul V. Peterson, a professor at Ohio State University, who compiled the major journalism enrollment survey annually. Peterson's surveys made it plain that journalism students were turning away from the news-editorial programs that traditionally occupied a preeminent position in the curriculum. In 1980 he observed, "When sequences are analyzed, there is a clear indication that a growing percentage of students are enrolling in the advertising and public relations sequences while the number in news-editorial is declining. The first two sequences are more heavily female populated as well" (p. 3).

Changing enrollment patterns cannot be attributed to any single cause. The closings of metropolitan newspapers, mushrooming communications industries, new forms of technology, low starting salaries, and declining patterns of readership all play a part in making news-editorial sequences less attractive to the majority of journalism students than previously. Still, the influx of women students itself cannot be overlooked in the relative fall of news-editorial enrollments.

Peterson concludes that the statistics clearly reveal "more females [than males] looking at non-traditional forms of journalism for careers." He also sees in the statistics a reflection of past discrimination: "I still think they [young women] see the newsroom as an all-male bastion" (personal communication, March 26, 1984).

Indeed, women graduates appeared to experience somewhat more difficulty than male graduates in finding journalism-related jobs, including those on daily newspapers, in the mid-1980s, the Maryland study reports. It uses these figures from the Dow Jones Newspaper Fund/Gallup Survey (1984) of 1983 journalism graduates:

- While women represented 64.1%, or 11,326, of the total of 17,670 graduates surveyed, they were less likely than male graduates to locate news-editorial jobs. While 14.6% of the graduates as a whole found jobs in news-editorial areas, only 11.8% of the women did so.

- Although 9.4% of the graduates found jobs on daily newspapers, women were less likely than men to be in this category, with only 6.9% of the women reporting jobs on daily papers.

- A higher percentage of women graduates were unemployed than the graduates as a whole, with 14.2% of the women continuing to seek media-related work six months after graduating compared to 11.8% for the total group.

The figures suggest that journalism schools were turning out an increasing number of graduates who would encounter sexual bias in their careers. Were these students being properly prepared to recognize sexism and to overcome it? Would the predominance of women graduates mean that journalism education would be perceived as a second-rate educational program (since occupational programs predominantly attracting women, such as nursing and elementary education, long have lacked the status of programs for men)?

These were questions the Maryland researchers attempted to address through the second major portion of their project—a survey of Maryland journalism alumni and students as well as their employers. Like those of other large state universities, Maryland's journalism program expanded greatly in the late 1970s and early 1980s. In 1968 the university had only 120 journalism majors, 80% of whom were men, but by 1984-85 there were more than 1,000 undergraduate majors, of whom 69% were women. In advertising and public relations sequences, women represented about 80% of the enrollment.

Headed by Kathryn T. Theus, associate director of the study, investigators sent out 642 questionnaires to a sample of male and female graduates beginning with the class of 1981 and including graduates of other classes at three-year intervals back to 1951. Of these, 356 were returned, yielding a 55% response rate. In addition, the researchers surveyed all potential graduates of the class of 1984, as well as an employer sample drawn from newspapers, agencies, or corporations where Maryland graduates were employed. There was a 60% response rate for the student survey of 280 persons and a 57% response rate for the 251 employers contacted.

Highlights of the alumni survey include the following:

- Males were more satisfied with their jobs, incomes, and chances for advancement than were females.

- Women were 13 times more likely than men to have had career interruptions due to family responsibilities and seemed to suffer substantial income loss as a consequence. Women were out of jobs slightly longer than men and were twice as likely to change jobs as were men.

- Alumni agreed that salaries of women doing journalism-related work were lower than those of men doing comparable work, and that men were promoted more quickly.
- Only 41-43% of respondents said that they would encourage their sons or daughters to study journalism.
- In general, men were more likely to have married and to have larger families than women (Beasley & Theus, 1988, pp. 55-57).

The student survey did not show widespread variances between males and females in attitudes toward their education, their careers, or sexual bias in the classroom and workplace. Almost one-third reported they had witnessed discrimination in the classroom based on sex. Curiously, in assessing their overall journalism experience, about 83% considered it very or extremely good, and 90% said they would major in journalism again. Yet less than half said they would encourage their children to study journalism and, of those, more would encourage their daughters than their sons (Beasley & Theus, 1988, pp. 57-58).

Women students perceived greater potential for discrimination in the workplace than men, although all recognized the presence of discrimination on the basis of sex. Women agreed more strongly than men with a statement on the questionnaire that women doing journalism-related work were lower paid than men doing comparable work. They also agreed more strongly with a statement that a man would be hired over an equally capable women (Beasley & Theus, 1988, pp. 57-58).

The employer survey showed that only slightly more than one-third cited journalism as the most important undergraduate major for communication-related jobs. Males and females were evaluated rather evenly on job skills, although males were usually evaluated a percentage point or two better than females. Women employers, however, evaluated women employees significantly higher than did male employers in several areas, including reporting and photography (Beasley & Theus, 1988, pp. 58-59).

Women employers more than men employers tended to agree with the statement that women doing journalism-related work were generally paid lower salaries than men doing comparable work. Employers were split on whether women were hired as a result of affirmative action policies. Slightly less than half of the employers reported they would encourage their sons to study journalism, while half would encourage their daughters to do so (Beasley & Theus, 1988, pp. 58-59).

To serve as a "reality check" on the statistical study, the Maryland researchers held two roundtable discussions in 1984. The first included women who had achieved substantial successes in journalism careers. The second involved students and recent graduates.

Among participants in the first roundtable were six women representing newspapers: Marcia Slacum Greene, a reporter for the Washington Post; Claudia Townsend, city editor on leave from the *Washington Post*; Nancy Monaghan, national editor, *USA Today*; Sharon Dickman, assistant metro editor, *Baltimore Evening Sun*; Mary Lou Forbes, associate editor, *Washington Times*; and Tonnie Katz, managing editor, *Baltimore News American*.

Comments included references to the competing demands of jobs and family life. Katz said, "I find at my office, which is very informal, that while I'm glad to have anyone go at any time to take a child here or there . . . I . . . don't do that. I wait until 10 p.m. till I get home for dinner. . . . women still put that pressure on themselves" (Beasley & Theus, 1988, p. 90).

Townsend explained, "I had sort of anticipated being pushed off into the corner . . . as somebody who had a baby. . . . And they [*Washington Post* editors] crossed me up by offering me a promotion. . . . I sit and think about whether I'm going to let the baby stay home [with a sitter] . . . and is that going to drive me crazy" (Beasley & Theus, 1988, p. 90).

Monaghan pointed out that women appear to be trying harder than men to succeed in newspaper jobs: "They're trying to prove that they can do the job that men think they can automatically do." Therefore, the panelists agreed, women sometimes were willing to settle for less than men (Beasley & Theus, 1988, p. 93).

Dickman and Greene spoke of the difficulties women have in getting hired and moving up the newspaper career ladder. Dickman said, "[We at the *Baltimore Sun*] have more women applicants than men for jobs, but recently we had some openings, and we made three hires, one white woman, one white man and one Black woman. . . . And that's generally how our hires go . . . . In companies like ours where there's a small number of women, it is the pioneering days" (Beasley & Theus, 1988, p. 97).

"The 1983 survey from the ASNE [American Society of Newspaper Editors] shows that of the major newspapers in the country in terms of editors there are 93 women and 1,027 men. . . . And the bottom line is there're 89.4 percent men compared to 10.6 percent of women in top management. I don't think that's going to change overnight," Greene pointed out (Beasley & Theus, 1988, p. 102).

Forbes urged women to develop their skills to compete successfully: "They [editors] cannot deny [you] if you're good and you constantly turn out a good product. You write the best obituaries in the office; you come up with a scoop out of police court every day. This is a great business for women because if you're good they can't deny it" (Beasley & Theus, 1988, p. 95).

The roundtable of students and recent graduates included two recent graduates employed by daily newspapers, Cristal Williams, *Easton* (Maryland) *Star-Democrat*, and Chris Harvey, *Prince George's Journal*. Both spoke of problems that they foresaw in combining careers with children.

As Williams put it, "One of the things I have thought about more since I have been working is, I guess, to postpone getting married" (Beasley & Theus, 1988, p. 113).

"I just couldn't picture myself in the job that I'm doing now and having children because you just work 50 to 60 hours a week, you work at night, you work on weekends," Harvey said. "To have little kids around, I would just have to take an easier job" (Beasley & Theus, 1988, p. 112).

Harvey also referred to pay scales in the field: "The thing that bothers me is the salary. I think maybe it's more noticeable on the littler papers especially because . . . there seem to be a lot more women. . . . Young women and people who are married and have come back to the field" (Beasley & Theus, 1988, p. 114).

From the roundtable discussions, the Maryland researchers identified four areas for amplification in the study. These pointed to the need for women journalism students to (1) acquire strong basic writing skills, (2) have suitable role models, (3) learn how to persuade employers of their worth so they are not forced to settle for less prestige and pay than men receive, and (4) plan how to combine family responsibilities successfully with their careers.

The question of women defining the news arose in connection with the issue of acquiring basic writing skills. The study cites work by Catherine S. Covert, a journalism professor at Syracuse University, who theorized that journalism is written in terms of winning and losing, conflict and controversy. Quoting examples from a journalism history textbook—"the press wins a beach-head," "the rise of the fourth estate," "the race for news"—Covert (1981) held that this is the language of male "winners," not that of women, a submerged group who have been conditioned to develop alternative values based on "concord, harmony, affiliation and community" (p. 4).

In Covert's opinion, the old newsroom sobriquet "sob sister" conveyed women's position in relation to male journalists, revealing the fact that women reporters and their human-interest stories are "only marginally relevant to the rational [male] business of the newsroom day." According to this line of thought, the preference of women journalism students for sequences other than news-editorial may reflect the social conditioning of many women and their avoidance of male-designed news formulas. The Maryland report contends that if women students are less conflict-oriented than men, they are likely to choose media fields outside the mainstreams of journalism (Covert, 1981, p. 4).

Consequently, the Maryland report recommends that journalism educators emphasize the blending of news and feature writing that has occurred in recent years. To a degree this represents a blurring of the sharp lines that used to denote "hard news" (the front-page news stories denoting action) and "soft news" (the feature stories appealing to the emotions). Calling attention to the blatant sexual overtones of these terms, the Maryland study urges that journalism schools not perpetuate old stereotypes by assigning women students feature stories, for example, while grooming males to be campus editors or by assigning male instructors general reporting courses and women instructors feature-writing classes.

The male orientation of the newspaper industry is apparent from studies cited in the report. One, conducted by Dorothy Jurney for the ASNE, showed that less than 12% of editors were women in 1985. Another, done in 1983, reported that top women newspaper managers earned about 60.1% of men's salaries for comparable jobs, with the actual dollar gap given as $18,147 annually.[1]

A 1982 study of 200 recent journalism graduates of the University of North Carolina with newspaper experience also is noted. This study used a six-point salary classification scale to compare men's and women's salaries; the average category for women was 1.98, while for men it was 2.34. At the same time, the men had more job experience than the women, indicating that the women had dropped out and returned or had moved more often than the men (McAdams, 1984, pp. 10-12).

In addition, the Maryland report mentions a study distributed by ASNE, which analyzes coverage by 10 leading newspapers of alimony and child support questions, enforcement of Title IX (the law prohibiting discrimination in education), the Equal Rights Amendment campaign, the 1977 National Women's Conference in Houston, pay equity, and the World Conference of the United Nations Decade for Women. The conclusion: News articles in some papers on these subjects were inadequate, unfair, or lacking in recognition of the issue (*New Directions for News*, 1983, pp. 3-4).

In light of this material, the Maryland study speculates that the nature of news itself might change, at least somewhat, if women become the majority in the newsroom—unless they are restricted to the prevailing male model for professional advancement. The report, however, chiefly concentrates on economic issues, noting that it is possible that journalism and related fields may become "pink-collar ghettos" on the lower levels, with salaries and status there lower than those of other major professions. It urges journalism educators to fight against discrimination, and warns, "If salary and status in journalism-related fields decline relatively and those fields become less competitive, some of the most important work of a democratic society will become less attractive to students gifted in intellect, resourcefulness and general ability" (Beasley & Theus, 1988, p. 140).

The preliminary version of the Maryland report made headlines in October 1985, following a press conference at the National Press Club in Washington, D.C., to unveil a five-year plan for upgrading the University of Maryland College of Journalism. A group of faculty members presented various research findings at the press conference. Media attention, however, focused on the "new majority" study instead of on either the college's plan for development or research described by male faculty members. (These topics included examinations of science writing and findings that the public gains news primarily from print, not from television.)

To aid reporters in covering the event, the University of Maryland prepared press packets including press releases. The release on the "new majority" study was not written by the women associated with the research. It was headlined "Maryland Study Warns Against 'Pink-Collar Ghettos' of Lower Pay and Status in Journalism-Related Fields," and it began, "Journalism and related professional fields are becoming principally female, with a danger that they will be 'pink-collar ghettos' offering lower salaries and status than they would as largely male fields, a new University of Maryland study says." The release said that "female-dominated fields such as teaching, social work, nursing and librarianship traditionally have been lower-income professions." It continued, "Although salaries in journalism-related fields (some of which already are noted for low pay) may not decline, there should be concern that they will not rise as they might if these fields remained predominantly male." It also pointed out that women are filling the ranks but are not yet well represented in management.

Some reporters at the press conference used the release as the basis for stories that sensationalized the issue. United Press International sent out a story beginning, "Women are quickly dominating the ranks of the news profession and their emergence threatens to keep both the money and the status of the industry low, a two-year study by the University of Maryland says." The story said that women constituted about 40% of the daily news force. It led to headlines like the following: in the *St. Louis Post-Dispatch* (October 15, 1986), "Study: Women May Devalue Journalism"; in the *Easton* (Maryland) *Star-Democrat* (October 15, 1985), "News Women Creating 'Pink Collar Ghetto'"; in the *Deseret News* (Salt Lake City) (October 16, 1985), "Women Are Taking Over Journalism"; and in the *Miami News* (October 15, 1986), "Journalism Seen Turning 'Pink-Collar.'"

Other newspapers handled the story more responsibly. The *Washington Post*, for example, headlined the story "Women Predominate in J-Schools" and used a comprehensive lead: "Women now make up 60 percent of all journalism students in the country and may soon outnumber men in communications, according to a University of Maryland study whose authors expressed fears that the shift will lower pay and the prestige of the field in comparison to male-dominated fields" (Arocha, 1985).

Headlined "Women the 'New Majority' in Journalism Schools," the story received balanced coverage in the *Evening Sun* of Baltimore. Sharon Dickman (1985) reported, "Women have taken over the classrooms of journalism and mass communications schools around the country, but they still face discrimination when they graduate and look for work, a new University of Maryland study shows."

Some of the news coverage of the press conference drew an inflamed response. In a column in the *Trenton* (New Jersey) *Times*, reprinted in part in *Editor & Publisher*, Linda Cunningham, executive editor of the Trenton paper, declared, "Not since conservative Patrick Buchanan's column, which said it was a woman's fault if she were raped, has anything in the newspapers raised my dander so much." She quoted a statement attributed to me at the press conference and carried in the UPI report: "If journalism joins other devalued professions dominated by women, such as nursing and teaching, the watchdog role of the news media might become trivialized" (quoted in Miller, 1985, p. 52).

"Hogwash," Cunningham wrote. "Spend 15 minutes in this newsroom [*Trenton Times*] and then tell me the women around there are less demanding or more inclined to believe unquestioningly what their sources tell them. Ask my bosses if I demur daintily when thwarted or sit quietly in a corner." Reacting to the suggestion in the study that the nature of news might change if women predominate in the field, Cunningham retorted, "I'm often asked whether women editors approach the news differently from their male counterparts. My answer is, invariably, no. News is news; it has no sex" (quoted in Miller, 1985, p. 52).

Excerpts from Cunningham's attack and other criticism of the Maryland study appeared in a column in *Editor & Publisher* by Susan H. Miller, director of editorial development for Scripps Howard Newspapers. She quoted from a letter by Judith Clabes, editor of the *Covington* (Kentucky) *Post*: "A seething anger is growing to a crescendo of outrage over the disservice the Maryland 'research' has done to a whole group of professional, hardworking and dedicated women journalists." In common with Cunningham and Clabes, Miller apparently viewed the study personally. She asserted it "adopted unwarranted and unsubstantiated assertions about the professional performance of women" (Miller, 1985, pp. 32-33).

In a reply to Miller, also published in *Editor & Publisher*, I blamed initial media coverage—as well as the emotional response from a few token women editors—for obscuring the point, which is that women are clustered in relatively low-paid, low-prestige journalistic positions, not because they want to be, but because of societal factors that historically have undervalued them economically. "The community press, where large segments of women increasingly are concentrated at low salaries, may not be in an economic position to embrace the watchdog function," I stated in my reply. And I concluded, "Let's see 'seething anger' and 'a crescendo of outrage' over discrimination in general and over low salaries in particular—whether men or women are being victimized" (Beasley, 1985, pp. 44, 33).

Defending the report's conclusions, Chuck Stone, writing in the *Philadelphia Daily News* in 1986, pointed out that women writers and journalists historically have not fared well at the hands of white males in terms of Pulitzer Prizes and other professional recognition. Calling attention to criticism of the Maryland research by Linda Cunningham, Stone commented, "But let the word go forth to Cunningham, women journalists . . . and women writers everywhere. Maybe you have come a long way, baby. But in 1986, male America is still dumping on you." Stone, who is Black, said the issue translated into power for white males and weakness for "everybody else."

The Maryland research did not directly take up the question of minority employment on newspapers, although minority representatives participated in the roundtable discussions. Yet it should be emphasized that minority hiring—of men or women—remains at a relatively low level. In 1988 newsrooms were 7.02% minority compared to 6.56% a year before, an increase of only .46%, according to the American Society of Newspaper Editors. Among other ASNE findings:

- Some 55% of U.S. dailies employ no minority newsroom professionals at all.
- Minority hiring activity of small newspapers declined form 24% in 1986 to 22% in 1987, and dropped to 20% in 1988.
- Only 4.1% of 12,600 management positions are held by minority journalists ("Newsroom Minority Employment," 1988).

Today there is little reason to think that the nature of news is changing dramatically. The coverage of the Maryland report itself speaks to that point. As the examples given in this chapter show, much of the coverage was biased and superficial. It conformed to the conventional male model of conflict, controversy, and "spicy" headlines. Those women in decision-making roles who criticized the report appeared determined to prove that they had absorbed the same news values as their male predecessors. At the same time, they displayed a "sob sister" response, attacking what they construed as personal aspersions on them instead of logically considering the issues. While a new majority may be moving into newsrooms, it appears it is continuing to encounter roughly the same old definitions of news even though there are occasional efforts to broaden coverage.

At this point three years have elapsed since the release of the Maryland report. Do the concerns that prompted the project still exist? Are women making a relatively smooth transition from journalism school into newspapers? Has the pay risen substantially? Are women moving up the newspaper ladder? Has the perception of discrimination been eliminated?

Unhappily, the answer to all these questions is no. In 1987, for example, women represented 66% of the estimated 26,350 graduates of journalism schools, but the proportion of all students specializing in the news-editorial field declined from 21.8% to 18.3%. The number who actually looked for full-time employment with a newspaper declined, with newspapers and wire services hiring only 11.5% of journalism graduates, a drop from 15.5% in 1986. Women students were much more likely to select advertising and public relations than news-editorial sequences (Becker & Engleman, 1988, pp. 4-5, 16).

Although newspapers and wire services hired more women than men from the 1987 graduates, they still tended to hire fewer women—58.9%—than the female percentage of the total graduates. Minority students, both male and female, represented 10% of the graduating class. Yet only 7.8% of the newspaper and wire service hires from the class of 1987 were minorities, a drop from 14% the previous year. Median yearly—starting pay at daily newspapers stayed at $13,900, the same as in

1986. On nondaily newspapers it was even less—$12,948 (Becker & Engleman, 1988, pp. 17, 14-15).

By contrast, starting pay in public relations and advertising was substantially higher. The median annual salary in public relations went up from $15,300 in 1986 to $16,744 in 1987. The median in advertising advanced from $14,700 to $15,028 (Becker & Engleman, 1988, p. 14).

Once hired on newspapers, women could look forward to a slow climb upward. According to Jean Gaddy Wilson (1988) of the University of Missouri School of Journalism, "Women are creeping ever so slowly toward the year 2055 when projections indicate they will attain levels in newspaper editorships on a par with their level in the population [53 percent]" (p. 1). Wilson bases her projections on a report compiled from the *Editor & Publisher Yearbook* that shows less than a 1% increase in directing editorships for women—from 12.4% in 1987 to 13.03% in 1987. It appears that it will be a long time before women as a group will be in a position to define the news. They may be a new majority at the lower levels, but at the upper echelons white males still wield the influence.

NOTE

1. A variety of studies in recent years have addressed the problem of women's slow progress into management, for example, see Jurney (1986), Ogan, Brown, and Weaver (1979), and Ogan (1983).

REFERENCES

Ackerman, Carl W. (1949, June 6). *The inside of a newspaper should be like the inside of a home*. Speech given at the American Press Institute, New York. (Box 164, Carl W. Ackerman papers, Library of Congress.)

Amrine, Abbie A. (1941). This is our day. *The Matrix, 27*, 15, 19.

Angelo, Betty. (1953). Career: Metropolitan vs. community newspaper. *The Matrix, 39*, 14.

Arocha, Zita. (1985, October 15). Women predominate in j-schools. *Washington Post*, pp. B1, B7.

Beasley, Maurine H. (1985, December 14). In defense of the "women in journalism" study. *Editor & Publisher*, pp. 44, 33.

Beasley, Maurine H., & Theus, Kathryn T. (1988). *The new majority: A look at what the preponderance of women in journalism education means to the schools and to the professions*. Lanham, MD: University Press of America.

Becker, Lee B., & Engleman, Thomas E. (1988, April). *1987 Journalism and Mass Communications Graduate Survey.* Unpublished report, Dow Jones Newspaper Fund/Ohio State University School of Journalism.

Covert, Catherine L. (1981). Journalism history and women's experience: A problem in conceptual change. *Journalism History, 8,* 2-6.

Dickman, Sharon. (1985, October 15). Women the "new majority" in journalism schools. (Baltimore) *Evening Sun,* p. D2.

Dow Jones Newspaper Fund. (1988, Summer). '87 survey shows increase in journalism graduates. *Advisor Update.*

Dow Jones Newspaper Fund/Gallup Survey. (1984, January). *Final tabulation of 1983 journalism graduates.* Princeton, NJ: Author

Dunn, Betty Hinckle. (1942, December). Matrix final. *The Matrix, 28,* 3.

Employers' symposium. (1940, October). *The Matrix, 26,* 7-8.

Jurney, Dorothy. (1986, January). Percentage of women editors creeps upward to 11.7—but other fields continue to progress faster. *ASNE Bulletin,* pp. 8-9.

Logie, Iona Robertson. (1938). *Careers for women in journalism: A composite picture of 881 salaried women writers at work in journalism, advertising, publicity and promotion.* Scranton, PA: International Textbook.

Marzolf, Marion. (1977). *Up from the footnote: A history of women journalists.* New York: Hastings House.

McAdams, Katherine C. (1984, June). [Paper on comparison of work patterns and starting salaries between men and women journalism graduates of the University of North Carolina—draft]. Unpublished manuscript.

Miller, Susan H. (1985, November 23). Was "pink collar" ghetto study deliberate sensationalism? *Editor & Publisher,* pp. 52, 32-33.

New directions for news. (1983). Washington, DC: George Washington University, Women's Studies Program and Policy Center.

Newsroom minority employment reaches 7 percent. (1988, June/July). *Minorities in the Newspaper Business,* p. 3.

Ogan, Christine L. (1983). *Life at the top for men and women newspaper managers: A five-year update on their characteristics.* Working paper, Indiana University.

Ogan, Christine L., Brown, Charlene J., & Weaver, David H. (1979). Characteristics of managers of selected U.S. daily newspapers. *Journalism Quarterly, 56,* 803-809.

Peterson, Paul V. (1980, January). J-school enrollments reach record 71,594. *Journalism Educator, 34,* 3-9.

Sherwood, Midge Winters. (1951, October). No such thing as part-time mother. *The Matrix, 37,* 9-10.

Stone, Chuck. (1986, January 22). Women are still being dumped on. *Philadelphia Daily News,* p. 36.

Wilson, Jean Gaddy. (1988, January). Only 68 years to go. *Press Women 51,* 1-3.

Women and the newspaper. (1924). (Journalism Series No. 30). Columbia: University of Missouri.

10

Magazines

Women's Employment and Status in the Magazine Industry

SAMMYE JOHNSON

There is no way of knowing how many magazines will celebrate the industry's 250th anniversary in 1991, because no one knows for certain how many different magazines exist in the United States. It has never been easy to define magazines, or to assign definitive figures to the industry. Even Frank Luther Mott's (1939) Pulitzer Prize-winning five-volume history of American magazines from 1741 through 1930 dealt only with certain important magazines, for "exact figures are impossible to obtain" (p. 341).

One key historical fact is that the first magazines were published in America within three days of each other in 1741: Andrew Bradford's *American Magazine, or A Monthly View of the Political State of the British Colonies* and Benjamin Franklin's *General Magazine, and Historical Chronicle, for All the British Plantations in America* (Mott, 1939, p. 24). Thereafter, magazine scholars and researchers are on their own. It is impossible to know how many magazines—even if there were agreement on what a magazine is—have been published since 1741.

Women have been active in the magazine industry as publishers, editors, writers, and readers since its beginnings. As early as 1787, letters from women were published in magazines, articles had feminine authors, and women were being wooed as readers. Noah Webster said in his December 1787 issue of *American Magazine*, "*Fair* readers may be assured that no inconsiderable pains will be taken to furnish *them* with entertainment" (Mott, 1939, p. 65). One of the earliest great magazine editors was a woman—Sarah Josepha Hale, who founded *Ladies' Magazine* in 1828. She merged her publication with Louis Godey's *Godey's Lady's Book* in 1837, and served as editor for 50 years, during which the magazine became famous for its elegant essays and hand-colored fashion plates (Mott, 1939, pp. 582-583).

Through the decades, magazine mastheads have listed women in top editorial positions. Women have always been recognized as important readers and subscribers, for magazines dedicated to women uniformly appear in the top 10 magazines by total circulation year after year, according to the Audit Bureau of Circulations (ABC) (1987).

Additionally, the 87.4 million women who read an average of 10 different magazines a month constitute the majority of the nation's magazine readers (94% of the U.S. population, 18 years of age and older, or 164.1 million adults, make up the magazine industry's audience) ("Magazine Almanac," 1988, p. 5). Indeed, women are involved as readers and editors across the spectrum of magazine types. They have always played important roles in this medium.

However, there is mystery surrounding the magazine industry, in terms of people involved, numbers of titles, and kinds of publications. Regardless of the time frame, the magazine universe is so complex and so changing that it shifts constantly, and is impossible to freeze into a quantifiable mass. So it should come as no surprise that the roles women play today—whether as magazine editors or advertising directors or circulation managers or writers—are as shrouded in swirls of mist as any romantic thriller. Unfortunately, finding out about the heroine is hampered by the environment in which she lives and works.

THE MAGAZINE ENVIRONMENT

Look at any current magazine study or mass media textbook and the problem becomes evident. There is no agreement on how to categorize magazines, much less how to determine the exact dimensions of the industry.

Most researchers use Mott's (1939) definition of a magazine "as a bound pamphlet issued more or less regularly and containing a variety of reading matter" (p. 7). However, Donald N. Wood (1983) points out:

> Derived from the French word *magasin*, meaning 'warehouse' or 'storehouse,' the modern magazine almost defies explicit description. About the only generalizations one dares to toss out are that the magazine is *usually* bound or stapled (unlike most newspapers) and is *normally* published on a regular schedule (unlike most books). The one characteristic common to the

magazine industry is that, with a few notable exceptions, magazines are aimed at specialized audiences. (pp. 83-84)

One result is that some textbooks divide magazines, also referred to as periodicals, into general consumer, special interest consumer, business, association, farm, and public relations (Click & Baird, 1986, p. 3). Others say there are four basic categories: consumer; business, technical, trade, and professional; association; and company publications (Baran, McIntyre, & Meyer, 1984, p. 138). There are those who say magazines divide into four principal areas—farm, business, consumer, and religious (Bittner, 1986, p. 69). Still others never attempt to categorize magazines, but instead list types—newsmagazines, city and regional magazines, women's magazines, controlled circulation magazines, political opinion magazines, and so forth. There simply is no consensus.

However, researchers who specialize in magazines (of whom there are very few) seem to be moving toward a three-part division: consumer magazines (publications of general or specialized interest sold to the public), business magazines (which deal in various specific aspects of particular industries, businesses, or professions, and which may be sold or given away free), and public relations magazines (which are published by corporations for specific internal or external audiences and which are almost always free). The problem here is that some publications, like farm and religious magazines, cross divisions, making classification difficult.

Numbers present a daunting situation. Since there is no standard magazine classification, the range becomes awesome. Depending on what reference you choose, you can make a case for just about any set of magazine numbers.

The *Standard Periodical Directory 1988* provides data on over 65,000 periodicals in the United States and Canada (Oxbridge Communications, 1988). To be included, a periodical need only be published at least once every two years. Periodicals listed range from consumer magazines and trade journals to newsletters, government publications, and yearbooks.

The *Gale Directory of Publications* (formerly *Ayer's*), often cited in magazine research and mass communication texts, lists 11,229 periodicals for 1988 (Gale Research, 1988).

The numbers become more manageable when you turn to the main source of information for advertisers. Standard Rate and Data Service, Inc. (SRDS) publishes data on consumer, farm, and business publications. It lists (as of July 1988) more than 1,700 consumer magazines and more than 250 farm magazines in *Consumer Magazine and Agri-Media Rates and*

Data (SRDS 1988b); more than 3,700 business magazines are classified in *Business Publication Rates and Data* (SRDS, 1988a).

The Magazine Publishers of America, with 207 member publishers representing 839 U.S. magazines, uses *Gale*, SRDS, and ABC figures in its consumer magazine research ("Magazine Almanac," 1988, p. 2). The Association of Business Publishers cites 2,776 magazines in the business or trade segment of the industry for 1988. Both organizations point out that there are still many consumer and business magazines that exist, but are not audited, surveyed, or even listed anywhere.

The Society of National Association Publications (SNAP) numbers only 200 publication members for 1988, although there are more than 3,500 associations in Washington, D.C., alone; most of them have some sort of publication. A survey by the American Society of Association Executives (1987) which has more than 16,000 members, revealed that 95% of the respondents issued periodical publications (p. 79).

The problem intensifies when you turn to the largest and hardest to identify category: public relations magazines. No census has ever been taken, so estimates range from 10,000 (Click & Baird, 1986, p. 5) to 100,000 (Paine & Paine, 1987, p. 15).

New magazines are started every day, consumer titles multiply at a rate of 150 to 300 a year, and only 10% survive a second year (Pattis, 1986, p. 4). Start-up figures for business publications and public relations magazines are not available.

Government data do not clarify the magazine industry, either. The *Statistical Abstract of the United States 1988* cites *Gale* figures, which include weekly, semimonthly, fortnightly, monthly, bimonthly, and quarterly periodicals (U.S. Bureau of the Census, 1987).

Furthermore, Bureau of Labor Statistics data are based on the printing and publishing industry as a whole, and include newspapers and books as well as printing establishments. Figures for periodicals are not always specified, and the editor/reporter occupation classification is not limited to magazines.

For April 1988, the Bureau of Labor Statistics listed 127,900 employees at periodicals (U.S. Department of Labor, 1988, p. 51). In the "printing, publishing and allied industries, except newspapers" category (a segment that encompasses more than just magazines), women were 44.1% of the total employed; Blacks were 6.9%, and Hispanics were 5.3% in 1986 (U.S. Department of Labor, 1987b, p. 190). In 1986, women were 50.5% of the editors/reporters employment category, with Blacks at 3.8% and Hispanics at 4.4% (U.S. Department of Labor, 1987a, p. 179).

Thus the magazine industry cannot be considered feminized, or racially balanced, and it does not appear to be moving in either of those directions. Interviews with women in the consumer magazine field support the concept of gender balance in the industry, which is documented by Bureau of Labor Statistics data. Most women do not believe that the magazine industry is flooded with females, and many can remember times when they were the only woman reporter or editor in the room. While women say men traditionally have held the top positions or have been better established in the corporate hierarchy of magazines, they point out that the field is balanced "at least fifty-fifty, including editors, writers, photographers, designers, production, circulation, and ad sales" (Valys, 1988). Jobs are there for women at all levels, but pay equity is not.

WOMEN AT CONSUMER MAGAZINES

While numerous studies have been made of magazine content, advertising, and readers, there is a paucity of institutional research on the structure and roles of those employed at consumer magazines. One reason for this is that the magazine industry is very volatile, and numbers of magazines fluctuate, as do the numbers of jobs and people employed. There is no consistency in job title and position description, which makes salary surveys difficult. An editor at one magazine may have the responsibilities of an associate editor at another; a circulation manager at one company may be a circulation marketing director at another. While all magazines need four kinds of personnel—editorial, advertising sales, circulation, and production—this doesn't mean that every magazine has four departments, or even four employees (Wright, 1987, pp. 480-481).

Early consumer magazine studies primarily counted names on mastheads to determine positions held by men and women. While studies of editorial mastheads in 1970 revealed that men held more of the top positions than did women, other research showed great variations among individual magazines (Butler & Paisley, 1980, p. 195). For example, a 1974 analysis of 18 well-known magazines found that 70% of the editors at *Redbook* were women, while just 25% of the top editors at *Ladies' Home Journal* were women (Butler & Paisley, 1980, p. 195).

A study of magazine editors listed in *The Working Press of the Nation* in 1973 found "that 11% are women, while 74% have men's first names, 13% give initials in lieu of a first name, and 2% have names used for both sexes. Women were most likely to edit technical magazines that have small circulations. Men edit the well-known women's and news magazines. Only 1 of the 25 listed news magazines was edited by a woman" (Butler and Paisley, 1980, p. 196). Research conducted at Stanford University in 1977 examined the numbers of women and men on the editorial staffs of business, news, analytic, women's, and popular magazines; across all types of magazines, 73% of the major editorships were held by men (Butler & Paisley, 1980, pp. 197-198). Yet other research has found that as many as 100% of articles in a single issue were written by women (Butler & Paisley, 1980, p. 224).

More recent data are not available, for a systematic analysis of those employed at consumer magazines—male or female—has not been made. Except for David H. Weaver and G. Cleveland Wilhoit's inclusion of newsmagazine writers and editors in their major study of American journalists, there has not been a complete look at who works at consumer magazines. Weaver and Wilhoit (1986) estimate that newsmagazine journalists make up only 1.1% of the full-time editorial work force in U.S. news media (p. 13).

Weaver and Wilhoit (1986) make the following comments about newsmagazine journalists: Women make up 31.7% of news magazine staffs, up a tad from the 30.4% reported by Johnstone et al. in 1971 (p. 21); minorities are less likely to be attracted to newsmagazines than to broadcast media or daily newspaper positions (p. 22); the newsmagazine journalist is, like the rest of the editorial work force surveyed by Weaver and Wilhoit, a white Protestant male (p. 12), but the newsmagazine journalist has a much higher median income than the "typical" journalist, at $34,750 compared to $19,000 (p. 84); and newsmagazine journalists, who constitute the most highly paid group in the news media, also have higher job satisfaction (p. 103).

Folio: The Magazine for Magazine Management has conducted salary surveys for various top management positions in the magazine industry since 1982, including editorial, circulation, advertising sales, and production. However, there does not appear to be any continuous survey of lower-echelon editorial staff, such as assistant editors, editorial assistants, or staff writers. Salary surveys conducted by the Magazine Publishers of America are confidential, and are available only to members.

Folio's first salary survey, appearing in 1982, states: "There has been very little published research in this area, although there has been a lot of informal asking around about what other magazines do" (Love, 1982, p. 88).

Folio points out several problems in doing a salary survey, problems that exist to this day:

> Survey results indicate the salary question is complex since many variables are involved. Management and editors of all rankings interested in these findings should use the data cautiously. Average salaries cannot be applied without adjustments made for region, total magazine revenue, the number of editorial pages produced (particularly for chief editors and art directors, who have total responsibility), and special factors at each magazine. (Love, 1982, p. 88)

Although not commented on in the survey, lack of consistent editorial rankings or title designations made the field harder to compare and quantify. But the major shortcoming of this survey is its failure to separate men's and women's salaries. *Folio* would make numerous changes in its next editorial salary survey, in 1985.

Folio's 1985 survey went directly to editors who were asked to report anonymously on their salaries and titles. And salary by gender was analyzed. The result: "Wide variations in salaries for people with same title; lower pay for women; general dissatisfaction with editorial compensation" (Love & Angelo, 1985, p. 69).

The 1985 findings are based on responses from 484 people (53% response rate) in six positions: editorial management, editors, managing/executive editors, senior/associate editors, copy editors, and art directors. The average salary for consumer magazine editorial management (which included editorial director, vice president-editorial, editor in chief, and editor-publisher) was $47,633. This time *Folio* broke out salary averages by nine variables: region, type of magazine, average editorial pages produced annually, number of editors on the staff, frequency, circulation, gender, number of magazines responsible for, and years of experience (Love & Angelo, 1985, p. 73).

When the average consumer magazine salary for editorial management was indicated by gender, women's compensation was 68% that of men's ($35,800 versus $52,350), or $16,550 less. And the same pattern of less money paid to women existed among editors, managing/executive editors, senior/associate editors, copy editors, and art directors, although the discrepancy was not as great. For example, women with the title of editor earned 81% of what men with the same title received ($28,560 versus $35,120) (Love & Angelo, 1985, p. 74).

In that 1985 survey, several women commented on differences in salary: "I'm still waiting for equal pay for equal work," and "Men make about 25% more, even if they work on less prestigious and smaller circulation magazines" (Love & Angelo, 1985, p. 71). Said a woman senior copy editor in the Northeast who was earning a salary in the high teens: "My salary is terribly low, considering the amount of expertise and work that go into this job. The discrimination against women in terms of monetary compensation in this industry is horrendous." Female copy editors in 1985 averaged $23,300 to males' $26,650 (Love & Angelo, 1985, p. 82).

Folio cautions readers about using the numbers:

> It should be noted that the data here have been presented in the form of simple totals (only one variable was studied at a time). The interaction that may exist between the totals has not been examined. For example, regarding salaries by region, it appears that editors working in the Northeast are paid higher salaries. But were there more males in the Northeast? Higher circulations? Editors with more experience? . . . Clearly, this survey reveals only what people *are* paid. When it comes to salary differences between men and women, for example, no one would argue that a woman with the same title as a man should be paid less. (Love & Angelo, 1985, p. 72).

Folio's 1986 editorial survey, with responses from 518 professionals (representing 45.6% of those surveyed), shows women continuing to receive less money than men in every level except copy editor. Male editors earned $14,204 more than females ($57,000 to $42,796), the greatest difference in the categories (Angelo, 1986, p. 80).

Comments from women are revealing: "I have on five occasions been paid less than male predecessors, peers or replacements in jobs where I was praised as 'The star,' or 'The best ever,'" wrote a woman editor in the Northeast with almost 25 years of experience, who earned a salary in the mid-$80,000s (Angelo, 1986, p. 82).

Folio changed its universe studied for this 1986 survey; no comparisons could be made to the salaries published the year before (Angelo, 1986, p. 90). Unfortunately, *Folio* changed its universe sample every time a salary survey was done.

For the 1987 survey, *Folio* had a 49% response rate, with returned questionnaires from 556 editorial and design professionals. Although the same nine factors were presented, *Folio* broadened its sample base, eliminating previous requirements. Therefore the survey could not be compared to any past ones (Zelkowitz, 1987, p. 94).

Salary range closed in 1987 in editorial management, managing editor, senior/associate editor, and copy editor categories, with women earning between 96% and 100% of what men earned. But the picture changed dramatically when consumer magazine editor and art director salaries were studied in terms of gender. A female editor made 78% of her male peer's salary, $35,620 versus $45,736. A female art director earned only 70% of the salary of a male director, $32,136 versus $45,627 (Zelkowitz, 1987, pp. 97, 103).

Folio's 1988 survey, of 559 editorial professionals (a 53% response rate), found that women continued to earn less than their male peers, from a low of 74% of men's salaries for editorial management to a high of 99% for managing editors (Steed, 1988, p. 103). For example, in editorial management slots, women earned $43,747 to men's $59,200; in the editor category, women took in $37,568 to their male peers' $45,320 (Steed, 1988, pp. 106-107).

Folio also has surveyed consumer magazine professionals in circulation, advertising sales, and production. Each year, and in each category, men were more highly paid than women, reflecting the same gap found in editorial. However, as mentioned above, a major problem with *Folio*'s surveys is that of changing samples; no consistency exists in the universe from year to year for comparison or longitudinal analysis.

Other salary data can be found in sources such as *Media Industry Newsletter*, *The Gallagher Report*, *The American Almanac of Jobs and Salaries*, and *Magazine Week*. The information is not gender-specific, and varies considerably, but job categories not surveyed by *Folio* can be found there, such as editorial assistant, assistant editor, paper purchasing manager, staff writer, and executive assistant. None of these sources indicates race, another variable that should be considered in studying employment patterns in the magazine industry.

Comments from women about salary discrepancy or discrimination are few in published surveys. Recent interviews with women in the consumer magazine field reveal that most believe there has not been overt discrimination against them, and that, in general, women are paid about the same as men in similar posts.

A woman in the magazine field for the past 10 years as a copy editor, associate editor, and managing editor at four publications, and whose salary peaked in the $20,000-$29,999 bracket, said:

> I was in top management positions, but I could not advance because the only position I could advance to was a man's—and I was propping him up. Partly the reason I got out of magazines is because they need mothers. They need somebody who will make a personal investment in the quality and integrity of the publication—that's well beyond the call of duty. I felt overly burdened by that.

This woman is now a free-lance writer for a variety of publications (Valys, 1988).

Another 10-year veteran who has been a staff writer, associate editor, business editor, editor, and senior editor at five different consumer magazines said, "Most of the power has been in the hands of men. I think a lot of women end up doing detail things like editing or fact checking. In general, I had the same title and the responsibilities as a man." She is now with a trade magazine as a writer, where she is making as much as she made at a glitzy consumer magazine as senior editor (Valys, 1988).

WOMEN AT BUSINESS/TRADE MAGAZINES

In all its salary surveys, *Folio* examined the pay scales of those working on business magazines as well as those at consumer magazines, generally surveying equal numbers of business and consumer magazine professionals. In its first survey, published in 1982, *Folio* points out that "whether a magazine is a consumer magazine or a business magazine is not an important factor, on average. But among the highest-paid editors (the top third), consumer magazine editors do better" (Love, 1982, p. 88).

At business magazines in 1985, women earned less than their male peers, except in the copy editor category, with an even greater gap in salaries by gender than was found at consumer magazines. For example, in the senior/associate editor category, female business editors earned just 74% of what male business editors made, while women in this position at consumer magazines earned 95% of men's salaries (Love & Angelo, 1985, p. 78).

The 1986 *Folio* report still showed female business editors making less money than males in all categories except copy editor, where women earned about $3,000 more. However, men earned as much as $22,000 more than women in other positions (Angelo, 1986, p. 82). A 10-year veteran woman editor in the Midwest, who earned $35,000 a year, wrote, "I am one of several magazine editors in a business publishing company. My peers are all about my same age, and have my same amount of experience. They are also all male. They all make more than I do" (Angelo, 1986, p. 82).

In 1987, *Folio* reported that

> those on consumer titles earn $62,295 versus $55,580 for their colleagues on business magazines, or 12.1 percent more. In the Northeast, those on consumer publications outpull their business magazine peers by 18.1 per-

cent—$78,959 compared to $66,875. . . . Although the difference in salaries
between the two types of magazines is small for men—with business magazine men outearning their consumer colleagues by 9.6 percent—women
managers on consumer magazines, at an average salary of $75,633, make
61.2 percent more than their sisters on business magazines. (Zelkowitz, 1987,
p. 91)

Analysis of the most recent *Folio* survey (1988) reveals that, across the
board, women continue to earn fewer dollars than men on business magazines (Steed, 1988, p. 103). The same patterns hold true for business magazine professionals in circulation, advertising sales, and production, according to *Folio* data. The survey makes no attempt to compare business
magazines within particular areas, either vertically or horizontally.

Finding complete published data about the people—whether male or
female—working at business, trade, or professional magazines is difficult.
The Association of Business Publishers releases salary data from surveys
in confidential reports to members only.

The Society of National Association Publications salary survey in 1987
reinforced some of the findings of the *Folio* surveys, although it was limited to association publications only. Working from a random list of 1,034
association publication executives, 485 completed questionnaires were
used—a 50.2% response rate (SNAP, 1987, p. 3). Two findings were particularly relevant. The first was that "the majority of positions held in association publications are held by women, although there are a majority of
males in the positions of publisher, editor-in-chief, and advertising sales-
person" (p. 6). The second was an analysis of average salary by sex and age.
Not surprisingly, males made more money than females in almost every
job category. No analysis was made of race (pp. 34-39).

Additional data can be found in papers presented by journalism and
mass communication professors at annual conventions of the Association
for Education in Journalism and Mass Communication (AEJMC). For example, Dennis W. Jeffers, in his 1987 paper *A Descriptive Study of Perceived Impact of Gender on Employment Status, Type of Work, Industry
Relationships, Working Environment and Job Satisfaction in Livestock Industry Magazines*, points out that gender concerns had not, to date, been
investigated in trade or business magazines. Instead, the main area studied
where gender predicts income, and where the problem has been clearly
identified, is in the public relations and business communications areas
(p.3). According to Jeffers, an associate professor at Central Michigan
University, "Many industrial publications are associated with industries
that, if linked to one gender, have been traditionally linked to males. . . .

for the the most part, the livestock industry is 'traditional' in that women play very narrow and specific roles" (p. 4).

Jeffers distributed questionnaires to 69 livestock magazine staffers attending an annual meeting in 1986 in Fort Worth, Texas. Although nearly 60% of the respondents were female, "women are underrepresented in editorial positions and about equal in other positions on the magazines scrutinized." Those other positions included advertising, design, and production (p. 8).

Jeffers's data, which were consistent with the findings of other gender studies, showed that "in spite of the influx of women in the field . . . men are the managers and women are the technicians at livestock magazines" (p. 8). Jeffers does not analyze salary, but nevertheless, his research adds reliability to results of other gender-related studies in mass communication.

Jeffers concludes:

> Finally, gender-related studies such as this one should be extended to other types of industrial magazines. In particular, researchers should investigate whether the same kinds of problems are present in magazines that cover *other* male dominated industries. What about industrial magazines covering *female* dominated industries? . . . do they have the same kinds of problems? Clearly, there are many opportunities for additional research. (p. 14)

Jeffers's research focused on a very narrow part of the trade magazine category. Kathleen L. Endres, an assistant professor at the University of Akron, broke ground on the category as a whole with a paper titled *The Business Press Journalists: Who They Are, What They Do and How They View Their Craft*, presented at the 1988 AEJMC Convention. Pointing out that surprisingly little is known about the business press or its journalists, Endres (1988) provides what is probably the most comprehensive demographic profile of business press editorial personnel to date, along with information about work patterns and perceptions of the field. Since no comprehensive list of full-time business magazine journalists exists, Endres drew her sample from SRDS's *Business Publication Rates and Data*. She ended up with 374 questionnaires (45% response rate), which "represent a cross section of journalists in the business press. They cover a number of different industries, live in different parts of the country and work for periodicals that span the circulation range of free to paid, the frequency rate of weekly to quarterly and the formats varied from magazine to newspaper" (p. 3).

Endres found that "the typical business press reporter or editor is a microcosm of U.S. journalists in general. Typically, the business journalists are likely to be white males in their mid-30s with bachelor's degrees" (p. 5). This finding supports Weaver and Wilhoit's (1986) research; however, Endres's research also goes a long way toward providing information about women in this area of the magazine industry.

Although men made up 54% of those responding to Endres's survey, females outnumbered males in periodicals covering certain types of industries:

> For example, women outnumber men on periodicals covering the retail and service industries, two areas where women dominate in the general labor force. Just the opposite was the case in periodicals covering businesses that traditionally hired men. In the periodicals covering the professions, building trades, industry, business/management, transportation and the other fields, men outnumber women. The only exception to this are the publications covering the medical/science field, where women outnumber men by a sizeable margin. (Endres, 1988, p. 6)

Endres found that men and women working on business magazines differed in several key respects, in areas corresponding to research done in public relations and that validate *Folio* salary surveys:

- Women have less professional journalism experience than men responding to the survey. On the average, men have 13.2 years experience versus 7.3 years for women (p. 7).
- Women are likely to get their professional experience in different ways from men. Men are more likely to work for a newspaper first, while more women start at other business publications or in public relations. "Those differences, while not statistically significant, may help explain why women and men hold different types of jobs" (p. 8).
- Women are less likely to hold the job of editor or senior editor than men, with men serving in those top positions 50% of the time to women's 25%. Only in the position of managing editor is there any parity. "Two explanations are possible for such a disparity. First, the relative inexperience of the women compared to the men. According to those responding to this questionnaire, women have about half the professional experience of men. The other explanation may deal with tradition. While none of the women reported discrimination as a weakness in the business press field, the small numbers of women employed in the top editorial positions seems to suggest that there may be more to this situation than mere inexperience" (p. 9).
- Women earn substantially less than men, with an average annual income of $25,658 versus $39,559 for men. Furthermore, such a differential is not

unique to Endres's survey; a salary survey by the American Society of Business Press Editors in 1987 found a substantial difference as well. "The disparity could be found across all editorial jobs. Whether managing editors, editors, senior editors or reporters, women are paid less than men" (p. 9). For example, female managing editors were paid an average of $26,666, while males received $36,379. Women editors earned $33,275 to men's $45,303. Differences in salaries tended to be smaller in entry-level jobs. Yet even the female assistant/associate editor, the most common job for women at business magazines, received less pay than her male peer, $21,956 to $24,714. The smallest differential was found in the reporter slot, where men received $27,500 and women $27,000 (pp. 9-10).

Endres's study also provides information about race, something that rarely has been covered in magazine studies. The overwhelming majority of business press professionals were Caucasian—98% of those answering the questionnaire. Only eight members of minority groups were identified: three Blacks, one Asian and four Hispanics (2%). Endres said the minorities were split between men and women, but, more disturbing, "That ethnic breakdown means that minority groups are more greatly underrepresented in the business press than the journalism field in general or the U.S. population" (p. 12).

WOMEN AT PUBLIC RELATIONS MAGAZINES

This, the largest category of magazines in the United States, is also the hardest to study. So it is not surprising that there has been very little research specifically dealing with house organs. The International Association of Business Communicators, an organization made up of approximately 11,000 communicators in the United States, does not identify how many of its members manage, edit, or produce either an internal or external magazine, nor are tabs kept on how many companies might be producing magazines. There is some information available about communicator titles, with editor being listed 15% of the time (International Association of Business Communicators, 1987, p. 6). However, as with titles at consumer and business magazines, titles in corporate communications or public relations areas are not consistent. A manager or director is just as likely to produce or edit a magazine as is an editor, coordinator, or specialist.

Interviews with women who have worked in this magazine field for several years provide some information as to their status as professionals.

Said one who has spent eight years as editor or senior editor at three different public relations publications:

> Women get up to be editors—which people on the outside think is a top slot. But the reality is that public relations magazines are likely to be headed by a president and board of directors. And these slots are typically held by men. So the problems for women at public relations publications are not magazine industry issues, but corporate structure issues. As senior editor, I probably do what an editorial assistant would do at a consumer or business magazine. I never make my own decisions; I am not autonomous. I have to clear things through management. Yet I'm not experiencing salary discrimination because I know a man would be paid the same as I because of the grade structure at my corporation. Whoever has this job is essentially a technician.

This woman's current salary is in the $30,000-$39,000 range (Johnson, 1988).

Another woman who has been senior editor for seven years on an external high-tech corporate magazine says:

> I really think women can get the same slot and have the influence. I believe that management is more concerned about talent than gender. Employers are looking for people who can do the job regardless of sex. However, the women I know who work in editorial jobs have—categorically—worked harder than the men. It seems like there's an unspoken rule that we must overachieve to stay on top.

Earning between $30,000 and $39,000, she adds, "The editor is a mystery person in the corporation. Top management has a hard time assessing the individual's worth as a writer/editor because it's hard to quantify words, layouts and designs" (Johnson, 1988).

This is an area that needs to be studied. Public relations research has not addressed the area of internal or external public relations magazines put out by corporations. However, it is likely that much of the material in Chapter 14 of this book applies to this aspect of the magazine industry.

MAGAZINE RESEARCH

Research about magazines, whether involving magazine journalism or the magazine publishing industry, has been scanty. Work on the demographics, attitudes, and beliefs of magazine professionals has also been neglected. Scholarly magazine research simply has lagged far behind the work being done on other aspects of the mass media by mass communication researchers.

Peter Gerlach (1987) has documented the infrequency of magazine research in publications on journalism and mass communication. Studying the years from 1964 through 1983 in *Journalism Quarterly*, a key refereed journal in the field, Gerlach found that only 6% of the articles published dealt with magazines. About half of these articles consisted of content analysis, followed by historical and economic topics. Others dealt with effect analysis, readership, communication analysis, and education (p. 179).

Gerlach surveyed 40 AEJMC members who had published one or more articles about magazine research in *Journalism Quarterly*, asking their opinion of American magazine research, among other questions (p. 178). With 32 surveys returned (80% response rate), Gerlach found, "All in all, 68.7 percent of the respondents thought that magazine research has been unsatisfactory in one respect or another" (p. 181).

Pointing out that descriptive content analysis and not studies of processes and effects have dominated magazine research, Gerlach's respondents also said that magazine research is not a well-funded area, that there have been too few systematic studies of the industry in general, and that the vastness of the field has made it difficult to study (p. 181).

Compounding the lack of magazine research has been a neglect of gender roles. With my colleague William G. Christ, I have pointed out the lack of research on how women newsmakers are presented in magazines (Johnson & Christ, 1987, p. 1). We analyzed the representation of women on the cover of *Time* from its beginning issue in 1923 through 1987 because *Time* has argued "that history is made by men and women, no matter how strong the forces and movements that carry them along" (Johnson & Christ, 1987, p. 2). Because of this, *Time* tends to feature personalities on its covers, as opposed to events, ideas, or themes. We used this characteristic to look at gender and to analyze which women newsmakers have been covered. Out of 3,386 covers published in the 64-year period researched, only 482 covers showed images of women on them, or about 14% (Johnson & Christ, 1987, p. 6).

SUGGESTIONS FOR THE FUTURE

Four areas need to be addressed before magazine journalism and publishing can be studied adequately: (1) articulation of what the magazine field involves, (2) definitions that tackle methodological as well as structural and theoretical problems inherent in the magazine industry, (3) linkages among researchers in the field, and (4) analysis of the demographic and social order of magazine professionals.

To address the first area, Marcia Prior-Miller, an assistant professor at Iowa State University, has begun to articulate what the magazine field involves, primarily, "the lack of conceptual clarity among both magazine professionals and academic scholars about the types of magazines available and the factors which might be considered principles common to all and the distinguishing uniquenesses among magazines"(personal communication, August 6, 1988). She is developing a typology, or theory of magazines, for "without an adequate typology, designing quality comparative studies of magazines and magazine organizations and the professionals working in them is not possible" (personal communication, August 6, 1988).

Regarding the second area, as can be discerned from reading this chapter, there are major difficulties in identifying the universe of magazine titles from which to draw samples for cross-sectional study. Prior-Miller points out that "directories both duplicate the listings of other directories and omit large numbers of publications. Descriptions of the criteria for the inclusion or exclusion of titles is often less than adequate from the scientific perspective. Thus, any effort to design a careful sample immediately is confronted with this weakness in the sampling frame" (personal communication, August 6, 1988).

Third, those interested in magazine research have difficulty building upon prior studies because of the lack of ongoing research. There is a great deal of fragmented research, or, as Prior-Miller puts it, "Existing studies tend to be discrete and atheoretical. New generations of scholars tend to be overwhelmed by the lack of a coherent body of research on the history of the development of the field, the on-going social order, and the problems of communications within the medium. Given the dominant model of research on other media and the intellectual and financial support for continuing to work within that dominant model, young scholars understandably turn their interests in those directions" (personal communication, August 6, 1988).

Finally, until these methodological and structural concerns are met with functioning definitions and terminologies, professionals working in the magazine industry cannot be studied systematically. There is no agreement on job titles, nor has there been an attempt to break down staff responsibilities to reflect size or type of magazine. What is needed is a project along the lines of Weaver and Wilhoit's (1986) study of American news journalists. Then, and only then, can issues relating to women and minorities be addressed clearly.

REFERENCES

American Society of Association Executives. (1987). *1987 policies and procedures in association management.* Washington, DC: Author.
Angelo, Jean. (1986, May). Editors' average salary: $52,240. *Folio: The Magazine for Magazine Management,* pp. 76-90.
Association of Business Publishers. (1988, August). [Report]. New York: Author.
Audit Bureau of Circulations. (1987, December 31). *FAS-FAX report for six months ending December 31, 1987.* Author.
Baran, Stanley J., McIntyre, Jerilyn S., & Meyer, Timothy P. (1984). *Self, symbols and society: An introduction to mass communication.* Reading, MA: Addison-Wesley.
Bittner, John R. (1986). *Mass communication: An introduction* (4th ed.). Englewood Cliffs, NJ: Prentice-Hall.
Butler, Matilda, & Paisley, William. (1980). *Women and the mass media: Sourcebook for research and action.* New York: Human Sciences.
Click, J. William, & Baird, Russell. (1986). *Magazine editing and production* (4th ed.). Dubuque, IA: William C. Brown.
Endres, Kathleen L. (1988, July). *The business press journalists: Who they are, what they do and how they view their craft.* Paper presented to the Magazine Division at the annual meeting of the Association for Education in Journalism and Mass Communication, Portland, OR.
Gale Research. (1988). *Gale directory of publications 1988* (120th ed.). Detroit: Author.
Gerlach, Peter. (1987). Research about magazines appearing in *Journalism Quarterly. Journalism Quarterly, 64*(1), 178-182.
International Association of Business Communicators. (1987). *IABC profile '87.* San Francisco: Author.
International Association of Business Communicators. (1988, July). San Francisco: Author.
Jeffers, Dennis W. (1987, August). *A descriptive study of perceived impact of gender on employment status, type of work, industry relationships, working environment and job satisfaction in livestock industry magazines.* Paper presented to the Magazine Division at the annual meeting of the Association for Education in Journalism and Mass Communication, San Antonio, TX.
Johnson, Sammye. (1988, July-August). [Interviews with women working at public relations magazines]. Unpublished.

Johnson, Sammye, & Christ, William G. (1987, August). *Women through Time: Who gets covered?* Paper presented to the Magazine Division at the annual meeting of the Association for Education in Journalism and Mass Communication, San Antonio, TX.

Love, Barbara, (1982, August). The *Folio* editorial salary survey. *Folio: The Magazine for Magazine Management*, pp. 88-100+.

Love, Barbara, & Angelo, Jean. (1985, July). Editors' average salary: $34,623. *Folio: The Magazine for Magazine Management*, pp. 69-84.

Magazine almanac . . . facts, trends and perspectives that can work for you. (1988, March). *MPA Newsletter of Research.*

Mott, Frank Luther. (1939). *A history of American magazines: Vol. 1. 1741-1850.* Cambridge, MA: Harvard University Press.

Oxbridge Communications. (1988). *Standard periodical directory 1988* (11th ed.). New York: Author.

Paine, Fred K., & Paine, Nancy E. (1987). *Magazines: A bibliography for their analysis with annotations and study guide.* Metuchen, NJ: Scarecrow.

Pattis, S. William. (1986). *Opportunities in magazine publishing.* Lincolnwood, IL: VGM Career Horizons.

Society of National Association Publications (SNAP). (1988, August). [Report]. Washington, DC: Author.

Society of National Association Publications (SNAP). (1987, October). *Society of National Association Publications salary and benefits surveys.* Washington, DC: Author.

Standard Rate and Data Service. (1988a, July 24). *Business publication rates and data.* Wilmette, IL: Author.

Standard Rate and Data Service. (1988b, July 27). *Consumer magazine and agri-media rates and date.* Wilmette, IL: Author.

Steed, Robert M. (1988, August). Editorial salary survey. *Folio: The Magazine for Magazine Management*, pp. 103-121.

U.S. Bureau of the Census. (1987). *Statistical abstract of the United States, 1988* (108th ed.). Washington, DC: U.S. Department of Commerce.

U.S. Department of Labor, Bureau of Labor Statistics. (1987a, January). *Employment and earnings: Employed civilians by detailed occupation, sex, race and Hispanic origin.* Washington, DC: Government Printing Office.

U.S. Department of Labor, Bureau of Labor Statistics. (1987b, January). *Employment and earnings: Employed civilians by detailed industry, sex, race and Hispanic origin.* Washington, DC: Government Printing Office.

U.S. Department of Labor, Bureau of Labor Statistics. (1988, May). *Employment and earnings: Employees on nonagricultural payrolls by detailed industry.* Washington, DC: Government Printing Office.

Valys, Susan. (1988, July). [Interviews with women working at consumer magazines]. Paper in progress.

Weaver, David H., & Wilhoit, G. Cleveland. (1986). *The American journalist: A portrait of U.S. news people and their work.* Bloomington: Indiana University Press.

Wood, Donald N. (1983). *Mass media and the individual.* St. Paul, MN: West.

Wright, John W. (1987). *The American almanac of jobs and salaries.* New York: Avon.

Zelkowitz, Suzanne. (1987, June). Editorial salary survey. *Folio: The Magazine for Magazine Management*, pp. 91-104.

11

Radio

A Woman's Place Is on the Air

JUDITH A. CRAMER

HISTORY

A woman's place in early radio was in singing, acting, and giving household hints. It was also in research, off-air interviewing, and writing. It was not, however, in announcing, or in reading the news, nor was it in managing or owning a radio station. World War II, affirmative action, and the contemporary women's movement of the 1970s combined to open those doors of opportunity.

Women in radio in the 1920s described their field as an excellent one—one where there was less sex discrimination than in other fields, and one in which the opportunities for moving into positions of greater creativity and responsibility were good (Marzolf, 1977, p. 123). Bertha Brainard, assistant broadcasting manager of New York City's WJZ in 1928, seemed to support this assessment when she said, "The pioneering state of radio gives men and women equal opportunities and equal pay for equal work" (Marzolf, 1977, p. 124).

Opportunities for women in early radio were a logical extension of their roles in the home. For example, Ruth Crane pioneered the "homemaker" program concept as host of *Mrs. Page's Home Economies* which aired six days a week on WJR in Detroit from 1929 until 1944. From there, Crane moved to Washington, D.C., to host WMAL's *Modern Woman* program. Prior to World War II, most stations employed one woman air personality, usually as host of a "homemaker" program that was anywhere from 15 minutes to an hour long. The women hosts, according to Crane, did not receive much respect.

> I've checked this with many other women who were in radio and TV too. You were really not supposed to know anything about food or household hints or any of the subjects you were broadcasting on. Our efforts were not taken very seriously by our associates even though the announcers and technicians were often veritable beginners on the staff. And the jokes directed at her were not always innocent. (Beasley & Silver, 1977, p. 88)

An accomplished magazine and newspaper journalist, Mary Margaret McBride, expanded the homemaker program concept when she began her radio career on New York's WOR in 1934. She not only offered household tips and recipes on her *Martha Deane Program*, but conducted human-interest interviews as well. Unlike other hosts of homemaker programs, she did not use a script. McBride played an important role in the creation of the radio talk show concept.

In 1933, the first radio news team was assembled at CBS. Paul White put together the team, which included one woman—*New York Journal-American* reporter Florence Conley. Conley reported on what, today, we term "society" news.

The broadcasting industry saw its first woman news commentator in 1936, despite the belief by many in radio that a woman's voice was neither low enough nor authoritative enough to be giving the news (Hosley & Yamada, 1987, p. 22). Kathryn Craven's 5-minute program, *News Through a Woman's Eyes*, aired on CBS radio until 1938, when the program was dropped.

World War II increased the opportunities for women in all areas of radio. Because of the wartime shortage of men, radio station management was forced, at least temporarily, to open doors to women for positions as news reporters, announcers, and managers. Marion Taylor, among others, signaled a turning of the tide when she took over the *Martha Deane* show in 1941. She chose not to focus on the "women's angle," believing good and bad stories were not gender-related (Marzolf, 1977, p. 132). In 1936, CBS radio, according to its then-Director of Talks Helen Sioussat, relaxed its corporate policy to include hiring women as assistant directors and producers. And more and more women were working as news reporters.

During the 1940s, women also entered the announcing ranks in larger numbers. However, although more women were employed in radio, men continued to receive top billing. Much of the women's programming was aired on weekends and reports by female war correspondents were usually last in the network newscast or were relegated to the weekend, when the male correspondents had time off.

In 1946, women made up 28% of the people in broadcasting. A year later, the *Labor Department Round-Up* predicted there would be many more opportunities in broadcasting for men and women with the conclusion of the war years. But this proved not to be the case for women. When the men returned from war, they assumed many of the positions women held during World War II.

Predictions were made that radio had reached its peak in growth and popularity during the World War II years, that with the advent of television and the ensuing competition between it and radio, women would have fewer radio career opportunities. After all, announcing positions for women were still almost nonexistent. The vast majority of radio's decision makers were male, and they still held to the beliefs that women's voices were "poor" and that radio announcing meant dealing with irregular hours and equipment that was difficult to operate (Marzolf, 1977, p. 145). Women's voices and abilities were good enough for homemaking programs, however.

In the 1950s, women slowly moved into other areas of radio. They found employment as "script girls," a position called "production assistant" when a man held it. Women also became interviewers on and coordinators of radio programs like *Nightline* and NBC's weekend program *Monitor*. However, it was routine procedure to rub the woman interviewer's voice off the tape so that an on-mike male announcer could ask the questions (Marzolf, 1977, p. 146). In addition, the late 1950s saw a few women move into music programming as coordinators of disc jockey shows. Women in general were poorly paid and were expected to maintain high levels of energy and resourcefulness (Marzolf, 1977, p. 146).

Less attention was given to researching radio trends with the inception of television in the 1950s. However, studies do show that women constituted 20% of all university and college broadcast course graduates in the 1960s. Yet, radio hired only 60 to 80 of those graduates a year (Marzolf, 1977, p. 149). In 1960, Smith and Harwood conducted the very first survey of men and women in broadcasting on behalf of the Association for Professional Broadcasting Education and the National Association of Broadcasters. The results were based on the responses of 156 women (72 in television, 84 in radio) and 1,573 men in radio and television. The survey results did not include the responses of broadcast managers, since there were only 3 women managers in the sample. Smith and Harwood (1966) found that about 90% (140) of the women surveyed were employed in clerical and secretarial areas, regardless of education, such as the continuity and traffic departments, and earned much smaller paychecks than men. In fact, 84% of the women but only 17% of the men in radio Smith and Harwood surveyed earned a weekly salary of less than $96. Out of every 10 women in radio, 7 earned less than $77 a week (p. 340). Only about one-fourth of the women in radio expressed dissatisfaction with their salaries. Other satisfactions they received from their jobs might have compensated for their low salaries (p. 354). One of those compensating satisfactions may have been the contacts these women had with other professionals.

According to the Smith and Harwood study, women 28 years ago entered radio by "chance" and worked in the medium an average of 3 to 4 years. Men, on the other hand, trained for the radio profession and worked in the field much longer—10 to 14 years. More than a fourth of the women and 47% of the men surveyed cited money and career advancement as reasons for leaving their last positions. Interestingly, only a quarter of the women cited family and personal considerations as reasons for leaving their last positions, perhaps putting in question the belief that family concerns are the most significant reason in job change for women—at least in radio.

The 1960s was a time of societal change, but bias against women still existed in radio newsrooms. In responding to a survey conducted in 1977, broadcast news directors offered the same old reasons for that bias: Men sounded more authoritative; women let personal problems affect their job performance; women could not handle assignments. This bias was reflected in the fact that only 4.7% of radio and television newsroom staffs were female (Marzolf, 1977, p. 149).

The 1970s signaled a turning point for women in radio. A 1972 survey of American Woman in Radio and Television (AWRT) members found women were moving into larger radio markets, receiving better salaries, and attaining more responsible and audible positions. According to the survey results, women were more satisfied with their jobs, but had become more conscious of discrimination, which they blamed on sex stereotyping. AWRT members, however, believed the status of women in radio would improve, but thought it was up to the individual to improve it (Marzolf, 1977, p. 150). (AWRT flourishes today, with more than 2,700 members nationwide.)

Women and Public Radio in the 1970s

The introduction of National Public Radio in 1971 brought with it increased opportunities for radio broadcasters in general. These new opportunities in radio emerged simultaneously with the second wave of the women's movement, thus offering the hope that public radio would open more career doors for women. In 1972, a survey of public radio stations by Barbara Patterson of WFCR-FM in Amherst, Massachusetts, and Elaine Prostak of WBFO-FM in Buffalo, New York, found that women were employed at 103 public radio stations, where women constituted 14% of management and 16% of all on-air positions (Butler & Paisley, 1980, p. 194). Two years later, women held 26% (3,452) of all public radio jobs.

In 1974, Caroline Isber and Muriel Cantor conducted a survey of 245 public television and 159 public radio stations on behalf of the Corporation for Public Broadcasting. A total of 306 men and 120 women in public radio responded to the survey. According to the Task Force on Women in Public Broadcasting report, 4 members of National Public Radio's 16-member board of directors were women (Isber & Cantor, 1975, p. 141), while women constituted just 16% of the membership on local boards of directors. The proportion of women holding radio management positions was even smaller—12%, just 1% more than in 1972. Such a small increase in the number of women in public radio management was especially disappointing because 80% of the public radio stations in 1974 had affirmative action plans and more than 70% of the stations were licensed to universities that had affirmative action policies (Butler & Paisley, 1980, p. 194).

The report goes one step further by suggesting that women were, for the most part, confined to the area of business management. In fact, women constituted 82% (9) of the business managers. They were 19% (6) of the operations managers, 17% (18) of all program managers, 12% (8) of the stations managers, and only 4% (2) of the general managers. At the highest managerial level, men outnumbered women 10 to 1 (Isber & Cantor, 1975, p. 105).

The Task Force Report also notes large disparities in the salaries, promotions, and assignments of women and men in public radio, which again is surprising, given the strong public scrutiny to which public radio is subjected. Of the full-time public radio employees who responded to the survey (1,535), 76% of the women and 44% of the men earned less than $9,000 per year, while no women and 8% percent of the men made more than $17,000 per year. The men made more money, but part of the explanation for this is that they had been in their present jobs longer than the women (Isber & Cantor, 1975, p. 131).

In the area of career advancement, a greater percentage of men than women in public radio received requested and unrequested promotions. For example, 80% (40) of the men who asked for promotions got them, compared to only 69% (8) of the women. Fewer women than men had moved beyond their entry-level positions (Isber & Cantor, 1975, p. 43).

The Task Force looked at 13 different kinds of adult public radio programs and found that 80% (375) of them had male narrators/moderators only, while just 10% (49) had female narrators/moderators only; 10% (45) had both male and female narrators/moderators (Isber & Cantor, 1975, p. 83). The men were much more likely to narrate/moderate discussions of business, economics, law, and government. The women narrated/moderated general human-interest discussions in most of their appearances (Isber & Cantor, 1975, p. 86).

Most of the men interviewed in the Corporation for Public Broadcasting survey said they were willing to employ women, but their specific responses to questions on hiring and promotional practices seem to contradict this "open" attitude. For example, most of the men responded with male names when asked who had been hired recently as managers. While a number of male managers said they were unable to find qualified women for management positions, the women executives interviewed said they had no problems finding qualified women (Isber & Cantor, 1975, p. 47).

Women and Commercial Radio in the 1970s

A 1974 study of station managers revealed that prospects for women were bleak. More than half of the managers still thought people did not like the sound of women on the air, even though earlier research refuted this stereotypical view (Marzolf, 1977, p. 150). Women, nevertheless, made great strides between 1972 and 1976 despite the dim outlook and some continuing large disparities in numbers and positions.

In 1976, Stone surveyed 330 commercial radio stations and found that the number of stations where newswomen were on the air had more than tripled, from 15% in 1972 to 49 % in 1976 (Stone, 1977, p. 7). However, women constituted just 15% of the newscasters and 18% of the on-air field reporters. The clear majority (208) of the stations did not have one female newscaster, while only 8% (26) did not have a male newscaster. A little more than half (55%) of the women worked as radio newscasters, but 82% of the men held that same position. Even though radio was not making full use of women, it was becoming commonplace for radio news staffs to have women on the air.

Not surprisingly, the number of women radio news directors also rose during the 1972-76 period, from 4% to 8% (Stone, 1977, p. 10). These women were young, usually in their 20s, and were college graduates with degrees in speech and broadcasting. This was quite a change from the 1960s, when women did not train to work in the radio profession. Stone predicted that the trend toward women news directors would continue as long as the number of women in radio increased.

The number of women in radio significantly increased between the 1920s and the 1970s. Women who held on-air positions went from being the hosts of homemaker programs in the thirty years preceding World War II to anchoring and reporting news primarily in the 1960s and 1970s. The 1970s saw the greatest improvement in pure numbers and positions of responsibility. Since there was only one study on public radio conducted during the 1970s, it is virtually impossible to track the employment trends of women. However, the number of women who worked in public radio, and their positions, salaries, and opportunities for promotion clearly did not compare favorably with those of male public radio employees. While women in commercial radio made large gains in numbers and positions, including significant movement into the management ranks, there was much room for improvement in terms of reaching parity with the men in commercial radio news.

THE CURRENT STATUS OF WOMEN

Women and Commercial Radio in the 1980s

Women have not continued to make the same kinds of large gains in radio they did in the 1970s in terms of pure numbers, type of position, and salary. Parity between men and women in the radio newsroom has not yet been truly realized at either the commercial network or local level. The least impressive gains have been at the radio networks. As noted in *Variety*, the number of women managers increased a maximum of just three percentage points between 1983 and 1986 ("Women in Broadcasting," 1987). ABC had the most women managers working for it in 1986, when they constituted 20% (120) of management. According to *Variety*, CBS was the only radio network to employ women as general managers in 1983 and 1985. In 1987, however, no woman held that position at CBS.

At the local level, improvement has been gradual. For example, women made up 29% (5,929) of commercial radio news anchors in 1986—a 9% increase over a 14-year period (Stone, 1987a, p. 11). Overall, the number of women employed (6,358) by local commercial radio station news departments grew by 30% during this period, with a little more than half of the local stations (177) responding to a survey reporting at least one woman on the news staff, while only 20% (33) employed at least one newswoman in 1972 (Stone & Dell, 1972).

Most of this growth took place in locally owned stations in large markets, where, presumably because the size of the news staff is larger, they were more likely to hire a woman. Furthermore, at the entry level, close to half of all new hires (47%) in local radio news in 1986 were women and half of these women were hired to work as reporters. In terms of sheer numbers, women constituted one-third (6,800) of the local radio news force in the 1980s (Stone, 1986a, p. 28).

Perhaps the most significant gains in the 1980s for women in local commercial radio have come in the area of management. One of every five (24%) radio news directors was a woman in 1987—a tremendous increase from 1972, when they constituted 4% of the news director population. Female news directors worked at 26% (94) of all commercial stations (Stone, 1988a, p. 32).

A comparison of the demographic profiles of the local radio news directors is also interesting. Women news directors are younger (average age 27) than their male counterparts (average age 32). Stone found that most commercial radio news directors had been news directors before. Women news directors, according to Stone's (1987b) survey results, are now close to reaching parity where salaries are concerned (p. 44). Female news directors, on average, earn $600 less than men ($16,400 versus $17,000). Stone suggests that the small disparity is not sex-role related, but rather has to do with factors such as age, experience, and news operation size. However, wage discrimination based on sex remains. One woman news director/anchor of a station in a large Midwest market said that she knows she's earning $4,000 per year less than a male anchor/reporter she supervises. She also said that she is waiting for the right time to use this disparity to her advantage.

Stone also found female news directors to be less ambitious in advancing their careers. Only 28% (27) of the women surveyed, compared with almost half of the men (132), aspired to become general managers. Stone

(1987b) attributes this finding to traditional sex-role expectations—that long-term career commitment continues to mean greater family sacrifice for women (p. 44). Kathy Lehr, a 30-year-old woman who has been the news director/morning anchor at WLW in Cincinnati, Ohio, for three years, agrees in part with Stone's assessment. She is a "working woman, wife, and mother" who is on call seven days a week, 24 hours a day. Lehr believes her greatest challenge is in "trying to do it all." But she thinks more factors than just family desires contribute to women apparently not wanting to move up the station management ladder. In a telephone interview, Lehr said, "Women quite often are in the lower-paying, lower-level positions. They may not think there's a chance of being promoted to general manager. They may discover they can earn more money doing something else which might motivate them to get out of radio before they've even worked the number of years necessary to be seriously considered for promotions."

Women and Public Radio in the 1980s

In the first survey since 1974 of public radio employment trends, conducted in 1987, Stone (1988a) found that three times as many women (39%) were working in the area of general news than had been 13 years ago (13%) (p. 30). Stone surveyed more than half of all public radio stations with working addresses (605) and found that while only one-quarter (159) of the public radio news directors were women, women were just a little less likely than men to hold public radio news managerial positions or to work as newscasters/anchors (p. 32). For minority newswomen, the news was good and bad. They made up just 7% of the public radio news staffs and 12% of the public radio news directors in 1987. Minority newswomen, however, were just as likely as minority newsmen and white newswomen to work as news directors (p. 32).

Stereotypes of Women in Radio

Walter Lippmann (1922) defines *stereotyping* as the act of categorizing behavior. This categorization allows people to organize the world around them (p. 59). Stereotypes are formed through the things people tell us before we experience them and through the things we imagine the world to include before we see them. If what we see or experience matches what is anticipated, then our stereotypes are reinforced. If what we see or experience is contrary to our stereotypes, then we can either dismiss them as exceptions or begin to feel unsure about all our accepted ways of viewing life and second-guess the things around us. According to Lippmann, a point is reached where our stereotypes and the facts separate because our image of how things are is more basic and fixed than the flow of events that surrounds us (p. 73).

Some stereotypes of women in radio have been slow to change in the 1980s. One such stereotype leads to the belief that it is possible to have "too many" women on the air. In 1981, Claire Cowley, then 22 years old, worked for $9,000 a year as news director/announcer at a small radio station in McMinnville, Tennessee; population 12,000. She supervised a two-person staff. "There were two female announcers, including myself. The program director would not allow us to go on the air back-to-back. He said there would be too many female voices so he hired a male announcer to come on the air for one hour, splitting the shifts (personal communication, Claire Cowley, WOSU-AM, Columbus, Ohio, July 1988)."

The stereotype that women's voices are not low enough and thus are not authoritative enough did not die with the 1960s or 1970s (Halper, 1987, p. 7). It is very much alive today. For example, in the early 1980s, Kathy Lehr was the only woman on the air at WLW in Cincinnati. She worked as an afternoon news anchor. "I had one program director who told me he was going to take me off the air because my voice wasn't low or controlled enough" (personal communication, Kathy Lehr, WLW-AM, Cincinnati, Ohio, July 1988). The program director left the station before Lehr could be removed from her on-air position.

WHAT NEXT?

In raw numbers, at least, women have made few gains in radio since World War II. Women today constitute just 5% more of the overall radio work force than they did at that time. Recent studies of employment trends in radio suggest that women fare slightly better working in public than in commercial radio news (Stone, 1988a, p. 31). As of 1988, women constituted 6% more of the paid work force in public radio and 2% more of the news director population. There are more minority women employed in public radio newsrooms than in commercial radio newsrooms, and minority women stand as great a chance of becoming news directors as do their white counterparts. However, while the number of white newswomen is expected to increase, the number of minority newswomen is not (Stone, 1988a, p. 32). White and minority newswomen can expect to earn more money in public radio. Overall, public radio salaries are 20-25% higher than commercial radio news salaries.

Numbers in and of themselves can be deceiving. One must wonder, for example, how much of an impact the addition of television and vastly improved radio technology have had on the numbers of both men and women entering the radio profession. The fact that not many more women (6%) are working in radio today than in 1946 does not reflect the strides women have made in securing positions as reporters, announcers, and news anchors. The contemporary women's movement, together with affirmative action, has helped open doors of opportunity for those women interested in radio careers. Today more and more women are training for and working in on-air positions. However, these advances have not occurred with the same speed and magnitude that they did in the 1970s.

Some attitudes toward women in radio have not changed much, either. For example, the assessment that women news directors are not as ambitious as men may not take into account all factors in the actual situation. Women may not see other women in management positions or may not be openly encouraged by management to seek promotions. Women may not perceive that it is possible to move up if support and encouragement are not forthcoming, and therefore may not display ambition.

Not to be minimized is the question of self-worth and its impact on ambition. Studies have found that women in all walks of life suffer from feelings of low self-worth. This often manifests itself in the amount of money women expect to earn in jobs. As was noted earlier, only a quarter of the women responding to a 1960s survey showed dissatisfaction with their salaries. Women of the 1980s may be having similar experiences. On the other hand, the contemporary women's movement may have served to empower women so that they are less likely to stay in low-paying, low-level positions. As Kathy Lehr points out, low pay and position remain factors in influencing the exodus of women from radio.

In the 1980s, women have made the largest gains in radio management. Research indicates they are not having difficulties in supervising men (Stone, 1976, p. 11). However, particular attention needs to be given to minority women, who are tremendously underrepresented in the managerial ranks. But care must also be taken that women are not promoted to managerial positions that offer title but no decision-making power or appropriate remuneration.

An interesting development appears to be that a small but increasing number of women are choosing not to "go the management route." Jane Evans, vice president and general manager of WBTH/WXCC in

Williamson, West Virginia, said in an interview in *RadioActive* that women are considering station ownership more seriously these days: "I believe women are going into ownership more than management because it is the quickest way of getting where they want to be. It is earlier, and eventually more lucrative to start their own concern" ("Women in Management," 1987, p. 14).

The more women there are working in all areas of radio, the more likely they are to become a strong, integral force. Evidence of this can already be found in such organized radio and television groups as Boston Women's Community Radio, Bridgeways Communications Corporation in Woodbridge, Connecticut, and Radio Free Feminists in Atlanta, Georgia. These groups, together with regular women's programming, like *Something About the Women*, which airs on WMFO in Medford, Massachusetts, and WWVU in Morgantown, West Virginia, and *Women's Magazine,* which can be heard on KZSC in Santa Cruz, California, provide greater employment opportunities and legitimacy for women interested in radio (Allen, 1988, pp. 41-43).

There is a dearth of contemporary research on radio, which may suggest that interest in radio as a viable and appealing medium is waning. Therefore, future research might include the impact of technology and television on the employment trends of women in radio. It might also be interesting to study the influence women in radio have on the coverage of women and women's issues, as well as whether the special concerns of minority women in radio are similar to or different from those of white women. Certainly, a more complete study of the employment trends of women in public radio is needed. Female role models in the industry and their impact on the socialization of young women into radio careers, factors that would increase the number of women at the network level, women who either own or are general managers of radio stations, and the future of women's programming and women's radio organizations are all areas that deserve further study. Obviously, however, much of the success of women in radio will depend on the future of the medium itself.

REFERENCES

Allen, Martha L. (Ed.). (1988). *1988 directory of women's media.* Washington, DC: Women's Institute for Freedom of the Press.

Beasley, Maurine, & Silver, Sheila. (1977). *Women in media: A documentary source book.* Washington, DC: Women's Institute for Freedom of the Press.

Burgoon, Judee K. (1978). Attributes of the newscaster's voice as predictors of his credibility. *Journalism Quarterly, 65*(2), 276-281, 300.

Butler, Matilda, & Paisley, William. (1980). *Women and the mass media: Sourcebook for research and action.* New York: Human Sciences.

Gallagher, Margaret. (1986). *Unequal opportunities.* Paris: UNESCO.

Halper, Donna, L., (1987). *Radio Active* (pp. 7-10). Washington, DC: National Association of Broadcasters.

Hosley, David, & Yamada, Gayle. (1987). *Hard news: Women in broadcast journalism.* New York: Greenwood.

Isber, Caroline C., & Cantor, Muriel. (1975). *The report of the task force on women in public broadcasting.* Washington, DC: Corporation for Public Broadcasting.

Lippmann, Walter. (1922). *Public opinion.* New York: Free Press.

Marzolf, Marion. (1977). *Up from the footnote: A history of women journalists.* New York: Hastings House.

Seigerman, Catherine (Ed.). (1987, June). Women in management, *Radio Active* (pp. 14-15). Washington, DC: National Association of Broadcasters.

Women in management. (1987, June). *RadioActive,* pp. 7-22.

Smith, Don, & Harwood, Kenneth. (1966). Women in broadcasting. *Journal of Broadcasting,* pp. 339-355.

Stone, Vernon. (1976, October). Surveys show younger women becoming news directors. *RTNDA Communicator,* pp. 10-12.

Stone, Vernon. (1977, February). More women reporting news on the air. *RTNDA Communicator,* pp. 7-10.

Stone, Vernon. (1986a, April). Women hold almost a third of news jobs. *RTNDA Communicator,* pp. 28-30.

Stone, Vernon. (1986b, June). News directors profiled. *RTNDA Communicator,* pp. 21-26.

Stone, Vernon. (1987a, August). Women gain, Black men lose ground in newsrooms. *RTNDA Communicator,* pp. 9-11.

Stone, Vernon. (1987b, December). Female news directors are younger, lower paid. *RTNDA Communicator,* pp. 43-44.

Stone, Vernon. (1988a, June). News operations at public radio stations surveyed, part I. *RTNDA Communicator,* pp. 29-34.

Stone, Vernon. (1988b, July). *Pipelines and dead ends: Jobs held by minorities and women in broadcast news.* Paper presented at the annual convention of the Association for Education in Journalism and Mass Communication, Portland, OR.

Stone, Vernon, & Dell, Barbara. (1972, August). More women in news broadcasting, according to RTNDA survey. *RTNDA Communicator,* p. 4.

Women in broadcasting. (1987, March 4). *Variety,* p. 110.

12

Television

Sex Discrimination in the TV Newsroom—
Perception and Reality

CONRAD SMITH
ERIC S. FREDIN
CARROLL ANN FERGUSON NARDONE

In the United States during the 1950s and 1960s, most television reporters and other journalists were men. Two unrelated events helped increase the proportion of women in these positions during the 1970s. One was pressure from the Federal Communications Commission (FCC) that began in 1971, when the commission added women to the list of minorities on its equal opportunity employment guidelines. Television station owners who ignored these guidelines risked losing their operating licenses. The other event was rapid growth of newsroom staffs during the 1970s, after owners realized TV news could make the same kinds of profits as entertainment programs while continuing to meet the public service goals mandated by the FCC. Thousands of new jobs were created as the number of journalists at the typical TV station grew from 10.5 in 1972 to 19.2 a decade later (Stone, 1987).

In the new regulatory climate, many of these job openings were filled by women. Between 1971 and 1982, the proportion of women in local television news tripled, growing to 33% (Weaver & Wilhoit, 1986, p. 21).[1] In the 1980s, this trend ceased after broadcast deregulation reduced affirmative action pressure from the FCC and after news became less profitable in face of competition from cable television, videocassettes, and new independent television stations. The proportions of women in local television news in 1987 (32%) was about the same as it had been in 1982, although more than 40% of newly hired local TV journalists in 1987 were women (Stone, 1988b).[2]

Local television news shops in the United States employed approximately 18,700 journalists in 1987. Women were much more prevalent in some specialties than in others—about 40% of local TV reporters and nearly half the local news producers were women, but only 14% of the news directors and an even smaller proportion of photographers (Stone, 1988a, 1988b). Female general managers of television stations were almost nonexistent.

The pattern was similar in national news organizations. A 1988 survey of 451 network television journalists by Victoria Fung, a fellow at the Gannett Center for Media Studies, found that about a third were women. A total of 39% of network news producers were female, but only 18% of correspondents and 15% of beureau chiefs, and only 6 of 29 network news vice presidents were women (Fung, 1988).

The Fung study also suggests that the networks hire male anchors on the basis of journalistic experience, but that female anchors are selected by male executives on the basis of cosmetic appeal. Male anchors in Fung's sample averaged 20 years older than female anchors, and they had about twice as much news experience. Male correspondents had an average of half again as much experience as female correspondents, and their average salary was 22% higher. Similar salary and experience gaps existed between men and women in other network news positions.

Despite the numerical gains of the 1970s, an internal study at ABC television news in the early 1980s revealed that some female employees were earning thousands of dollars a year less than men performing the same work (Sherr, 1986). A 1984 study by the National Organization for Women showed that female network correspondents were much less likely than male correspondents to receive air time during evening national newscasts (Flander, 1985).

Current census figures show that professional women often earn less than men doing the same work (U.S. Department of Commerce, 1984). Studies of the legal and medical professions, both of which traditionally have been dominated by men, indicate that women lawyers and physicians tend to perform less prestigious tasks and to be in less prestigious specialties (Epstein, 1982; Patterson & Engleberg, 1978). If television follows the same pattern, we would expect women television journalists to earn less than men and to receive less prestigious assignments.

The rest of this chapter examines the extent and nature of sex discrimination and discriminatory attitudes among local television news organizations in the United States. How have women fared in this formerly male bastion? Do female reporters earn as much as their male peers? Do they receive the same kinds of story assignments? Do their stories fill the prestigious newscast-leading position as often? Are they as likely to aspire to management positions? To what degree do sexist attitudes exist among today's reporters and their supervisors? How does morale differ between male and female reporters?

We address these questions through multivariate statistical analysis of data from national random samples of television reporters and news directors.[3] Because sex discrimination can occur in many different ways, we used three criteria for assessing it: earnings, morale, and reactions to a newsroom scenario that pits discrimination against other values.

We did not look for the specifics of one instance, or the story that seemed particularly unusual or compelling. Instead, we tried to get behind the unusual and the unique story to find the typical set of relationships between attributes, such as gender or experience, and other workplace conditions, such as earnings or the belief that a woman should not be given a dangerous assignment.

EARNINGS AND STORY ASSIGNMENTS

The median income for males in our national sample of local TV news reporters is $470 a week, compared to a median of $385 for women, including typical overtime pay. This amounts to about 82 cents for women against each male dollar. But the story does not end there, because the earnings gap ignores any effect of the relatively recent influx of women into the profession. In our sample, the typical (median) female reporter is 27 years old and has five years of experience. The median male is 30 and has seven years of experience.

Other factors can also influence pay. The "human capital" perspective emphasizes the importance of individual investment in such things as education and experience, and key questions focus on the "rate of return" for such investments. For example, is the increase in earnings for each year of experience the same for men and women? Parcel and Mueller (1983), in a national study of employment in general, found that differences in the rate of return for resources were the principle source of differences in pay between men and women. Compared to men, women generally had a lower rate of return for the resources they had.

The human capital perspective, however, tends to ignore social processes and social structures that can affect differences in earnings—processes and social structures over which the individual has little control. Parcel and Mueller, for example, found that the type and extent of discrimination depended partly on the makeup of the local labor market, the type of industry, and the type of occupation. We have attempted to adapt their approach by taking into account structural factors that seem to apply to local television reporters.

We conceptualized these structural factors as occurring at the market and the organizational levels. Our market-level concept is market size, here measured by the logarithm of the number of households in the market. One of our organizational-level concepts is the proportion of the reporting staff that is male—one measure of possible tokenism or of relative slowness in increasing the number of females. The other is the ratings for local newscasts, a key means of assessment in the industry.[4]

The bulk of differences in reporters' earnings in our sample were accounted for by structural variables such as market size and by human capital factors such as experience. Although our analysis indicates there is no systematic, pervasive discrimination of women in terms of earnings, there are some indications of discrimination. These explain about 2% of earnings variance, a relatively small but statistically significant amount. For example, women are rewarded less than men as they get older or as market size goes up, or both, suggesting greater age discrimination against women than against men. Women are rewarded more than men for changing news shops often or for moving to larger markets, or both. This suggests that women may be in demand in larger markets more because of their gender than because of their journalistic qualifications.

Another possible indication of tokenism is that, after controlling for market size, all reporters earn more in newsrooms that have a higher proportion of male reporters. Women in these shops receive greater earnings advantage than men as the proportion of male reporters increases, suggesting that some television newsrooms employ only a token number of women, but pay them the same wages as male reporters.

Women also receive more financial reward than men for winning news awards. Since news awards are judged predominantly by men, this could mean that women have to be better reporters than men to earn news awards, and that the better-paid women who have won awards are being paid for their superior journalistic skills.[5]

Perhaps it is more significant that the earnings of all reporters, in real dollars, have been going down as more and more women pursue successful careers in journalism. The human capital model indicates that on a macroeconomic scale, discrimination shrinks the pool of available labor. If only men are hired, news organizations may have to pay higher wages to obtain this scarcer human resource. Hiring women can therefore help drive down wages. Although men and women in our sample receive similar earnings and essentially equivalent story assignments, both groups may receive lower earnings because of women entering the field.

In public relations, for example, salaries and status have decreased as increasing numbers of women entered the occupation (see Chapter 14, this volume, and Cline et al., 1986). In broadcast and print journalism, the inflation-adjusted median salary declined about $7,000 between 1970 and 1981 as the proportion of women increased by 60%. The decline in reporters' buying power was greatest in television, where the proportion of women tripled (Weaver & Wilhoit, 1986, pp. 17-22, 82-87).

We also studied story assignments, using the same human capital model. Differences in assignments for 10 types of stories[6] were not statistically significant, except for education. Women covered more education stories than men, but the difference was rather small. We also found that there was no statistically significant difference in the number of newscast-leading stories reported by women and men during the previous 10 working days, although women had reported slightly more.

Our analysis does not mean that instances of favoritism do not exist. The typical picture, however, is that they do not. This, too, may be related to the basic notion that discrimination is a cost to the employer, who must hire more employees if some are restricted only to certain tasks.

ATTITUDES ABOUT SEXISM

Sexism can be expressed in other ways, as some women were quick to point out in their critiques of our initial study of earnings and story assignments. For several reasons, we thought the nature and extent of discriminatory attitudes might be revealed by having respondents react in some detail to a hypothetical incident in which a news director does not give a woman a major assignment she requested.

The idea of posing a hypothetical scenario was taken from Schuman's study of racial attitudes in Detroit in the late 1960s. Schuman (1972) notes that the issue of discrimination often does not emerge by itself; rather, it emerges when values clash in a particular situation. Schuman argues that the proportion of respondents giving a prodiscrimination answer depends largely on the values that clash with it. Schuman used this scenario in his study:

> Suppose a good Negro engineer applied for a job as an engineering executive. The Personnel Director explained to him: "Personally I'd never given your race a thought, but the two men you would have to work with most closely—the plant manager and the chief engineer—both have strong feelings about Negroes. I *can* offer you a job as a regular engineer, but *not* at the executive level, because any serious friction at the top could ruin the organization." (p. 348)

A total of 85% of Schuman's respondents said employers should, in general, hire employees without regard to their race. But 50% said the personnel manager was right to ask the other men how they felt about working with a Black and in deciding whether or not to hire him on the basis of their wishes. Further, 39% said it was right to refuse to hire the Black as an engineering executive in order to avoid friction.

Asking a person whether or not he or she favors sex discrimination makes assumptions that can be insulting, and some answers are clearly more acceptable than others. We thought that placing the questions in the context of a decision that can be seen as involving a conflict of values might produce more honest answers. Finally, we thought reporters, and news directors, would tend to think in terms of stories; that is, in terms of specific incidents rather than abstract concepts, hence the scenario might more accurately reflect the kinds of thought processes generally used on the job. With these issues in mind, we constructed the following scenario, which was timely in 1986:

> A news director receives authorization for two out-of-town trips for local interest stories. He decides to send one reporter to Honduras with a local National Guard unit going there on maneuvers. The reporter will also attempt to accompany a contra rebel unit on a border raid into Nicaragua.

> One reporter who wants the assignment is a woman. The news director says no, although he considers her one of his best reporters. He says he is concerned about her safety in a contra combat zone. He also feels that as a woman she will have less access to male sources in the National Guard and in Central America. Instead, he offers to send her with the mayor to the National League of Cities convention in Phoenix, which the mayor will chair.

We presented the scenario to reporters and news directors, and asked how strongly they agreed or disagreed, using a 9-point scale, with the following statements: (1) The news director is justified in not sending the woman because of the danger involved. (2) The news director is justified in not sending the woman because being a woman may compromise her news-gathering ability in Central America. (3) Given that the news director will not send the woman to Honduras, he acted appropriately in offering her the National League of Cites story as an alternative. (4) In general, story assignments should be given without regard to the sex of the reporter.

We also asked reporters how they thought "most reporters" and "news directors" would respond to each statement, and asked news directors how they thought "most reporters" and "other news directors" would respond. This approach allowed us to compare self-reports with perceptions of others in a number of ways.

The first three statements were designed to assess individual respondents' news-gathering values that might conflict with support in principle for equal treatment of men and women, described in the fourth statement. We assumed most respondents would support egalitarianism in principle, but that they would be more equivocal when this abstract principle conflicted with the other values. Based on this assumption, we have four measures of egalitarianism: one in the abstract, and the other three based on the degree to which respondents supported basing an actual story assignment on a reporter's gender.

Although the scenario was meant to be hypothetical, a female reporter from Texas wrote, "I went to Honduras with our local National Guard unit. It was my second trip to Central America, probably my tenth to Latin America. I was the *only* female reporting for television among statewide crews, although there were some females from the print media."

In response to the "danger" issue, a 25-year-old woman from North Carolina wrote, "During four years of reporting I have had only one supervisor believe a woman should not be sent on a dangerous assignment. In fact, even in eastern North Carolina, an area where professional women are not generally taken seriously, I was usually sent on dangerous assignments before male reporters." Several female respondents said men were more likely than women to agree that danger was a justification for not sending a woman on the story.

On the idea that the female reporter's news-gathering ability might be compromised, a 31-year-old woman from Louisiana said, "That is the oldest excuse in the world for not giving a woman certain stories."

A 26-year-old male reporter from Florida, on the other hand, wrote: "This entire question is purely ivory tower stuff. News directors don't make decisions this way. If they do send a man instead of a woman—they sure won't try to compensate the woman with an obvious 'consolation trip.' If you want working journalists to complete long surveys—at least give us 'real world' situations to ponder. This series of questions was written by a feminist masquerading as an objective researcher."

Overall, reporters and news directors were strongly egalitarian in describing their own reactions to the scenario: 54% of reporters and 49% of news directors registered the strongest possible *disagreement* on our 9-point scale with the idea that the woman should be kept home because of the danger; 46% of reporters and 41% of news directors selected the strongest *disagreement* score with the idea the woman should not be sent because her news-gathering ability might be compromised; 21% of reporters and 30% of news directors indicated the greatest possible *disagreement* with the idea the woman should be given a consolation assignment. In the same spirit, two-thirds of reporters and news directors marked the greatest possible *agreement* with the idea that, in general, news directors should assign stories without regard to gender.

However, both reporters and news directors rated their peers as less egalitarian than themselves. The differences are statistically significant, except for reporters on the issue of assigning stories without regard to gender.

The persistent gap between self-assessments and assessments of peers can have at least two interpretations. One is that both assessments are accurate, and thus that there is a systematic misperception of one's peers. This kind of misperception is referred to as "pluralistic ignorance," and has been found in the attitudes of Caucasians toward Blacks.[7] Another interpretation is that many respondents exaggerate their egalitarianism, and that something closer to the truth is projected in their assessments of peer attitudes.

A definitive interpretation cannot be made in a single study. However, we suspect the pattern is largely due to projection. This conclusion is based on our two independent measures of the attitudes of reporters and news directors. Each respondent assessed her or his own group, and each respondent assessed the other group as well. These two assessments are generally quite close. That is, when news directors and reporters assess reporters in general, the results are often equivalent. The same is true when news directors and reporters assess news directors in general. This is in contrast to the consistent gaps between the self-assessments and assessments of one's own group.

For each issue or statement in Table 12.1 the three assessment measures are listed in the sequence that gives the range within which true value for

Table 12.1. Self-Assessments and How Each Group Evaluates Peers and the Other Group

1 = Strongly Disagree 9 = Strongly Agree		Assessment of Reporters (Mean, N = 352)		Assessment of News Directors (Mean, N = 131)	
(1) Danger justifies not sending the woman reporter to Central America.					
self-assessment	—	2.57	ns	2.68	—
	|	***		***	|
assessment by respondent's own group	***	3.41	***	4.83	***
	|	ns		*	|
assessment by the other group	—	3.52	***	5.34	—
(2) Compromised news-gathering ability justifies not sending the woman reporter to Central America.					
self-assessment	—	3.09	ns	3.10	—
	|	*		***	|
assessment by respondent's own group	**	3.45	***	4.29	***
	|	ns		ns	|
assessment by the other group	—	3.56	***	4.63	—
(3) If not sent to Central America, the woman reporter should be given a consolation story.					
self-assessment	—	5.21	***	3.89	—
	|	***		***	|
assessment by respondent's own group	ns	5.27	ns	5.34	***
	|	***		ns	|
assessment by the other group	—	4.10	***	5.70	—
(4) In general, stories should be assigned without regard to a reporter's gender.					
self-assessment	—	7.89	ns	8.20	—
	|	ns		***	|
assessment by respondent's own group	***	7.32	***	6.61	***
	|	ns		***	|
assessment by the other group	—	7.62	***	5.37	—

NOTE: A 1 in the original scale represents "strongly disagree" and a 9 represents "strongly agree," therefore the larger means in this table represent greater agreement than the smaller ones. A 5 is neutral. Probabilities of statistically significant differences between pairs of means should be interpreted only as a rough indication, as each pair was tested separately.

$p \leq .05$; $**p \leq .01$; $***p \leq .001$; ns = not significant.

the group most likely lies. Generally, the most egalitarian result is from the self-assessment, and the least egalitarian is from the assessment made by members of the other group. For this reason, we suspect the true attitudes of each group are closer to the more sexist values attributed to others than to self-descriptions by individual respondents. Because of the small number of overtly sexist responses, results of all measures generally range from strongly egalitarian to neutral.

Alignment of the three measures for each group and each question facilitates comparison of reporters and news directors. News directors are significantly less egalitarian than reporters on seven of the eight measures that are not self-assessments. Reporters' perception of news directors is significantly less egalitarian than news directors' perception of reporters. News directors' perception of news directors in general is also significantly less egalitarian than reporters' perception of reporters, with the exception of the consolation issue. In terms of mutual perceptions there is a persistent difference in egalitarian values, but both news directors and reporters basically support egalitarian values.

Data from this scenario can also be used to study differences in attitudes between male and female reporters. Data presented in Table 12.2 indicate that, generally speaking, men are significantly less egalitarian than women. These differences hold when controlling for structural factors of market size and the ratio of men to women in the news organization, and when controlling for individual traits of experience as well as interactions among these variables.[8]

Most reporters of both genders agreed that, in general, assignments should be made without regard to the gender of the reporter, although the degree to which female respondents agreed was significantly greater (see Table 12.2). Men were significantly more likely than women to agree with each of the three specific reasons for not sending a female reporter on the Central America assignment.

Men and women agreed about equally that most other reporters would, in general, reject the idea of considering gender when stories are assigned. But women were significantly less likely than men to agree that most other reporters would accept the three specific reasons for not sending the female reporter to Central America. This lends further credence to idea that opinions projected to peers may actually reveal the respondent's own true attitudes.

Female reporters were less likely than male reporters to agree that news directors would, in general, consider the gender of a reporter before making story assignments. However, both women and men evaluated news

Table 12.2. Evaluation of the Decision Not to Send a Female Reporter

1 = Strongly Disagree *9 = Strongly Agree*	*Men*		*Women*	
	N	*Mean*	*N*	*Mean*
The news director is justified in not sending the woman because of the danger involved.	253	2.86	193	2.14***
The news director is justified in not sending the woman because being a woman may compromise her news-gathering ability in Central America.	253	3.39	193	2.65**
Given that the news director will not send the woman to Honduras, he acted appropriately in offering her the National League of Cities story.	250	5.54	189	4.76**
In general, story assignments should be given without regard to the gender of the reporter.	253	7.67	193	8.19**
Most reporters would agree that the woman should not be sent because of the danger involved.	251	3.70	192	2.99***
Most reporters would agree the woman should not be sent because her news-gathering ability might be compromised.	248	3.72	192	3.08**
Most reporters would agree the news director acted appropriately in offering the alternative story.	246	5.62	189	4.79***
Most reporters would agree that, in general, story assignments should be made without regard to sex.	252	7.21	191	7.50
Most news directors would not send the woman on the Central American story because of the danger.	250	5.28	192	5.43
Most news directors would not send the woman because her news-gathering ability might be compromised.	249	4.47	192	4.81
In these circumstances, most news directors would offer the reporter an appropriate alternative story.	247	5.82	190	5.53
In general, most news directors assign stories without regard to the sex of the reporter.	251	5.53	192	5.16

*$p < .05$; **$p < .01$; ***$p < .001$ (two-tail t-test).

directors as significantly more likely than themselves to agree with the specific reasons for not sending a woman.

MORALE

Pay is one general means of judging sexism, and it has a precision and objective quality that makes it attractive. However, the data on the Central America scenario indicate that attitudes favoring at least some discrimination toward women can be found among reporters, particularly male reporters, and among news directors. There are ways besides pay and story assignment for discriminatory attitudes to be expressed—as many anecdotes indicate.

One way of getting at the less tangible but still very real aspects of the workplace is to study employee morale. We treated morale as a summary judgment, that is, as an overall evaluation made up of many components, each weighed and balanced against the others.[9] The statement used was: "Reporter morale is good in this shop." Respondents marked their degree of agreement on a 9-point scale.

Morale is an interesting question for several reasons. It is an assessment of the entire group of reporters. We presume that a good deal of the respondent's own level of morale is being reported, just as it appears that a good deal of the respondent's attitude toward sex discrimination is reported in assessments of "most reporters." When the morale question is considered alone, no significant difference between male and female reporters was found. For both sexes, morale was low. On the 9-point scale, in which 1 means "strongly disagree," 15% of all respondents marked 1 in response to the morale statement, and 52% disagreed to some extent.

Given these kinds of figures plus anecdotes underscoring the precariousness of holding a television reporting job, it would seem quite possible that morale would decrease as experience increases. However, the relationship between morale and experience might be different for men and women. If news directors act on attitudes that are more sexist than those of reporters, particularly the women, then morale may decrease more rapidly for women than for men as experience increases. Of course, it may be that men reap some kind of benefit from sexist behavior, hence their morale might increase with experience.

Other processes may act against this. For a variety of reasons, morale would increase with market size. Working in a larger market is more prestigious. Larger markets may give reporters more benefits of one type or another, such as more interesting stories, better pay, and greater challenges. Morale might be better in larger markets, particularly if pay is good and news ratings are high.[10]

News shops with a greater proportion of male reporters may have higher morale, all other things being equal, perhaps because news directors generally tend to be seen as discriminating somewhat against females.

A number of important personal traits could affect morale. Receiving awards is one. The most straightforward interpretation would be that awards increase morale. On the other hand, morale may decrease because winning an award may change nothing in the daily routine, hence the award might function to make salient the disadvantages of the job.

Morale presumably would be affected by two general characteristics of the job: the amount of autonomy the reporter thinks he or she has, and the extent to which the reporter thinks pay raises and promotions in her or his particular news shop are fair.

Morale could also be influenced by attitudes of reporters toward day-to-day news decisions, such as when to use "live" coverage,[11] and toward the effectiveness of television as a medium for conveying journalistic facts, such as information about political candidates and election issues.[12] Both kinds of attitudes could surface during day-to-day work decisions about what to cover and how to cover it, providing endless ways in which general attitudes about "live" coverage and facts in the news can be expressed.

Differences in attitudes uncovered in reactions to the Central America scenario may also affect morale. We decided to use variables based on two of the statements: that the woman should not be sent because of the difficulty of dealing with sources, and that, in general, assignments should be made without regard to gender. The respondent's own attitude was used as well as the respondent's assessment of how news directors would respond to the questions. Also, the difference between the self-assessment and the assessment of the news directors was used as a variable.

In the case of these attitudes, as in other traits, the effect on morale for men may be different from that for women. Differences in attitudes have been found with regard to sex discrimination, hence men and women reporters are coping with environments that are somewhat different even if they are in the same newsroom.

The analysis strategy for morale paralleled the procedure used for pay. Because the hypotheses were quite general, backward stepwise multiple regression was used to identify statistically significant variables.[13] In all, 48 variables were entered and tested. Of these, 16 were found to be significant. About 32% of the variation in level of morale was explained by the variables we used. Following the backward stepwise regression, the variables were entered into a hierarchical regression (see Table 12.3). In general, structural variables were entered first, followed by individual traits.

Table 12.3   Regression Analysis of Morale for Local Television
                 Reporters

Variable	*Adjusted R^2 = .317* B	Standard Error	R^2 Change	F Ratio
Market- and shop-level variables			.051	
market size[a]/news ratings[b] interaction	.030	.0077		14.716 ***
proportion of reporters that is male	1.540	.7067		4.749 *
Individual reporter characteristics			.029	
weekly earnings[c]	−1.489	.8946		2.770 ns
years of TV reporting experience	−.163	.0617		6.976 **
news awards (0 = no, 1 = yes)	−2.233	.7180		9.669 **
Market size/reporter interactions			.019	
market size/weekly earnings	.342	.1367		6.257 *
market size/news awards	.712	.2823		6.362 *
Reporter attitudes			.213	
perceived fairness of news shop[d]	.238	.0406		34.272 ***
autonomy[e]	.304	.0482		39.695 ***
attitude toward "live" coverage[f]	−.104	.0604		2.987 ns
attitude toward news facts on TV[g]	−.148	.0575		6.588 **
value comparison with management[h]	−.108	.0487		4.910 *
Market/egalitarian attitude[i] interaction	−.038	.0183	.005	4.285 *
Gender	−1.537	.4957	.001	9.610 **
Gender-related interactions			.023	
gender/reporting experience	.242	.0711		11.578 ***
gender/egalitarian management[j]	.109	.0566		3.708 *
Constant	4.132	1.7602		5.510 *

a. Log, thousands of television households.
b. Rating for the weekday 10 p.m. or 11 p.m. newscast.
c. Logged.
d. "Promotions and pay raises in this shop are based on ability. In other words, if you
   do a good job, your chances of advancement here are good."
e. "I can usually do my job the way I want to do it."
f. See text note 11.
g. See text note 12.
h. A composite scale formed by subtracting the reporters' self-evaluations of the scale
   "The news director is justified in not sending the woman because being a woman
   may compromise her news-gathering ability in Central America" from the reporters' assessments of news directors, "Most news directors would not send the woman because her news-gathering ability might be compromised." Strongly disagree =
   1, strongly agree = 9; thus the bigger the composite variable, the more egalitarian
   the reporter compared to the news director.
i. "The news director is justified in not sending the woman because being a woman
   may compromise her news-gathering ability in Central America."
j. "Most news directors would not send the woman because her news-gathering ability might be compromised."

*p ≤ .05; **p ≤ .01; ***p ≤ .001; ns = not significant (one-tail test).

Sex-related variables were entered last in order to make their testing more severe.

We found that morale increases as the ratio of male reporters increases within shops. The more that reporters are opposed to "live" shots, and the more that reporters think television does a poor job of conveying journalistic facts, the lower the morale. The more the autonomy and the greater the perceived level of fairness in promotions and pay raises, the higher the morale.

The effect of awards is slightly more complicated. Receiving awards results in lower morale, but this effect is lessened as market size goes up. The higher the pay, the lower the morale, but this effect, too, is reduced as market size increases. Because these findings are in some ways contrary to conventional wisdom, they merit additional discussion.

The morale-depressing influence of news awards, all other things being constant, could be interpreted to mean that reporters who win awards have higher standards for themselves, which they less often achieve. Failure to meet these higher standards could result in lower morale. The fact that news awards depress morale more in small than in large markets could mean that awards are less likely in small markets to be recognized by peers and managers.

The effect of earnings in reducing morale could have a similar explanation. Since other variables are held constant, the measured increase in earnings is not accompanied by any change in other aspects of the job. A pay raise in these circumstances may bring heightened expectations that are not met. Marlene Sanders, for example, describes her own low morale while she was earning a very good salary as the first female network vice president at ABC television news (Sanders & Rock, 1988).

Experience also works in a complicated fashion. The effect of experience depends on the gender of the respondent. When considering experience with all other factors in the analysis held constant, the following occurs: On average, morale is significantly lower for males than for females, but for females, morale decreases slightly as experience increases. For males, morale increases as experience increases.

News ratings themselves have no significant effect on morale, but as ratings and/or market size increases, morale increases. In general, market size appears to have an ameliorating effect in that it reduces the negative effect of news awards and pay.

This ameliorating effect extends to some assessments from the Central America scenario. We discovered this by looking at the difference between how reporters responded to the idea that a female reporter should not be sent because she would have poorer access to sources, and how reporters predicted news directors would respond. The greater the difference, the more sexist the news director was relative to the respondent. We found that as the gap increased and/or as the market size increased, morale decreased.

The last variable is more puzzling. For males, the more news directors are seen as favoring egalitarianism, the higher the morale. The gap does not affect morale for females.

OTHER NEEDED RESEARCH

In late 1986, we presented our research about earnings and story assignments to the Columbus chapter of the Society of Professional Journalists, Sigma Delta Chi. After our remarks, three local television anchorwomen responded, suggesting concerns we had not addressed. Two of the three anchors talked about the difficulty of having both a family and a television news career:

> Another issue for women in television is that it is extremely difficult to handle a family. In the news business, men in the decision-making positions have wives who are not forced by economics to work outside the home. These same men are the ones who are making decisions about your workday. (Michelle Gailiun, WSYX-TV)

> Very few local markets provide maternity leave. When you get into the larger markets, some do provide for maternity leave although it's very limited. That makes it difficult for a woman to stay in the business if she is considering having a family. (Theresa Lukenas, WBNS-TV then, WJBK-TV now)

The concerns of women with families are another important issue, discussed at length by Sanders and Rock (1988). Local stations generally make few provisions for employees who must care for children, but the problem is even greater at the network level, where reporters are expected to travel anywhere in the world on short notice.

A central concern of the human capital context is that women receive lower rates of return because they are not consistently in the job market. They may leave to start raising a family, then return. Our data do not include information on marital and family status, but the young age and short experience of the typical (median) female reporter in the sample suggest that female reporters may be leaving the business to get married and raise families.

Issues concerning family, however, may be too narrowly defined if interpreted only in terms of sex discrimination. The notion that women might be discriminated against because they require special treatment to meet family demands assumes that a necessary part of this responsibility cannot or should not be shared by men. These issues are part of the more general problem of allocating the economic costs of raising a family, a problem that may be exacerbated by real wages falling in some fields, partly because more women are working in order to increase family income.

Angela Pace of WCMH-TV expressed other concerns:

> All the little things like my news director being more concerned with my cosmetic appearance than he is with my journalistic ability bother me. And those are the kinds of things that are not addressed in the study. I also think it would be very interesting to talk to people who are no longer in the business to find out why they left. But the big problem is that television news is still being run by white males. This means that the white male fantasy is going to be played out on television every day.

Cosmetic factors have always been a part of television news, and concern about them dates at least as far back as Edward R. Murrow's 1959 speech to the Chicago convention of the Radio -Television News Director's Association.[14] But many in the industry believe the stress on personal appearance in television news has increased, now that both local and network news are important profit centers. Sanders and Rock made this observation in their book about women in television news, and Roger Mudd (1988) talked in a recent essay about the "slowly crumbling wall" between television journalism and show business.

Another important test of sex discrimination may be occurring among women who are reaching the point where they are competing directly with men for positions as news directors. In television, where 86% of news directors and an even larger proportion of general managers are male, there are few female role models. The literature on sex-role socialization suggests that women are less likely than men to seek management positions. Other research suggests there are fewer rewards for female managers, and that women are less likely to advance to the top of a management hierarchy. Our data indicate that female reporters are just as likely as male reporters to say they plan to stay in television news, and just as likely as males to aspire to television management positions.

At the time of our survey, only 10% of news directors were women, certainly a low proportion. On the other hand, the average age of a news director was 38, and the average news director had 14 years of TV news experience (Stone, 1985). Among reporters in our sample who have more than 11 years' experience, 10% are women. If it is assumed that a median of 14 years' experience is needed to qualify as a news director (the figure would vary by market size), then the question is whether the female proportion of news directors will increase during the next decade or so as the proportion of women with enough experience increases.

Our study found little evidence for tangible sexism of the kind that would be grounds for legal action, but our findings suggest that sexist attitudes persist. Until women acquire equity with men at the highest levels of management, it seems likely that these attitudes will continue to affect the working lives of women in television news.

NOTES

1. The Weaver and Wilhoit figures do not include news photographers.

2. Stone's figures include news photographers.

3. The research is based on a 1986 mail survey. A total of 200 randomly selected network-affiliated television stations were asked for the names of all full-time reporters, and 87% complied. From the list of 1,453 reporters, 793 were selected randomly to receive our six-page questionnaire. A separate questionnaire was mailed to each of the 200 news directors. Up to three questionnaires were mailed to each respondent.

The 512 responding reporters (65%) represent 152 network-affiliated television stations in 45 states and the District of Columbia; 307 were male, 199 were female, and 6 declined to reveal their gender. We also received completed questionnaires from 131 of the 200 news directors (65.5%).

Of the 30 reporters among our respondents who were hired before 1971, only 3 were female. In 1971, the Federal Communications Commission started pressuring television stations to hire more women. The pressure was apparently effective, judging by the proportion of women among those hired more recently: 47% of reporters with five years' experience or less were female.

For our analyses, we used only reporters hired in 1975 or later. There were 53 males and 6 females who reported being hired earlier than 1975. Our reasoning was that if all data were used, separate earnings for men and women would not be comparable because the model for men in effect covers much more time.

4. Ratings figures are for the 10 p.m. or 11 p.m. weekday local news.

5. We are indebted to Theresa Lukenas, then of WBNS-TV and later of of WJBK-TV, for suggesting this perspective on news awards.

6. The 10 categories were (1) education, (2) health/medicine/science, (3) consumer news, (4) courts, (5) local/state government, (6) entertainment/culture/arts, (7) minority or women's issues, (8) labor/business/economy, (9) disaster/accident/spot news, and (10) human interest/people/features.

7. For a more detailed explanation, see O'Gorman with Garry (1976). For a different pattern of misperception, see Fields and Schuman (1976).

8. Details not shown. This analysis was done with hierarchical multiple regression, with sex entered after all other controls except interactions between sex and the other variables.

9. In many respects, salary was considered in a similar way. Various aspects of the job, and what the individual brings to it, were weighed and a figure arrived at.

10. Interactions between market size and all other variables were tested, since market size can have such diverse results. Also, reporters and anchors have often noted that stations in larger markets are quite different from those in smaller markets.

11. Factor analysis revealed three related attitude scales that we used as a composite variable. The three scales were as follows: (1) "A lot of non-news stories get on local TV news because they're so easy to do 'live'"; (2) "Some news operations use live capability primarily for promotional purposes"; and (3) "Some critics charge that the emphasis on 'live' shots has degraded newscast content. Do you agree?"

12. Another factor analysis revealed three additional related attitude scales, which we used as a composite variable. The three scales were as follows: (1) "Television has a tendency to overdramatize the news"; (2) "Television is better at conveying the emotional aspects of a story than at conveying facts"; and (3) "Television election coverage stresses visual hoopla at the expense of information about candidates and issues."

13. We investigated differences by using the same procedure we did for earnings, a stepwise backward multiple regression involving 54 variables. Stepwise regression was used because the generality of our hypotheses was such that no particular set of linear effects or interactions seemed to take precedence over any others. A more common regression technique is hierarchical regression. It is a conservative approach in that variables introduced at the end of an equation are tested to see what variance they explain after all variance they hold in common with other variables in the equation is allotted to those other variables. However, the hierarchical system effectively involves "peeking"—trying one equation, then another. For details, see Smith, Fredin, and Ferguson (1988).

14. Murrow described broadcast news as "an incompatible combination of show business, advertising and news." For details, see Sperber (1986).

REFERENCES

Cline, Carolyn Garrett, Toth, Elizabeth Lance, Turk, Judy VanSlyke, Walters, Lynne Masel, Johnson, Nancy, & Smith, Hank. (1986). *The velvet ghetto: The impact of the increasing percentage of women in public relations and business communication.* San Francisco: International Association of Business Communicators Foundation.

Epstein, Cynthia Fuchs. (1982). *Women in law.* New York: Harper & Row.

Fields, James M., & Schuman, Howard. (1976). Public beliefs about the beliefs of the public. *Public Opinion Quarterly, 40,* 427-448.

Flander, Judy. (1985, March). Women in network news: Have they arrived or is their prime time past? *Washington Journalism Review,* pp. 39-43.

Fung, Victoria M. (1988, October). Sexism at the networks: Anchor jobs go to young women and experienced men. *Washington Journalism Review,* pp. 20-24.

Mudd, Roger. (1988, June). After the television machine got hooked up to the money machine. *Radio-Television News Directors Association Communicator,* pp. 6-8.

O'Gorman, Hubert J., with Garry, Stephen L. (1976). Pluralistic ignorance: A replication and extension. *Public Opinion Quarterly, 40,* 449-458.

Parcel, Toby L., & Mueller, Charles W. (1983). *Ascription and labor markets: Race and sex differences in earnings.* New York: Academic Press.

Patterson, Michelle, & Engelberg, Laurie. (1978). Women in male-dominated professions. In Ann H. Stromberg & Shirley Harkes (Eds.), *Women working: Theories and facts in perspective* (pp. 266-292). Palo Alto, CA: Mayfield.

Sanders, Marlene, & Rock, Marcia. (1988). *Waiting for prime time: The women of television news.* Urbana: University of Illinois Press.

Schuman, Howard. (1972). Attitudes vs. action vs. attitudes vs. attitudes. *Public Opinion Quarterly, 36,* 347-354.

Sherr, Lynn. (1986, October). You asked me back as a reporter. *Radio-Television News Directors Association Communicator,* pp. 33-36.

Smith, Conrad, Fredin, Eric S., & Ferguson, Carroll Ann. (1988). Sex discrimination in earnings and story assignments among TV reporters. *Journalism Quarterly, 65,* 3-11, 19.

Stone, Vernon A. (1985, July). Male and female news directors compared. *Radio-Television News Directors Association Communicator,* pp. 151-153.

Stone, Vernon A. (1987). Changing profiles of news directors of radio and TV stations, 1972-1986. *Journalism Quarterly, 64,* 745-749.

Stone, Vernon A. (1988a, July). *Pipelines and dead ends: Jobs held by minorities and women in broadcast news.* Paper presented at the annual meeting of the Association for Education in Journalism and Mass Communication, Portland, OR.

Stone, Vernon, A. (1988b, August). Minority men shoot ENG, women take advancement tracks. *Radio-Television News Directors Association Communicator,* pp. 10-14.

U.S. Department of Commerce, Bureau of the Census. (1984). *Census of population: Vol. 2. Subject reports: Earnings by occupation and income.* Washington, DC: Government Printing Office.

Weaver, David H., & Wilhoit, G. Cleveland. (1986). *The American journalist: A portrait of U.S. news people and their work.* Bloomington: Indiana University Press.

13

Advertising

Women's Place and Image

a. A New "Genderation" of Images to Women

LINDA LAZIER-SMITH

A boy in a mass communication research project is asked what he would like to be when he grows up if he were a girl. "Oh," he exclaimed, "if I were a girl, I'd have to grow up to be nothing."

Advertising—15- or 30-second broadcast sales blurbs interrupting *Oprah, Monday Night Football*, or *General Hospital*; 7-by-10-inch pretty magazine page messages—brief, small, terse, seemingly simple. No one *really* takes these concise capitalistic communications seriously, do they?

Not even if the messages are part of a $100-billion-a-year communication industry?

Not even if the average person, every day, is exposed to somewhere in the neighborhood of 1,800 messages?

Not even if these brief blips are "pervasive and persuasive, environmental in nature, persistently encountered and involuntarily experienced" (Pollay, 1986, p. 18)?

Not even if the ubiquitous messages pervade all the media, forming "a vast superstructure with an apparently autonomous existence" (Williamson, 1978, p. 11)?

Not even if ads make up "the most consistent body of material in the mass media" (Leiss, Kline, & Jhally, 1986, p. 3)?

Not even then?

ADVERTISING: INSTITUTION TURNED ENTITY

Critics and commentators from every discipline have grappled with advertising's potential for power. It has been called "the most potent influence in adapting and changing habits and modes of life, affecting what we eat, what we wear and the work and play of the whole nation" (Fox, 1984, p. 97). It has been compared with "such long-standing institutions as the school and the church in the magnitude of its social influence" because it "dominates the media, it has vast power in the shaping of popular standards, and it is really one of the very limited groups of institutions which exercise social control" (Potter, 1954, p. 167).

McLuhan (1951), who has said that advertising reflects our "collective daydreams," also has commented that "ours is the first age in which many thousands of the best-trained minds have made it a full-time business to get inside the collective public mind . . . to get inside in order to manipulate, exploit and control" (p. v).

Criticisms and concerns have been vented by psychologists, who view advertising as a source of learning or conditioning, with cognitive and affective results; by sociologists, who speak to the role-modeling aspects and advertising's impact on social behaviors; by anthropologists, who examine the rituals, symbols, and cultural meanings involved; by educators, who question the influence on development; and by communication specialists, critics, and commentators, who often address the propagandistic role of advertising and fret over its influence on media content (Pollay, 1986).

The critics concur on one point. Advertising is its own force, an institution turned entity. Society has not put it on a pedestal—indeed, many consumers still scoff, claiming they are unaffected by ads—but the evidence more and more suggests that society has elevated advertising to an invisible podium from which we learn and by which we are influenced.

THE CONNECTION TO WOMEN

The gender perspective on advertising is dual. A central gender concern is that advertising is a shorthand form of communication that must make contact with the consumer immediately, establishing a shared experience or identification. Perhaps the best-known way advertising does this is by using stereotypical imagery. Stereotypes, we also know, are standardized mental pictures that *Webster's* defines as representing an oversimplified opinion or uncritical judgment.

The crux of stereotype "theory" comes compliments of Walter Lippmann (1922) who claims that the abbreviated communiques offer an "economy of effort" because they "substitute order for great blooming, buzzing confusion of reality" (p. 63). As such, they become "the cores of our personal tradition, the defenses of our position in society," which give "an ordered, consistent picture of the world to which our habits, tastes, capacities, comforts and hopes have adjusted themselves" (p. 63).

Stereotypes, or "pictures in our heads," can save interpretive effort. Others argue that stereotypes short-circuit or block the capacity for objective and analytic judgment in favor of well-worn, catchall reactions. This could lead to shortchanging. It also leads to the first connection to gender concerns: Advertising to women has consistently been filled with stereotypes.

Considerable evidence exists to indicate that advertising has in the past stereotyped women in traditional portrayals.

> There is overwhelming evidence that advertisements present traditional, limited, and often demeaning stereotypes of women and men. It is recognized, of course, that stereotypes in advertising can serve a useful function by conveying an image quickly and clearly, and that there is nothing inherently wrong with using characterizations of roles that are easily identifiable. However, when limited and demeaning stereotypes are as pervasive as those involved in advertising's portrayal of the sexes, it becomes important to question whether those stereotypes might result in negative and undesirable social consequences. (Courtney & Whipple, 1983, p. 45)

In print advertising, the results of more than a dozen studies, almost all conducted in the 1970s, have shown the messages of advertising to be astonishingly similar: Woman's place is in the home; women are dependent upon men; women do not make independent and important decisions; women are shown in few occupational roles; women view themselves and are viewed by others as sex objects.

The issues and the findings from television content analyses were similar to (and as debilitating as) those found in the print studies. Taken together, the television studies do two things: (1) point out three prevalent female roles—maternal, housekeeping and aesthetic; and, (2) point out flagrant discrimination—women and girls were seen far less frequently than men, they were shown to have different characteristics from males (less authoritative, active, powerful, rational, and decisive, and more youthful and concerned with attractiveness), they were housewives or in restricted, low-status, subservient occupations (and fewer roles), and they were depicted as less intelligent than males.

The anomalous fact is that while images of women as documented in advertising research hardly changed from study to study throughout the 1970s, both demography and attitudes among women changed dramatically (Courtney & Whipple, 1985). This embodies the second connection to gender concerns.

THE "THIRD AMERICAN REVOLUTION"

When advertising agency D'Arcy Masius Benton & Bowles asked people to "name your ideal job," what topped the list for women was "to be head of my own company." That, a senior editor of *Working Woman* magazine said in that publication's 298-page tenth-anniversary issue titled "How Working Women Have Changed America," "goes to show just how far women's ambitions now stretch: no more mere room of one's own, if you please. . . but a bustling business will do nicely" (Hellwig, 1986, p. 150).

That also is indicative that women, long socialized to be the homebodies, are now not only in the work force, but they sometimes own pieces of it, entrepreneurially and via stock portfolios, corporate boardrooms, and management titles.

This "surging tide of women into the workforce over the past 15 years is what economists are calling the most profound change of our century" and what sociologists and feminists are tagging the "third successful revolution in American history" (after the war for independence and the Industrial Revolution), a revolution that has "reached beyond women's own lives and changed the very way America lives, works, and even thinks" (Hellwig, 1986, p. 129).

What started as a dramatic shift in the labor market (in 1970, about half of all women between the ages of 25 and 54 years had jobs; by 1986, 70% of women in that age group did) "soon sent tremors through the entire economy and then beyond" (Hellwig, 1986, p. 129). Even Harvard professors of political economy note the benchmark: "We haven't seen anything like it in this century," says Harvard's Robert Reich, Ph.D. "If I were to list the social changes as they have affected the economy and the culture, I would place first the changing role of women, including the influx of women into the workplace" (p. 130).

These work-force changes have dramatically altered the employment, financial, and familial aspects of American life. New doors have opened to women, with more opportunities, more social visibility, more voice, more decision-making power, and more all-around societal impact.

WOMEN IN ADVERTISING

As in other communication areas, advertising has experienced a "feminization," at both university and industry levels. The U.S. Bureau of Labor Statistics reports that the percentage of women in advertising grew from 42.2% in 1971 to 47.9% in 1981, or from 49,400 women in 1973 (when the first study reported in this chapter was conducted) to a nearly tripled 149,070 in 1986, the year of the updated study. That growth is likely to continue, considering that females made up 63% of university advertising enrollment figures in 1986, according to Peterson's ongoing national study.

Historically, women have always been involved in advertising, although the number of "significant" women whose careers or contributions are detailed in Fox's popular advertising history book *The Mirror Makers* (1984) can be counted on the fingers of both hands (and almost on one). Women traditionally have not reached the upper echelon of agency management, but have been concentrated in areas such as media, traffic, and creative (both art and copy), according to *Adweek* magazine surveys.

Starting and early-career agency salaries for females have equaled males' in recent years, also according to *Adweek*—in the upper teens ($17,000-$19,000) for both creative and account personnel. Discrepancies of from $5,000 to $10,000 between the sexes are still experienced at the middle and upper-management levels.

Now that there are more women in the work force in general and in advertising in particular, we can (and must) ask if advertising has kept pace with societal change. Does "contemporary" advertising reflect woman's "contemporary status"? That is the central question of this chapter, which is an examination of "modern" ad messages to women.

NEW RESEARCH REPLICATES PAST STUDIES

Three past studies have been considered benchmarks in advertising stereotype/role research: the Consciousness Scale for Sexism study, Goffman's (1979) "gender advertisements," and Kilbourne's (1987) film on female ad images. The research reported in this chapter centers on the replication, via content analysis, of the three in what is believed to be the first print stereotype study of the 1980s. First, the original studies will be discussed; then, the findings of the new research will be given.

In the central study, the Consciousness Scale for Sexism was developed by Butler-Paisley and Paisley-Butler (1974); it was further elaborated by Pingree, Hawkins, Butler, and Paisley (1976). The original scale was applied to advertisements portraying women in four national magazines—*Ms.*, *Playboy*, *Time*, and *Newsweek*—coding 10 ads in each monthly issue for one year. The scale attempts to "measure" sexism by analyzing ad visuals via five levels:

- *Level 1: Put her down.* Presentations of women at this level include the dumb blonde, the sex object, and the whimpering victim. The woman is portrayed as being less than a person, a two-dimensional image. Examples of such images are common in men's magazines such as *Playboy*, in advertisements where the woman's body is included as a decorative object, and in situation comedies where the woman relies on others to do her thinking for her.

- *Level 2: Keep her in her place.* Traditional strengths and capacities of women are acknowledged, but tradition also dictates "womanly" roles. Women are shown functioning well as wives, mothers, secretaries, clerks, teachers, nurses. Negative Level 2 images show women struggling with roles that are "beyond them" (business executives, doctors, editors, and so on) or in which they develop "unwomanly" traits.

- *Level 3: Give her two places.* Consciousness Level 3 represents the level of many "progressive" media images of women. In entertainment (e.g., television drama), the woman can be a lawyer or an architect as long as she has dinner on the table for her husband at 6:00. In reportage, for example, the woman executive is described as "grandmotherly," and the interview eventually turns to her favorite recipes. It is the career that is often viewed as the "something extra." Housework and mothering come first. The image is that women may sometimes work outside the home professionally, but they always work in the home. An example is the ad with the woman Ph.D. in biochemistry discussing what she gives her children for breakfast.

- *Level 4: Acknowledge that she is fully equal.* These are rare among media images. The important distinction between this level and Level 3 (which also allows women to be professionals) is that Level 4 images do not remind us that housework and mothering are nonnegotiably the woman's work as well.

- *Level 5: Nonstereotypic.* Individual women and men are viewed as superior to each other in some respects, inferior in other respects. The dogmatism of Level 4 (women shall be equal to men) is unnecessary, because individuals are not judged by their sex (Pingree et al., 1976, pp. 194-195).

The 1973-74 study found 75% of all ads to be at the two lowest, or most sexist, levels—48% at Level 2, considered by the researchers to be the status quo, and 27% at Level 1. The researchers found 19% of the ads were at "equality" Level 4, but only 2% were at nonstereotypical Level 5; 4% were at Level 3.

The second benchmark study was conducted by sociologist Erving Goffman and has been popularized in his book *Gender Advertisements* (1979). In that book, Goffman concludes that women are weakened by advertising portrayals via six categories:

(1) relative size (shown smaller or lower, relative to men)
(2) feminine touch (women constantly touching themselves)
(3) function ranking (occupational)
(4) family scenes
(5) ritualization of subordination (proclivity for lying down at inappropriate times; women using bashful knee bends, canting postures, puckish, expansive smiles)
(6) licensed withdrawal (women never quite a part of the scene, possibly via far-off gazes)

In essence, Goffman finds that ads are highly ritualized versions of the parent-child relationship, with women treated largely as children.

The third "study" is a film that uses examples reflecting the findings listed above and that includes examples from Jean Kilbourne's qualitative assessment of advertising. Her first film, released in 1976, was titled *Killing Us Softly*. Her second film, a much-awaited and -demanded update released in late 1987, is titled *Still Killing Us Softly*; the *still* summarizes her assessment of a lack of improvement in imagery toward and about women.

Kilbourne's is a provocative collection of examples selected purposefully to show the extent of, and problems with, advertising's sexual imagery and its implication that sexual access to the female is the reward for buying many products. Scientifically-drawn samples have illustrated virtually the same conclusions as does Kilbourne's film. The film achieves dramatic impact by running hundreds of ads before the viewer, leaving Kilbourne's conclusions inescapable.

AD SEXISM "IMPROVES" BY TWO PERCENTAGE POINTS

The 1986 study replicated the method, categories, and procedures of the Consciousness Scale for Sexism and of Goffman's sexist categories (Lazier-Smith, 1988). All ads in the four magazines from July 1986 to June 1987 were coded to the sexism scale (intercoder agreement was 93.5%); all Goffman traits within these same ads were also coded. The findings from both analyses were then applied to Kilbourne's film.

The conclusions from the 1986 replication of the Consciousness Scale for Sexism study are simple:

The images of women in 1986 ads *did not* significantly change from the images found in 1973 ads. Portrayals did not "improve" overall to reflect women's increased social status.

Given the statistical analyses of the data, it can be concluded that not only has sexism *not* improved, but the 1986 ads, in the aggregate, are slightly more sexist than those in the 1973 sample. Kruskal-Wallis one-way ANOVA [hereafter K-W] mean rank: 1973 = 495.4; 1986 = 483.6. Higher score = less sexism. K-W chi-square = .47, p = .490.)

Central tendency showed median level (score) for both samples to be Level 2, the traditional sphere; mode level actually worsened, from Level 2 in 1973 to Level 1 in 1986; mean level remained virtually constant, from 2.21 in 1973 to 2.28 in 1986. A median statistical test showed no significance (chi-square = 1.28, p = .257).

The critical finding is that although distribution of ads by level *has* shifted (Kolmogorov-Smirnov [hereafter K-S] Z = 1.485, p = .024), the shift has not improved the overall level of sexism in ads—or that "improvements" such as a higher percentage of portrayals at the "best" level, nonstereotypic Level 5 (from 2% in 1973 to 11% in 1986), are offset by the 10% increase in portrayals at Level 1, the sex object/decoration/male adjunct category (see Table 13.1).

However, it must be noted that the distribution of ads, by level, creates different dispersion shapes, indicating a leveling of sexist tendencies. Fewer 1986 ads were coded to Level 2 (status quo—women in the home, in womanly occupations, or coupled with a male), the level that ties women to the traditional nurturing/public versus private sphere/role, the role the social statistics show is no longer primary. Fewer also fell at Levels 3 and 4, levels that put woman in "man's" world.

Table 13.1   Comparison of Female Portrayals in 1973 and 1986

Advertising, Using the Consciousness Scale for Sexism
(in percentages)

Level	1973 (N = 447)	1986 (N = 530)
(1) Put her down.	27	37
(2) Keep her in her place.	48	35
(3) Give her two places.	4	3
(4) Acknowledge that she is fully equal.	19	15
(5) Nonstereootypic.	2	11

In summary, the 1986 ads showed significant differences from 1973 in distribution by level (chi-square = 48.73, 4df, p = .000), specifically at Levels 1, 2, and 5. It should be noted that even though Levels 1 and 2 fluctuated over the two studies, cumulative percentages of ads in the two lowest or most sexist levels improved only marginally—from 75% in 1973 to 72% in 1986.

Levels were coded by "type" (e.g., Level 1 could be decoration, sex object, or total incompetent). The largest type for all female ads was "decoration" (Level 1) with 28% (N = 148) of all female ads. Second was the "couple" portrayal (Level 2) at 21% (N = 113).

Goffman traits did show some improvement, with three categories—relative size, function ranking, and family scenes—appearing so infrequently that they could be considered to no longer apply. Unfortunately, the largest coded category, ritual of subordination, could also be considered the most limiting or trivializing.

The findings of these two analyses support the contentions of Kilbourne's film of ongoing sexist tendencies. They also support the findings of Alice Gagnard, who looked at body images in magazines over several decades, and found women becoming increasingly slimmer. (See her work in part b of this chapter.)

THE ADVERTISING/MARKETING PERSPECTIVE

These findings are troublesome for several reasons. A central reason is that advertising is supposedly market-driven. The advertising industry has long been dependent on demographics and market/consumer research as the basis for construction of advertising messages. This "math" or "market" or "monitoring" orientation is what allows advertisers to develop messages recognizable to the consumer and her life-style, to create a "shared experience" with the consumer, one that provides a relatively accurate semblance of society, especially of the "new woman" and her multiple roles and responsibilities.

It would seem that this demographic or math approach would eliminate the "myth" found in former studies, since ads based on the market perspective would seemingly reflect both the social changes of the past decade (the demographics of women entering the work force) and the social ramifications of those changes (an increase in social status, which should lead to a decrease in sexist/limiting imagery).

THE CONCLUSIONS

In the final assessment, it seems to be a case of demigoddesses (mythical beings that seem to approach "perfection" or the divine) versus demographics. With nearly three-fourths of the female ads in the 1986 study coded to the two most sexist, stereotypical levels of the scale, we can paint the following portrait of the American woman:

> She is athletic, but never sweats. She is beautiful, but wears no makeup. She is working, but never tired. Aging, but not wrinkled. Breathtaking, but brainless. Intelligent, but humorless. She is everything. She is nothing. She is advertising to women. (Sharkey, 1987, p. WR4)

The increase in both sexist Level 1 images and nonsexist Level 5 images causes conclusional confusion—have things worsened or improved? Or do we simply seem to have a new "genderation" or sexism, perhaps a "Ms. Bimbo"?

Demographics—in all its mathematical, statistical, percentaged glory—evidently is no match for old-fashioned sexism. The numbers don't count. The demographics- and data-driven marketing-based perspective doesn't hold.

Coming to conclusions means coming to grips with an almost shocking, blatant sexism, an unexpectedly unnerving smack from an unexpected "reality."

Coming to Terms with Social Reality

We expected to see the *new* "social reality" reflected in the "modern" ads—a reality markedly different from the reality reflected in the academic analyses of the 1970s. However, our first conclusion must be that "social reality" was not the correct term. To expect it was wrong. And, with hindsight, we can see that what we actually wanted "reflected" was a cultural faithfulness—an accuracy in details about our beliefs, social forms, and traits. The critical question, then, should be this: Are today's ads culturally faithful in the depiction and portrayal of women?

Unpowering Instead of Empowering

Culture is central to communication, according to Dervin and Clark (1988). Communication, they say, is thought of in three fundamental ways—as content, structure, and procedure. "The content of communication comprises the 'what' of a culture. The structure comprises the institutional entities designated as 'keepers' of the what. The procedures of communication are the norms/rules about 'how to do' the keeping (the constituting and reconstituting)."

Gerbner explains the apparent lag between social or cultural fact and imagery; he says that culture's main function is to cultivate resistance to change, to get its members to accept the norms and values (cited in Tuchman, Daniels, & Benet, 1978). Should a culture encounter a social movement (the threat or promise to restructure a particular set of social relations—as is the case with women's entry into the work force), Gerbner suggests it will "manage" it in one of two ways: by resistance or by images.

If, as Gerbner suggests, we recognize media images of women as an area that defines/portrays either status or domination, then we must realize that the issue is not one of imagery but one of power. This leads to my first major conclusion: Advertising *does* reflect a cultural faithfulness, but not to demographics or to being "true to the facts of customary beliefs, social forms and material traits." Instead, the ads reflect the traditional balance of power. They reflect critical components of our culture—its stereotypes, its bigotries, its biases—its dominant values, a tendency toward the status quo, and ongoingness of the traditional. But, even more, they reflect its chauvinism and its sexism.

The ads reflect, but they reflect the mythical more than the mathematical: flawless, poreless, decorative females; young, thin, perfect; couple or mated; America's ideal woman.

The ads reflect the confusion in our culture of what women are. In advertising, as we grope with what we'll let today's woman *do* or *be*, we at least agree on how she will *look*.

Although the demographics (the math) has changed dramatically; the attitude (the mentality) has not. This, then, is my second conclusion. We seem to be suffering from a cultural lag—our culture's beliefs and attitudes and opinions on women are lagging behind the reality about women. The ads reflect that lag.

WHAT CAN BE DONE?

We must realize and then remember (and then re-vision) something critical about these messages: Status quo ad messages come from another basic source—work routines and traditions in advertising agencies.

Media organization and production routines add deadlines and performance pressure to the media mix. Message makers need to make messages quickly—messages that need not be reworked or rewritten, for time and especially for profit reasons (and profit to the multiple parties involved); messages that will gain in-agency and client approval with the least amount of hassle; messages that will be lauded and will lead to bigger and better assignments; messages that might win awards, new accounts, or some other type of attention; messages that are "safe."

These various production "needs"—along with the quirky matter that message makers simultaneously "work" for three parties: themselves (to outshine other writers and secure the best assignments, pay raises, or other perks), the agency, and the client—point toward a fast, nonthinking, go-with-the-known, "the way we've always seen/done/believed it" approach.

Content is also influenced by journalists' socialization. Most message makers' socialization includes a history of virtually uninterrupted sexist ads, as documented by the previous studies of both print and broadcast media. A steady diet of flawless, poreless limited-function females most likely encourages similar traditional expectations.

Past ads have been the socializers of the message maker, who makes similar ads and sends them out to society, which then sends the messages to women, clients, and future message makers. Thus distorted ads beget more distorted ads, resulting from "the way we've always seen/done/believed it" mentality.

THE FINAL CONCLUSION

So what does this all mean?

If we believe that magazines have a great impact on American society (the Magazine Publishers Association estimates that 94% of Americans read 11.6 magazines each a month) and if we believe that magazine ads are modern-day Lewis Carrollesque looking glasses (where spending is saving and being an individual means being just like everyone else and all women are beautiful and childish), and if we believe that the institution of advertising has great power, as discussed earlier, then we must now sit back and sigh. Cultural lag and dominant ideology are no small issues to "fix."

It seems that ongoing sexist ads will continue the ideology, which will continue the lag, which will continue the sexism, which will continue the circle—genderation after genderation. To break the cycle we must change either the messages or the message makers or both.

Perhaps it is with research realizations such as these that we can start. We can ask the message makers (an increasing number of whom are women) to rise to new levels of awareness—from Level 1 to Levels 4 and 5.

REFERENCES

Bullock, Alan, Stallybrass, Oliver, & Trombley, Stephen. (1988). *The Harper dictionary of modern thought*. New York: Harper & Row.

Butler-Paisley, Matilda, & Paisley-Butler, William J. (1974, August). *Sexism in the media: Frameworks for research*. Paper presented at the annual meeting of the Association for Education in Journalism, San Diego, CA.

Courtney, Alice, E., & Whipple, Thomas W. (1983). *Sex stereotyping in advertising*. Lexington, MA: Lexington.

Courtney, Alice, E., & Whipple, Thomas W. (1985). Female role portrayals in advertising and communication effectiveness: A review. *Journal of Advertising, 14,* 4-8, 17.

Dervin, Brenda, & Clark, Kathleen D. (1988). *Communication as cultural identity: The invention mandate*. Paper presented at the annual meeting of the International Association of Mass Communications Research, Barcelona, Spain.

Fox, Stephen. (1984). *The mirror makers*. New York: Morrow.

Goffman, Erving. (1979). *Gender advertisements*. New York: Colophon.

Hellwig, Basia. (1986, November). How working women have changed America. *Working Woman*, pp. 129-150.

Kilbourne, Jean. (Producer and Moderator). (1987). *Still killing us softly: Advertising images of women* [Film]. Cambridge, MA: Cambridge Documentary Films.

Lazier-Smith, Linda. (1988). *The effect of changes in women's social status on images of women in magazine advertising: The Pingree-Hawkins sexism scale reapplied, Goffman reconsidered, Kilbourne revisited*. Unpublished doctoral dissertation, Indiana University.

Leiss, William, Kline, Stephen, & Jhally, Sut. (1986). *Social communication in advertising: Persons, products and images of well-being*. Toronto: Methuen.

Lippmann, Walter. (1922). *Public opinion*. New York: Free Press.

McLuhan, Marshall. (1951). *The mechanical bride*. Boston: Beacon.

Merton, Robert K., & Barber, Elinor. (1963). Sociological ambivalence. In Edward A. Tiryakian (Ed.), *Sociological theory, values and sociocultural change* (pp. 91-121). London: Free Press.

Pingree, Suzanne, Hawkins, Robert P., Butler, Matilda, & Paisley, William. (1976). A scale of sexism. *Journal of Communication, 26*, 193-200.

Pollay, Richard W. (1986). The distorted mirror: Reflections on the unintended consequences of advertising. *Journal of Marketing, 50*, 18-36.

Potter, David M. (1954). *People of plenty: Economic abundance and the American character*. Chicago: University of Chicago Press.

Sharkey, Betsy. (1987, July 6). The invisible woman. *Adweek*, pp. WR 4-8.

Tuchman, Gaye, Daniels, Arlene Kaplan, Benet, James. (Eds.). (1978). *Hearth and home: Images of women in the mass media*. New York: Oxford University Press.

Williamson, Judith. (1978). *Decoding advertisements: Ideology and meaning in advertising*. London: Marion Boyars.

b. A Sociocultural Close-Up:
Body Image in Advertising

ALICE GAGNARD

Media critics often allege that stereotypes portrayed in advertising represent unrealistic goals of wealth, beauty, and success that most people cannot attain. One such stereotype is that of the excessively thin models used in ads, particularly in ads targeted to women. In the absence of an adequate explanation of the origins of the increasingly prevalent eating disorders of anorexia nervosa and bulimia, some experts point to elements of the "sociocultural milieu" as contributors to America's preoccupation with thinness and the desire to be thin. And while it is widely held that social factors such as parental pressure to succeed and socioeconomic status are correlates of eating disorders, mass media also are believed to play a major role in perpetuating cultural definitions of attractiveness and success.

How have the mass media portrayed body types in advertising? A study that analyzed 1,327 models featured in a random sample of women's magazine ads since the 1950s revealed the following:[1]

- The most commonly occurring body type, or "Thindex," for all decades studied was "average" (77%), followed by "thin" (15%), "overweight" (7%), and "obese" (1%).

- The proportion of thin models increased each decade since the 1950s, reaching a high of 46% in the 1980s.

- The incidence of overweight and obese models decreased with each decade, from a high of 12% in the 1950s to a low of 3% in the 1980s.

- More overweight and obese males than females were found for all decades studied, suggesting greater acceptance of male obesity.
- Thin models were featured as most attractive and successful of all body types.
- Obese models were portrayed as happiest of all body types, suggesting a "jolly and fat" stereotype.
- The combined ratings of attractiveness, success, and happiness yielded a "Yendex," or desirability index, that showed thin models to be the most desirable of all body types.

Though disagreement exists over the extent to which the media *shape* American values or simply *reflect* those values, results of this study are clear: The message makers in women's magazines have placed increasing emphasis on the desirability of a thin physique if a woman is to be considered attractive or successful. When compared with the actual incidence of body types in our society, it becomes apparent that women's magazine advertising in the 1980s has served a diet of unrealistically thin ideals. In the case of young women, who constitute the majority of eating disorder victims, and who have been shown to be especially "media conscious," advertising's contribution to the sociocultural milieu may not be a healthy one.

NOTE

1. For the complete results of the content analysis, see Gagnard (1986).

REFERENCE

Gagnard, Alice. (1986). From feast to famine: Depiction of ideal body type in magazine advertising: 1950-1984. *Proceedings of the American Academy of Advertising.*

14

Public Relations

The $1 Million Penalty for Being a Woman

CAROLYN GARRETT CLINE

A woman's place is no longer in the home, but in the communication department. It is obvious from our applications for jobs, from our graduating classes, and at our professional meetings that communication jobs are turning into women's professions.

Professions that have been feminized in the past, such as certain areas of banking, teaching, and nursing, have seen a reduction in salary and status already. The fear has surfaced that public relations has become, in the words of *Business Week,* "the Velvet Ghetto of affirmative action" (1987). Will this mean a decrease in salaries and a lowering of status for public relations?

In late 1984, the International Association of Business Communicators (IABC) Foundation commissioned a study to examine this trend. For more than a year I headed a research team that included two past presidents of IABC/Austin, Hank Smith and Nancy Johnson; Dr. Elizabeth Lance Toth of Southern Methodist University; Dr. Judy VanSlyke Turk, formerly with the University of Oklahoma and now at Kent State University; and Dr. Lynne Masel Walters, then at the University of Houston.

To examine the trends in the field, we looked at the profile studies of IABC for the last six years, which detail salaries and jobs (IABC, 1987). We also combed through written material concerning trends on women in management. We conducted nearly 40 in-depth interviews of senior-level practitioners, including Harold Burson, Herb Schmertz, and Edward Bernays. We arranged focus groups that were held throughout the United States and Canada. We talked to communicators in middle- and senior-level management.

Since then, we have supplemented this information with additional studies in Canada and the United Kingdom. We also used the traditional academician's measurement—students.

The first issue was the most basic: Is there a problem? Certainly there has been a dramatic increase of women in the workplace in general, but communication shows an increase that is far out of proportion. Of the entire U.S. work force, 44% is female. In the IABC profile in 1985, women were 63% of the respondents. Student groups and classes in public relations are now more than 80% female. We are coming close to 90% female at the universities in Texas.

Some professionals report that the increased number of women in public relations and business communication simply reflects a trend toward more working women and is not something to worry about. One man in San Francisco summed up the position: "This profession is growing. There are a lot more positions available. There are a lot more women in the work force these days, and if they gravitate toward this profession, fine. Let the people do the work that they feel comfortable doing."

But the bottom line—salaries—tells us that the situation is not fine. Researchers Glen Broom and Dave Dozier from San Diego State University have been studying public relations professionals and the roles they fill for over six years (Broom, 1982). They report that practitioners say their activities fall into two basic roles—manager and technician. They report that women are most often found filling the technician role, and that this role segregation depresses salaries.

Moreover, between 1979 and 1985 the situation got worse. The men in the study moved into management and the women stayed in the technician roles. This is not necessarily negative. Those practitioners who stayed as technicians expressed greater job satisfaction than many of the managers. However, the bottom line was still significant and negative. Women were and are paid less than men. Sex is one of the strongest, if not the strongest, predictor of a low salary. Other studies support the San Diego findings.

Controlling statistically for such factors as education, experience, and professional development, in 1985 a man earned $6,600 more than a woman with the same qualifications—a $6,600 bonus for being male. However, in the IABC profile studies, the salary gap has been improving over the past six years. Although there has been a slight improvement in IABC data over time, other studies suggest that the improvements might even be bad news. A 1986 survey in *pr reporter* showed a second straight decline in the median annual salary of public relations respondents, mainly Public Relations Society of America (PRSA) members.[1] For the second year, the median annual salary dropped $1,000—from $43,000 to $42,000. These were high-level PRSA members. Two trends, according to the editors, accounted for the drop: the increase in younger, lower-paid professionals, and the feminization of the profession.

Younger men were paid less than women their age, according to *pr reporter,* but the salary difference among the older professionals was staggering. The difference at the 50-59-year-old level was a whopping $25,000 a year.

But the Broom and Dozier (1985) study was even more discouraging. They found a difference of approximately $33,000 a year—controlling for all other variables. Based on these numbers, it is fair to say that a woman will make between $6,000 and $30,000 a year less than an equally qualified man. If a woman works for 45 years and loses $6,000 a year, this means she will earn about $300,000 less than a man at best. At its worst, if she loses $30,000 a year, the figure is close to $1.5 million—a million-dollar penalty for being a woman.

So the answer to the first question is yes, there is a problem.

But the numbers don't tell the whole story. If communicators had wanted to become rich they would have studied engineering or medicine. So we looked at why women are going into the public relations field in record numbers and what this might mean to the practitioners and to the whole field of public relations.

First, the study did not equate positions in management with success. Technicians are often more satisfied than managers. Several people who participated in the focus groups reported that they had been unhappy as managers; they missed writing and they missed being creative. Some went back to being technicians. Technicians can also be very highly-paid—especially for such skills as speech writing.

But what about those people who want management or upper-management positions? What about those who want a stronger say in corporate or organization decision making? Is the road to top management closed to them if they stay in communication? Will it close even further if it is identified as "a woman's job"?

That is what we asked the senior-level practitioners in the focus groups. The answers fell on a continuum. At one end were those who said that things were fine and that there was no problem. One top executive explained, "We don't have men and women at this company; we just have people." A Canadian woman said that the question of feminization was a "nonissue." And a male counterpart agreed: "I don't see any problem. The fact that they are 80% or whatever doesn't have me up at nights until three in the morning in a cold sweat. I never really thought about it. I really don't care."

Others welcomed the increase of women in their departments. They thought that women would bring in unique skills, such as empathy and understanding.

We found women who fit the definition of a "queen bee." They have the attitude, "I made it, so why can't other women?" One highly honored woman had a message for women in communication. She said, "Don't waste any time or energy thinking about what's different about women in this field. And, don't look under the bed at night to see if anybody discriminated against you today. The field is too demanding and challenging and you don't have that kind of time to waste. The women's issue has no role in professional success."

At the other end were those who thought a woman's place was anywhere but in management. "I don't like to hire women managers since they'll take time off when the kids are sick." "They'll only get pregnant and quit." "In the past my clients wouldn't accept a woman executive and I don't want to get them angry."

In between are those who worry. A woman executive reacted very strongly to the fear that public relations was becoming feminized. She said, "I think it's dangerous and I'm appalled. I'm afraid of it because I'm afraid of any profession becoming known as a female profession. It always has less money or less status involved with it than when it's mixed or mostly male."

A woman in senior management said the business world still thinks in stereotypes: "You think of nurses as being women. You still think of secondary teachers as being women. There's still that stigma that if a particular profession or career is primarily women, then for whatever reason, it's a less desirable kind of career."

A former president of the PRSA, also a woman, worried that feminization might be seen by men as an opportunity to put public relations down a notch in the corporate hierarchy. "I think it will go back to being seen as a position that you can get rid of. . . . It might be seen as an area that could be done better by someone at the top level or by someone who isn't in our profession. . .maybe someone in the legal, marketing, or finance departments."

A study done by Ted Joseph (1985) reports comments from a North Carolina public relations agency owner, a man, who says that feminization "could lead to decreasing influence for the profession as male CEOs give the position no more regard than that accorded to a secretary."

We found women and men worried about the impact of feminization. The practitioners discussed their fears that the misunderstanding of the communication role and function by top management threatens the place of public relations and communication in the corporate world. Male and female practitioners alike said they were ill equipped for management and sometimes unsure of where to go for training. They also feared that management bias against communication would make public relations a dead-end job. The president of a major public relations agency advised women, "If you want to get into top management, not just public relations management, get out of public relations all together. Go into some other line or area such as finance or whatever is the route to the top of that particular organization."

Another concern of the profession was bias, whether blatant or subtle. Women recalled discrimination when they were—or were not—hired. A Texas woman said that, although she thinks things have gotten better since she first started working, she still has vivid memories of bias. She said, "I was told one time I wasn't getting a job because I wasn't married. Therefore, I was unstable. I didn't get another job because I was married and my husband might move. Another time, I didn't get a job because I didn't have children and it was likely that I would have children. People actually had the nerve to tell me that they were rejecting me for these contradictory reasons."

Communicators reported that women were being hired at lower salaries and at lower positions than men. One smaller agency president, who recently quit one of the major public relations agencies, reported, "Now graduates are coming out with public relations degrees, but if they are women, larger agencies start them out as receptionists. They never start a man out as a receptionist. They're always junior account executives."

Moreover, women are often welcoming these jobs. The president of one IABC chapter reported that he was shocked at the number of recent graduates—all women—who were calling him for job ideas, saying that they would take a secretarial job just to "get a foot in the door."

Organizations are also actively recruiting men, as are schools, to counter the image of the communication department as a bunch of "girls"—a powder-puff department.

A friend recently described a position from which she stepped down, and in which she is being replaced by a man: "I'm really frustrated. If a man follows a woman into the job, it looks like a woman screwed up. If a woman follows a man into a job, it looks like they've downgraded the position. If a woman follows a woman into a job, it looks like it's become a ghetto."

It is almost a no-win situation. Even when they do break into management, some women are threatened by a phenomenon we found across the country—the male power structure, or the "old boys" network.

A woman in Atlanta summed up her experience. She said, "I think more and more women are managers, but I wonder how seriously they are being taken. I can really relate to this 'good ol' boy' syndrome. When I was director of communications in my company, I never felt I was taken as seriously as the person who had had my job previously. I didn't go out for breakfast with all the guys or go out drinking or anything like that, so I wasn't in that inner circle. I always felt kind of excluded and I wonder if that's not the way it is for a lot of women."

For a lot of women, that is the way it is. One man explained that he is a more effective manager—more effective than any woman could be. "I get done what the previous woman couldn't. I can go in and nudge and pal around and get what I want. And I do."

Communicators across the country echoed this problem. Women are not taken as seriously as men. They cannot be part of the gang. This stands in their way of becoming real members of the management team. The assumption is that men would rather work with—and for—men. One man explained that "men are more comfortable talking with other men and women are more comfortable talking with other women."

One agency women said, "Men seem to feel more comfortable having a male report to them and they feel that they speak the same language. Men are singing out of the same page in the hymn book. Females are considered to be in a different denomination, much less the same hymn book."

The most frequently addressed problem was the concept that women are not good managers. The problems of women as managers, according to the people we interviewed, are either inherent with women or are the result of their socialization. Right or wrong, the following are the perceptions that women in the public relations and other communications communities are facing, among men and women peers alike.

The first perception is that women are nurturers. When women say, "I like people," they are really saying that they are natural nurturers and like to encourage people. There seems to be a widespread belief that women work well with clients. There's also the assumption that women are especially suited to small agency work because they are nurturers—caring, sympathetic, and understanding. One woman in an agency said that she found women drawn to agency work because of "something that I find very natural to the female culture and that is nurturing skills. It's kind of a natural, nurturing capability that women have and it's very important in consulting."

But what this also means is that women are viewed as not tough enough for corporate life. One woman said, "Frankly, my blood boils when I read an article by a woman in business who says, 'I think I bring more to the job because I think women are sympathetic and intuitive.' That's the kind of thing that has set women back two decades."

An Atlanta woman agreed, and she discussed her first experience as a manager: "I wanted people who worked with me to be happy. I wanted to identify and sympathize with their problems and give them as much slack as I could in dealing with them. . . . I got walked all over. That was the worst-run office you could imagine." She said she was able to become tougher on her next job because she had been raised in a military family and therefore knew all the "codes" for male behavior.

The second assumption was that women are too emotional. Several men remembered working for a woman as an unpleasant experience because women were emotional. Women agreed with them. A Dallas woman said that women are harder to work for because they feel less secure in their positions.

A lot of this goes along with the issue of legitimization. Men are comfortable in the corporation because corporations have always been male. Men have been there and they belong there. Women have gotten into corporations by virtue of specific skills. No man got into a corporate training program on his typing scores. Women had to have specific skills. Now they have the skills for doing the newsletter, doing the press release, and making the press contacts. For many women this has legitimized their role in the company. When individuals move into management, it often means they must let go of the skills and delegate tasks. This means casting off the legitimization and relying on self-esteem and self-worth.

That seems to be the critical point in a woman's career—letting go of the skills and still feeling that she is part of the management team. Being a manager does not mean you never have to edit a newsletter, but it means you can let that task go and still be worthwhile.

There is also the assumption that women have children. They surely don't do it alone, but there is the idea that children are a "women's" problem. Men and women agree that children are "a bad thing" for a woman in corporate life. A woman spoke of the "threat of children" to her career. Several women reported leaving corporations for agency work because there was no way they could combine a corporate career and children. One man agreed, saying to a woman, "If you're going to lead a normal life you are simply going to have to take time out of work. You can't concentrate on your career."

A male manager defended paying his female employee less than her male counterpart by saying that she missed work because the kids get sick or they have to go somewhere. For men, children are a reason to ask for a raise; for women they may well mean the end of the climb to management.

This problem is not unique to communication. In 1984, a survey of executive women showed that 52% either had never married or were widowed or divorced; 61% had no children. A 1979 survey of executive men showed that 5% had never married or were divorced and 3% had no children. Executive women paid the price.

There is also the assumption that women cannot "play the game." Women have never learned the team spirit—the corporate spirit—that men learn on football teams or in the armed services.

Breaking into the management circle and getting onto the fast track are secrets that most women do not learn in male-oriented, male-dominated companies. The women reported that corporations are fraternities all over again and women cannot be accepted. So they are forming small agencies or "old girls networks" to try to emulate, not penetrate, the clubs.

There may be some validity in that approach. Look at the glamour sports for women—gymnastics, skating, swimming, and tennis—all individual-process sports. Many involve competing for a subjective number, not a goal or a bottom line. The score is some number a judge holds up at the end of an individual performance. These sports require individual, not team efforts, usually involving some nebulous goal.

Perhaps women need to examine what men did learn in team sports. They learned competitiveness as a team, not as individuals. Or perhaps they learned deferring—handing the ball off to your boss—and not getting all the glory that day because the team had to win. They learned to take criticism and they learned to accept getting yelled at. They learned to relate to a coach or a captain. There really may be something to the team analogy. It is too late for some of us to go try out for football teams, but women can look at what men have learned.

In the study, we did test two assumptions on our students. The first assumption was that women are just not aggressive enough; the second was that women are not career-minded. Traditionally, a woman's occupation has been something to fall back on. It has been a second source of income for a family. Despite the need for many women to work and the increasing number of women who are single parents, there is still the feeling that a woman does not need the work or money as much as a man needs to work.

She does not need a career, she needs a job once in a while. Her lack of aggressiveness impedes her from asking for her real worth.

We tested these assumptions on 500 students in the United States and Canada using a variety of standard psychological tests. The first measure was assertion comfort. These students—men and women—were absolutely over the top on the aggression scale. There was no significant difference between the men and the women: They were all pushy. There was also no significant difference between the men and women we surveyed in conflict avoidance or in planning orientation.

However, there was a significant difference in serious-mindedness. Men scored significantly higher than women in their orientation toward a challenging business career. This bears out a lot of the earlier literature. In addition, we asked them to rank the skills on the IABC matrix for professional development. Women were most interested in the skills at the entry-level end in the technical and creative. Men went right for the management categories. This may be a reaction against the "superwoman" image of the past decade—a reevaluation of the concept that you can have it all. There is currently a backlash against trying to do everything.

If women are looking for a career that combines reasonable status with time flexibility and the chance for creativity, public relations and corporate communication fit that image. These fields can be very, very rewarding. It is possible to drop out and then come back in. Although this is not the fast track to a corporate vice presidency, it is certainly a legitimate way to have a career in these areas. This flexibility does fit what some women are looking for. This type of career also allows women to work with people as nurturers.

Women in the focus groups reported that since communication is seen as a "soft" career in a corporation, women have more flexibility than they would in other departments to drop out, raise a family, and then come back. Public relations and business communication can be a rewarding career for the trained specialist. Yet, for some communicators, the route to management is still of critical importance.

It appears that as women enter the field, men *are* going elsewhere—into marketing, middle management, and top management. Women may become directors of corporate communication and managers of communication, but will the higher positions be closed to someone coming from corporate communication? Many of the senior- and mid-level practitioners said that communication would become a dead-end position unless things change. The ghetto may be real and a lot closer than we think.

As salaries keep declining, communicators may find themselves in a "polyester ghetto." It seems clear that it is time to start looking at what can be done to resolve some of the issues. With a second grant from the IABC Foundation, we are looking at what might be done to keep public relations a respected profession.

Betty Friedan addressed this issue in 1963 with *The Feminine Mystique*. She said that a woman should not expect special privileges because of her sex, but neither should she "adjust" to prejudices and discrimination. She must learn to compete—not as a woman but as a human being. Friedan was echoing the sentiments of Susan B. Anthony, who 95 years earlier had advised women to make their employers understand that women are in employers' service as workers, not as women.

The big question is, How?

First we must recognize that there is a problem. Not all of the media coverage of this study has been favorable. There has been backlash, questioning if there really is a ghetto and if this is good or bad. Some will not want to accept that there is a problem or that a million-dollar penalty for being a woman in this business is a meaningful figure. They keep saying, "I know you've looked at six research studies, but they've all messed up in the same direction." They do not want to see it. We have professional groups that do not want to hear anymore about that "damn ghetto." We have practitioners who fear that if we somehow recognize the problem we will cause it to come into being.

We also have people who fear that our concerns will be labeled a feminist issue, and will, therefore, be controversial and unacceptable in a postfeminist age. This is not a woman's issue. This is not a man's issue. The basic issue of the salary and status of the professional communicator cuts across such parochial limits as sex and roles. And it affects us all. Benjamin Franklin once said, "We must indeed all hang together or, most assuredly, we shall all hang separately."

RECOMMENDATIONS

Beyond a call for communication professionals to unify in dealing with this issue, we must begin to define success individually. Is it the satisfaction of writing? Working for a nonprofit organization? Helping people? Is it balancing a satisfying career with other aspects of life? Is it enough disposable income to finance a getaway weekend in Vail?

There is nothing wrong with being a good technician. The roles of manager and technician should be symbiotic. The technician must not be seen as a failed manager or as a woman who is afraid to take a risk. We need to recognize that the creative side of public relations is much more than a stepping-stone to management. It is a solid, valid, and wonderful part of the field. We also need to admit that the best corporate writers in the world still need to know how a corporation operates and how to communicate with their bosses. Those who want to be technicians are affected less by the findings of the "velvet ghetto report" than those want the fast track, or even the medium fast track—the 55 mph track—to management.

But for those women who are top-management bound, our research suggests some recommendations. For women, combining career and family is proving almost impossible on the fast track, so that choice must be made early. A woman cannot wait until she is 40 to make that decision, because it is too easy to panic about priorities then. For those who decide that they want it all, studies show that the best way may be to put the fast track first, and then find the husband and children. Women must be careful in making this choice, of course; dealing with 3:00 a.m. feedings can wear pretty thin after 40.

Women aiming for top management must develop career plans and select employers with care. Some respondents told us that luck or being in the right place at the right time played a major role in their careers. This passive role is more typical of women than of men. It is a role that any upwardly mobile communicator must reject. Women have to get into the game and be as aggressive and determined as any male counterpart. They must do what women traditionally do not do—they must have a game plan.

First, they must look at the corporation or the organization. What is the corporation's attitude toward women? What positions do women hold? They must look at the corporation's career tracks—some of the major agencies have very defined career tracks. Women must find out how people who have made it to management made it. They must find out the rules, concentrating on the long term, not the short term. What is valued by the organization? What does it take to get promoted? Is it 42 feet of newspaper coverage in the next month? What counts? What are the rules? What is the code? What is the uniform?

The importance of management skills was brought up time and again in our focus groups, where mid-level managers were reporting their own difficulties in learning how corporations work. Those who think of management only as "supervising other people" would be well advised to broaden their scope. Management is more, much more. It is a comprehensive process that includes goal setting, analysis, planning, research, program execution, measurement, and evaluation.

Public relations education has been criticized for turning out students who do not know how a corporation works and yet are planning careers in management. They do not know how to communicate with and like other managers. One woman expressed it beautifully:

> There has to be more of a business approach to communication. I think as time goes on, and this is especially critical for women, communicators are going to have to think like managers, talk like managers and communicate with other managers. And I mean this from the standpoint of the nitty-gritty of budgeting and business planning, of being able to look at a project and not think in terms of, well, can I win an award for this? But think in terms of what is my audience and what message do I have to convey? How many dollars will it take and what are the steps to get that done? And that kind of planning, which is what you always get from higher management, is bottom line results.

In its June 1987 issue, *Ladies' Home Journal* published a study that validates the same figures we have been getting for the past 15 years (Barrett & Greene, 1987). When women project what salary they will be making in 10 years, they project 60% of what men project. The figure is almost unchanging. Nationally, women are making about 64 cents for every dollar men make.[2] *Ladies Home Journal* suggests that women make the 60% ratio because women will accept less. They undervalue themselves.

Women with management ambitions should research the salaries in the area and in the type of business before accepting an offer. They should look at IABC profile studies, look at what *pr reporter* says, and check to see if the local IABC and PRSA chapters do salary surveys. They should talk to people, already working in the field, and find out what the salaries are and what the perks are. They should investigate the economic health of the area, as well as the company's economic health. If it is a public corporation, they should look at the annual reports—not just the president's messages, but the numbers as well.

And women should not be so quick to accept inadequate offers. We found with our focus groups that a lot of women were forgetting about the perks—the things that can be substituted when a company cannot or will not budge from a particular starting salary figure. Can the corporation pay PRSA and IABC dues or conference fees for the employee, for example?

Finally, study participants warned us about turning out "Miss America, the public relations major," the woman whose only articulated reason for going into public relations is "Because I like people." To steal a line from the president of the IABC Foundation, Wilma Mathews, liking people is a job requirement only for cocker spaniels. It's time that public relations practitioners stopped being cocker spaniels and started being professionals.

NOTES

1. The 23rd annual *pr reporter* survey of the profession in 1987 found that the U.S. median salary had risen $3,000 to $45,000, reversing a three-year decline. In this survey, women were found to account for 44.9% of all practitioners, which represented an increase of 2.3% from 1986. The median salary for women in this report is $35,000, compared to $50,812 for men. The data base for this study is a random sample of members of the Public Relations Society of America, the Canadian Public Relations Society of America, and *pr reporter* subscribers. The twenty-fourth annual survey in 1988 reported that the male/female ratio was almost even and that the median salary remained at $45,000.

2. The U.S. Census Bureau study released figures in September 1987 that reported that women now earn 70 cents for every dollar earned by a man.

REFERENCES

Barrett, Katherine, & Greene, Richard. (1987, June). Small expectations. *Ladies' Home Journal,* p. 78.

Broom, Glen M. (1982). A comparison of sex roles in public relations. *Public Relations Review, 8*(3), 17-22.

Broom, Glen M., & Dozier, David M. (1985, August). *Determinants and consequences of public relations roles.* Paper presented to the Public Relations Division at the annual meeting of the Association for Education in Journalism and Mass Communication, Memphis.

Friedan, Betty. (1963). *The feminine mystique.* New York: W. W. Norton.

International Association of Business Communicators. (1987). *IABC profile 87.* San Francisco: Author.

Jackson, Pat. (1987, September 17). 23rd annual survey of the profession, part I: Salaries and demographics. *pr reporter,* p. 1.

Jackson, Pat. (1988, September 12). 24th annual survey of the profession, part I: Salaries and demographics. *pr reporter,* p. 1.

Joseph, Ted. (1985). The women are coming, the women are coming. *Public Relations Quarterly, 30*(4), 21-22.

Mann, Judy, & Hellwig, Basia. (1988, January). The truth about the salary gap(s). *Working Woman,* p. 61.

PR: The "velvet ghetto" of affirmative action. (1987, May 8). *Business Week,* p. 122.

Section B. A Voice and Vision for the Future

15

Women's Movement Media and Cultural Politics

MARILYN CRAFTON SMITH

In the late 1960s, women's movement media began to appear in the United States. Destined to play an important role in the contemporary women's movement, these early media projects represented the means with which women could publicly challenge society and state their visions for the future. Producers of these media sought to create not only alternative forms of communication but also fundamental social change. For this reason, the women's movement media offer us a means of understanding the subtleties, shifts, and currents of the movement over the past twenty years.

Although it is frequently referred to in its singular form, the women's movement actually comprises many diverse groups. Ideological diversity in the movement also exists in forms that have been variously referred to as liberal, radical, or socialist feminisms, or those feminisms identified with women of color or Third World women (Hooks, 1981, 1984; Jaggar, 1983, Moraga & Anzaldua, 1981). Rather than focus on the ideological content of media representing any one of these forms specifically, this chapter will address feminist media that are primarily alternative or independent, meaning those that maintain either an ideological or structural distance from mainstream social relations and media institutions.

The first section reviews the context for the formation of women's movement media, the founding of which can be significantly attributed to the relations feminists had with the mass media. I will examine the ways in which feminist media, particularly print media, opposed the mass media to offer alternatives to women's movement supporters. The next two sec-

AUTHOR'S NOTE: I am grateful to Nina Gregg for her careful reading and suggestions during the preparation of this chapter. I also wish to thank H. Leslie Steeves for her supportive comments and discussions, and Pam Creedon for her helpful editorial suggestions. The prior work on women's movement media by Mather (1973), Armstrong (1981), and Allen (1988a) has provided much of the initial legwork in accounts of the early feminist media projects.

tions delineate the organizational and operational practices that characterize women's media: their collectivist and collaborative processes, and the political implications of separatism (in its various forms) for these media and their diverse audiences. The fourth section briefly provides examples of networking activities of feminist media workers and media formats other than print media. A review of previous studies on women's media is undertaken in the final section, with primary emphasis on print media. Here, I focus on the need for more rigorous analyses of the feminist implications of women's media and offer directions for future research.

POLITICAL PRECEDENTS:
THE FORMATION OF WOMEN'S MOVEMENT MEDIA

In the mid-1960s, there seemed to be little indication of widespread support for, or knowledge about, a social movement directed at women. Appellations such as the "women's movement," the "feminist movement," or even the more radical "women's liberation movement," had not yet been formulated. Often represented in today's mass media as the women's movement itself, the National Organization for Women (NOW), founded in 1966, was only in the beginning stages of establishing its chapter network. Moreover, little contact existed among women working for other causes such as the peace or civil rights movements. Working often in isolation from one another, groups of women engaged in various forms of political action, networking, theoretical development, and consciousness raising (C-R). Through this work they attempted to educate themselves and others about the inequities they experienced as women. Some sought to define women's oppression as a "class condition of women," using position statements and other rhetorical strategies (The Feminists, 1973), while others wished to share their experiences of oppression, discrimination, and politics surrounding gender. Expressing this emerging consciousness, in all its many levels, became the basis for the founding of the women's movement media.

Initiators of the women's movement came to it with diverse experiences in either politics or media. Jo Freeman (1973) and others have suggested that there were two distinct branches, referred to variously as the "reform" and "radical" components, or as those representing "women's rights" and "women's liberation" (Hole & Levine, 1971), which characterized the early women's movement. These two styles defined to some extent not only the political strategies that each branch pursued but also the approach each took in the media it produced.

Freeman (1973) contends that distinctions in structure and style more accurately differentiated the two originating branches than did ideology (p. 795). The style of organizational structure of the "reform" branch has been traditionally formal, with elected officers,[1] boards of directors, and the use of by-laws. This top-down leadership structure may have caused the slow development of a mass base of support for the early national reform organizations (p. 796). Trained in traditional forms of political action, the "reform" feminists pursued conventional avenues for social change through legislative means.[2]

Periodicals or newsletters were published by the nationally organized groups as a service to their various memberships. NOW-affiliated groups at the state and local levels also published periodicals. Much like *The Woman's Journal*, which was the official publication of the National American Woman Suffrage Association,[3] these periodicals continue to be a significant record of the members' actions and of the directions taken by the groups working within the framework of organized institutional feminism.

In contrast, proponents of the second branch of feminist activism in the 1960s, the women's liberation component, came to feminist politics with experiences gained in other social movements and groups associated with the Left. Thus they had participated in a variety of "liberation" movements such as the radical student movement, the anti-Vietnam war/peace movement, and the civil rights movement. Increasingly dissatisfied with their status in Left organizations,[4] and the sexism that was predominant there, these activitists left to form their own political groups.

The women's liberation branch had little organizational contact among the many small groups of which it was constituted. In fact, its participants frequently condemned traditional organizational structures, which they associated with the constraints of the establishment in general, and with hierarchical, elitist leadership in particular. Attempting to avoid what they considered to be the patriarchal replication of top-down power structures, these feminists adopted a style that often appeared spontaneous and leaderless.

Proponents of this branch had neither the resources nor the desire to form national organizations. However, their accumulated experience in local organizing enabled them to utilize the infrastructure of the radical community (Freeman, 1973, pp. 801-802); they transported their knowledge of grass-roots organizing and underground media to the women's movement and the founding of its media. Their periodicals represent the more radical or "alternative" publications within 1960s feminism.

Although feminist media developed along with the women's movement, additional factors contributed to the formation of feminist media projects. One such factor was the reactions feminists had to the mass media's representation of women. Portrayed either in a degrading manner or in almost total absence, women and their concerns were rarely treated with any seriousness. Consequently, although numerous institutions became the focus of feminist criticism, such as religion, politics, capitalism, and marriage, analysis of the mass media was a top priority to many feminists because of the blatantly oppressive representations of women they projected. Throughout this period, feminist writings reflect an awareness of the ideology around sex roles and the pervasive manner in which mass media representations contributed to this ideology (Friedan, 1963). Research on media representations in traditional women's magazines indicated that, although their audiences were primarily women, these publications, in contrast, gave little attention to altering the status of women (Flora, 1971; Franzwa, 1974).

The reproduction of sexist ideology, however, was not the only reason for feminists in both branches to distrust the mainstream media. Much of their disillusionment was derived from the mass media's coverage of the women's movement itself. In *The Politics of Women's Liberation*, Freeman (1975) shows how media antagonism was directed toward feminists by the press, either through the use of unflattering portrayals or through trivialization of feminists' political interests by focusing on marital status or mode of dress in interviews. As a result, the political messages underlying feminist actions and concerns, as conveyed by the mass media, were inaccurate, distorted, or trivialized (pp. 112-113).

Since the founding members of the larger institutionalized feminist organizations, such as NOW, had prior experience in working with the mainstream media, they were able to gain the publicity they needed to increase their memberships. Their organizations also represented the type of complex, legitimated institutions with which the news media were willing to collaborate for news coverage (Tuchman, 1978, p. 134). In the late 1960s and early 1970s, when the national news media simultaneously began to cover the women's movement, their professional news conventions mandated that reporters seek hard news "events" and people who could act as spokeswomen for the movement (Tuchman, 1978). Such practices ensured the omission of coverage of the symbolic, issue-oriented problems that were central to the radical movement's development. Additionally, the selection of certain "media-nominated leaders" (such as Gloria Steinem and Betty Friedan) limited the public voice of the movement to those who met the news media's criteria for spokespersons, a practice contrary to the feminist belief that no one feminist could speak for all others (Tuchman, 1978, pp. 139-140).

Feminist hostility toward the mass media is expressed in the founding issue of *off our backs*, a feminist monthly newspaper first published in 1970. The editors state, "The women's movement can no longer afford to be naive about the nature and function of the mass media in this society. . . . We no longer need to use the mass media to tell people we exist." Further, they call for a "halt to all dealings with the mass media—no more interviews, no more documentaries, no more special coverage. We don't need them and we don't want them" (Ferro, Holcolm, & Saltzman-Webb, 1977 pp. 117-118). A recent study of feminist periodicals (Allen, 1988a, p. 62) found that these early periodicals allocated editorial space in each issue for analysis of the mass media.

One major feminist objection to the mass media centered on the sexist portrayal of women in advertising. Such an objection was evidenced by the more than 8,000 letters on advertising that *Ms.* magazine received after its first issue. These letters were subsequently turned over to advertising firms so that the advertisers who portrayed women positively might be rewarded while others might be made aware of their audience's objections (Mather, 1973, p. 155). Members of various feminist editorial groups developed advertising policies that opposed sexist advertising, a practice characteristic of many feminist publications (Mather, 1973, p. 157). David Armstrong's (1981) study of alternative media also suggests that sexist attitudes and practices prevalent among 1960s alternative presses, such as the "selling of sex" to finance these publications, caused feminists to form their own alternative media (pp. 54-55).

A primary condition for the successful launching of a social movement is the ability to communicate with potential adherents. The media outlets developed by the women's movement activists became central organizing tools, with their capacity to relay information about political actions, to create a space for discussion about their concerns, and to offer support to and seek input from their readers. In these ways, feminists' overtly political media stand out in comparison to traditional mass media offerings. Features of organizational style, membership, and operating practices characterize feminist media projects, several of which are discussed below.

COLLECTIVITY AS ORGANIZATIONAL STYLE

The women's movement media grew out of a specific historical period characterized not only by the richness of its protest and dissent, but also by its desire for alternative ways of living and working. This was evidenced by the estimated 5,000 alternative grass-roots cooperative businesses that were reported as of 1976 (Gardner, 1976, cited in Rothschild-Whitt, 1979). The formation of these businesses was particularly prolific in fields requiring low capital needs (Rothschild-Whitt, 1979, p. 510). The development of low-cost offset printing, plus the use of typewriters and transfer lettering, made a publishing venture highly feasible for feminist groups with little capital.

The early feminist publishing groups were collectively owned and operated. Activists in them chose the medium of print to produce newspapers, newsletters, magazines, and journals. Although most of the periodicals were published initially in a newsletter format, dozens of these generically titled the *Women's Liberation Newsletter*, over 132 other newspapers, magazines, and journals were in existence by 1973 (Mather, 1973, p. 2). The newsletter format is still prevalent for feminist periodicals today.

Many feminist media workers, familiar with consciousness-raising groups, viewed the publishing collective as an extension of their own developing political awareness. The principle of equal participation became an operating goal of the early feminist publishers. As in the C-R groups and other collectivist organizations, the feminist collectives stressed a consensual process over majority rule, and collective formulation and resolution of problems. Collective control and loosely structured staffing characterized the feminist media as they had the alternative media that preceded them (Allen, 1988a, pp. 55-56, 121; Mather, 1973, p. 145).

Rothschild-Whitt (1979, pp. 511-512) shows that collectivity entails an alternative view of authority. Whereas bureaucratic organizations tend to locate authority with individuals, either through incumbency or expertise, in collectively run organizations authority resides explicitly in the collective as a whole.[5]

Rothschild-Whitt (1979) also notes three levels of incentives that sustain potential members of cooperative work organizations. In contrast to bureaucratic incentives, which are remunerative in nature, collectives' incentives include the fulfillment of values, solidarity (friendship), and material gain (p. 515). The primary reason, however, is purposive. Rothschild-Whitt notes that people join collectives to gain substantial control over their work, which enables them to structure both the product and the work process in accordance with their values and political goals. These findings were substantiated by both Mather (1973, p. 199) and Allen (1988a, p. 122) in their studies of women's movement media workers and by Armstrong's (1981) study of alternative media (pp. 22, 231). Indeed, staff members of many early feminist periodicals indicated that primary among their reasons for joining a collective were the opportunity to work with other women in a positive atmosphere and the need for women to develop their own media as a "forum" or vehicle for exchange of ideas (Mather, 1973, p. 199).

Although collaboration has been central to feminist media projects at the operational level, it also underlies the mutual sharing that goes on in the communication process itself. Feminist communication requires that women gain access to the communication tools themselves and that they actively participate in the communication process (Freeman & Jones, 1976, p. 5). A primary role of feminist periodicals has been the establishment of a space where members of the editorial collective and readers are able to exchange views.

The avenue for exchange may be extended space for letters to the editor or editorials collectively written by staff members. Feminist publications emphasize reader participation that allows readers to speak for themselves. Mather (1973) has shown that an average of 6% of each issue of feminist periodicals in her study was devoted to pages written by readers (p. 200). She contrasts this figure with the percentages taken six years earlier of five traditional women's magazines, in which no magazine exceeded 1%.[6] In contrast, *Ms.* allocated 5% of its pages to its readers.[7] Another means by which individual women are able to speak for themselves is through the use of interviews. In regular interview sections, feminist periodicals such as *off our backs* counter the mass media's use of movement spokeswomen and its treatment of movement issues (Allen, 1988a, p. 79).

Feminist periodicals are also distinguished by their inclusion of content not commonly found in mainstream media (Allen, 1988a, p. 82). Attention to issues such as the politics of abortion, sexuality, women's health, violence against women, pornography, and race and class analyses, which are frequently ignored in the mass media press, commonly appear in feminist publications. Additionally, these publications have included in their pages news of other publications and the formation of new media, news of the women's movement itself, and occasionally collaboratively shared editorial content with other publishers (Allen, 1988a, pp. 124-128). In this respect feminist publishing has represented a collectivist effort on the part of the many media producers within the movement.

SEPARATISM AS POLITICS

Feminists also have attempted to seek control of the production of their periodicals. Reappropriating the knowledge and meaning of their life experiences and advancing new ways of visioning the world lie at the heart of feminist media production. To some, the goals may be simply the daily dissemination of information that is deemed vital for a particular legislative action; to others the entire production process itself becomes a political act, a process whereby questions can be raised regarding the ethics and goals of publishing. Such a reclamation, however, has a subversive component in its allegiance to separatism.

Separatism has remained a prominent and constant component within feminism. In her discussion of separatism and power, Marilyn Frye (1983) shows that insofar as the theme of separation may occur in various manifestations and roles, it offers different meanings relative to different situations (p. 96). And although it may exist in a variety of forms, feminist separatism has implicitly assumed a position outside patriarchal institutions, a separation from "institutions, relationships, roles and activities which are male-defined, male-dominated and operating for the benefit of males and the maintenance of male privilege" (p. 96). More important, this separation is one that has been initiated by women.

Frye argues that asymmetric access is the basis for differences of power. That is, those with power have unlimited access to those without power. To Frye, total power is manifested in the unconditional access that men have historically had to women. As women choose to separate themselves from men, through the establishment of women-only projects or activities, they deny access to men and thus claim the assumption of power.

Through its power to give women control over their own ideas and words, a separatist dimension is inherently a part of the women's media movement. Media projects undertaken by contemporary feminists have primarily been women-only endeavors, established and operated by women for women. Frye (1983) argues further that, as women assume control over "what is said and sayable," over the nature of information imparted and to whom, they also assume the power to define. By controlling both faces of power, access and definition, women are "doubly insubordinate" (pp. 105-107).

The exclusivity of women-owned and -run media projects is unique to the contemporary women's movement. In her recent study of women's communications networks developed between 1963 and 1983, Allen (1988a) notes that contemporary women's media projects are rarely subsidized by or operated with males, as was the case with two feminist publications at the turn of the century: Susan B. Anthony's paper, the *Revolution*, funded by George Francis Train, and *The Woman's Journal*, established by Lucy Stone, her husband Henry Blackwell, and a few other reformers (p. 1).

The strain over finances also raises the controversial question of whether to do business with mainstream media (primarily, but not solely, publishers), who are considered by some feminists to be the patriarchal press. Doing business with mainstream publishers, for example, through the sale of subsidiary rights, may enhance the financial status of a particular feminist press and ensure the possibility of producing more feminist works in the future. However, some feminist publishers view this collaboration as a betrayal, as was the case with the editors of Persephone Press, a lesbian publishing house (now defunct). A clause was included in its publishing contracts that stated explicitly that the publishers would not sell rights to male publishing houses (Rich, Greenfield, McGloin & Snow, 1980, p. 83). By including this clause, the publishers attempted to validate feminist publishing in its own right, by precluding women authors from perceiving their press "as an elementary experience before the real thing" (p. 83). More important, initiating business collaborations with a patriarchal press was seen as equivalent to relinquishing the goal of establishing an autonomous lesbian network in publishing.

Although more radical feminists may view separation as an unconditional expression of radical gender politics (Frye, 1983, p. 96), separatism has an alternative meaning for women of color. For Black women, in particular, separatism may involve separation from whites, the dominant group in race relations, rather than separation from Black men, who also are, and historically have been, oppressed by whites (Combahee River Collective, 1983, p. 275)[8].

It should be noted that the majority of participants in the women's movement and the media that it spawned were white women. Many Black women, for example, supported the ideology of feminism (advocacy of social equality for all women), but rejected participation in the women's movement, which they perceived as being made up of middle- and upper-class college-educated white women working to meet their own needs. Bell Hooks (1981) has noted that the racism and classism of the liberal feminists were particularly apparent in their suggestion of paid work as the key to liberation. Additionally, because the women's movement developed in a period of organized struggle for civil rights for Blacks, support for the liberation of women could be construed as a threat against gains made for Blacks (p. 176).

Black and other women of color have developed their own media projects; although fewer in number, these media outlets voice the perspectives of Black, Native American, Asian, Hispanic, and Third World women. In her recent study of the media of women of color between the years 1963 and 1988, Kimberlie Kranich (personal communication, September 10, 1988) has identified 84 publications whose primary focus has been women of color.[9] Many of these publications no longer exist. As of this writing there are currently 20 publications focusing on women of color, the majority of which are aimed at Black women (M. Allen, personal communication, September 10, 1988). Only two newspapers for Black women are publishing currently: one for the Black Women's Health Project in Atlanta, and *Up Front*, a Washington, D.C., newspaper that, after several issues in 1984, reappeared again last year (Kranich, personal communication, September 10, 1988). Other publications include newsletters associated with research organizations and a scholarly journal, *Sage: A Scholarly Journal about Black Women*. In 1981 Kitchen Table: Women of Color Press began publishing books by, about, and for women of color, the first of which was *Cuentos: Stories of Latinas* ("Kitchen Table Press," 1982).

Although Black women's periodicals began to appear in the early 1970s, it wasn't until the mid-1970s that any significant numbers were produced, with the majority established in the 1980s. Martha Allen (personal communication, September 10, 1988) reports that many of the early Black women's media projects produced only one issue, which would not be followed by subsequent issues until one or two years later. The majority of Black women's periodicals, like those published by white feminists, are newsletters published by centers or associated with Black women's organizations, such as the Association for Black Women Historians, which publishes the newsletter *Truth*.

FEMINIST MEDIA NETWORKING

Feminist publishers organized in a national network have become identified with the women-in-print subculture, or "women-in-print movement," as it has been called. Charlotte Bunch attributes the organization of the first Women in Print conference, held in Omaha, Nebraska, in 1976, to the efforts of June Arnold (Doughty & Bunch, 1980, p. 72). Arnold wanted to bring together women involved in all aspects of feminist publishing—presses, journals, newspapers, bookstores, and distributors. The conference attracted representatives from about 80 publications, presses, bookstores, and distributors ("200 Women's Media," 1982, p. 1). Although only "130 white feminists" were reported in attendance, this first conference was an extremely important event for dispelling the isolation felt by so many feminist publishers. Bunch notes that this conference generated excitement similar to that found in the early periods of the women's liberation movement, when young feminists discovered each other (Doughty & Bunch, 1980, p. 72). It also encouraged the development of lines of communication among the different branches of the feminist media movement.

There are numerous reasons feminist authors might select a feminist publisher over one in the mainstream media (Jay, 1986a). Feminist writers turn to feminist publishers specifically because they seek a unique type of support and feminist publishers are likely to share the political goals of feminist authors, a criterion important to both. Additionally, unlike a corporate firm, which may promote only a small number of the books it actually publishes (one out of six, according to Jay), feminist publishers tend to put more effort into promotion and distribution and to backlist books, thereby keeping them in print indefinitely.

Mainstream publishing options are still not widely available for feminists. A buyer at Walden Books admitted that most publishing on women today falls in the "superwoman syndrome" category, for example, books about women who are both gourmet cooks and successful career women (Armstrong, 1987b, p. 10). To the major publishing houses in the 1980s, the radical side of feminism, which raises difficult questions and seeks radical social change, is over, boring, nonexistent. This erasure, however, attempts to construct a reality. As Tuchman (1978) has shown, the media continue their thinly veiled effort to collaborate in the symbolic annihilation of women, and, in this case, of the women's movement itself. Feminists who have started their own publications and presses know that strong, assertive feminist ideas never make it to the mass media unless diluted or contained.

A network similar to one that developed around the women's publications and presses also coalesced around women's music. A number of music festivals are held annually as a means to promote women's music as well as the messages of feminism (see Tilchen, 1984). The first of these, the National Women's Music Festival, was held in the summer of 1974 at Champaign-Urbana, Illinois. In 1982, this festival, an annual event, moved to Bloomington, Indiana, where it has continued to be held (Tilchen, 1984,

p. 294). In 1976, the Michigan Womyn's Music Festival, produced by the We Want the Music Collective, was begun by a group of women who rented land on which to hold the event. Since the first festival, which attracted 2,500, attendance has increased. This festival is an annual event during which women live for four or five days in a women-only environment, surrounded by women's culture. Other large regional festivals include Sisterfire, produced by Roadwork in Washington, D.C., a West Coast Women's Music and Comedy Festival, and more recently, the Southern Women's Music and Comedy Festival, both produced by Robin Tyler Productions.

Although several independent women's record labels promote the work of one or two artists,[10] Redwood Records and Olivia Records, Inc., are two of the larger recording companies representing a greater number of artists. Several independent companies produce specific types of music, for example, Musica Femina and Leonardo (classical) and Rosetta Records (lost blues and jazz recordings).

An example of an independent production company that focuses on the gathering and reporting of women's news is the Women's International News Gathering Service (WINGS). Since 1986, WINGS has produced and distributed 29 minutes of news a month, headlining major news stories about women that are ignored by the mass media ("WINGS Radio Service," 1987).[11] In addition to WINGS, the *1988 Directory of Women's Media* (Allen, 1988b) lists five other women's news services in the United States and five from other countries.

RESEARCHING CULTURAL POLITICS

As early as 1973, Anne Dudley Mather cited three reasons for researching feminist periodicals: the dearth of research in this area, the importance of women's media as a resource for research on the women's movement, and the need for research that makes more rigorous distinctions between media produced by "feminists" and those produced by "women." These concerns are still valid today.

Mather's (1973) study of early feminist publications was the first of its kind to review comprehensively the earliest publications of the current women's movement, those published between the years 1968 and 1973. This study also included a survey of suffrage publications and a brief analysis of *Ms.* magazine in its first year (1972) in comparison with other feminist publications of that year.

At the time of her research, Mather noted that there had been no significant work on the feminist press. Indeed, the omission of feminist media has been characteristic of much of the literature about the "press of protest." This omission is exemplified by two studies noted by Mather that examined the development of the alternative and underground press of the 1960s: Robert J. Glessing's *The Underground Press in America* (1970) and Laurence Leamer's *The Paper Revolutionaries* (1972). Although both provide a rich and important background on the period that spawned the women's movement, neither of these studies was sensitive to the struggle over gender politics that was emerging at the time.

A 1984 study by John Downing, *Radical Media: The Political Experience of Alternative Communication*, examines, through the use of case studies, a collection of alternative media organizations, with emphasis on selected collectives in the United States, Portugal and Italy, and Eastern Europe. Potentially interesting is the case study of Third World Newsreel, an alternative film collective. In it, Downing alludes minimally to the "women's struggle" within the organization as well to the struggles that surfaced over the inclusion of Black films. Of the eight case studies from the United States, however, none is representative of the feminist political struggle of the past 20 years.

In *The Dissident Press*, Lauren Kessler (1984) includes a chapter that surveys briefly the historical context of feminist publishing, from the suffrage periodicals of the 1840s to the variety of publications of the 1980s. However, this work is limited by the brevity of the analysis of the publications and by its scope, since it does not consider the plethora of periodicals associated with the recent women's movement. Additionally problematic is the unexamined assumption that magazines such as *Savvy*, *Working Woman*, and *Working Mother,* although directed at women, are equally representative of feminism.

In contrast, David Armstrong's study, *A Trumpet to Arms: Alternative Media in America* (1981), includes a chapter on sexual politics that is distinguished by its separate discussions of media aimed at disparate radical groups: women's liberation activists, lesbian-feminists, and gay men. Additionally, Armstrong recognizes significant links between the underground press and the feminist media that succeeded it.

More recently, Martha Leslie Allen (1988a) has examined media that have been produced by and for women since the inception of the contemporary women's movement, from 1963 to 1983. Allen, who is currently editor of the *Directory of Women's Media*,[12] focuses primarily on the many multi-issue, single-issue, and special-identity women's periodicals of the period, although she includes a section on other women's media formats: music, film, video, and radio. She identifies eight characteristics that define the various components of the women's communication networks: (1) women speaking for themselves, (2) collective structures, (3) sharing, noncompetitive, (4) critical of mass media portrayals of mass media, (5) a nonattack approach toward others in their reporting, (6) emphasis on the "open forum," (7) inclusion of information not found in the mainstream media, and (8) an activist orientation (p. 50). Allen's study is rich with anecdotes and personal interviews with founders of media projects.

These two studies by Mather and Allen represent the only in-depth research available that focuses primarily on print media. Further research is needed on feminists' use of various media formats such as video/film, music, radio, graphics, presses, printers, and news services as well as case studies of individual projects.[13] Of particular importance are the media produced by women of color, insofar as little information exists on these projects. Analyses of their organizational styles and formations could additionally be addressed.

Because many publications are short-lived, it is imperative, as Mather argues, that feminist media history be recorded. Although there are some feminist periodicals, for example, that have endured 10 years or more, and although many new periodicals emerge to replace those that cease to exist, the problems of burnout, financial strain, internal disagreements, or changes remain and contribute to the short life cycle and ultimate demise of many of the media projects. These media products and their history are invaluable sources for future research on the feminist movement, and yet many groups often come into and go out of existence before they are appropriately archived or recorded. Additionally, the dynamics of this formation process need to be recorded, along with reasons for the projects' demise.

Many archives categorize feminist periodicals, as well as other feminist media, with other materials classified as "women's media." Mather's call for research that distinguishes feminist media from other alternative media, particularly those designated as being "by women," points to a still unresolved area within feminism. In addressing this distinction in relation to feminist novels and feminist art, both Rosalind Coward (1980) and Michelle Barrett (1982) caution against the confusion of women's experience with women's politics. Coward notes, in reference to women's novels, that while such media products may have recognizable roots in the women's movement, "their relation to feminism is not the necessary outcome of taking women's experience as central" (p. 58). She argues further that "feminism can never be the product of the identity of women's experience and interests—there is no such unity. Feminism must always be the alignment of women in a political movement with particular political aims and objectives. It is a grouping unified by its political interests, not its common experience" (p. 63).

Making such a distinction is not to imply that there is nothing progressive about "women's media" (Coward. 1980, p, 61). The reclamation of women's history and experience can contribute to a sense of unity for the producers and consumers of women's media, and we have seen how women's media producers have challenged the traditions and conventions of the mass media with alternative organizational structures, practices, and content. However, the conflation of feminist periodicals and women's periodicals into a single category of the "dissident press," when uncritically addressed, does little to illuminate our understanding of the radical texts of the women's movement. In her appeal for us to move beyond women's experience, Coward argues for us to "discover its 'representativeness' which would show the workings of ideology and its relation to objective, material structures of oppression" (p. 63).

Media researchers suggests that alternative media, such as that aligned with the women's movement, play a key role in raising issues of concern to women that the mass media may then pick up and carry to a larger audience (Allen, 1987, p. 20; Kessler, 1984). Allen (1987) states that while "the mass media may not tell it our way—that articulation is still our job," they "open up the questions for consideration by the public" (p. 20). Yet the mass media themselves represent a "field of allowable images" (Jaddou & Williams, 1981, p. 121), a field that comprises a core of traditional images and those newly incorporated or on their way to incorporation. The process of incorporation is one of dilution, whereby images of feminist struggle that are taken in by the mass media are made to conform to dominant values and representations. As Jaddou and Williams (1981) point out, images on their way to incorporation do not come out of thin air, but rather arise within the field of the unallowable, those marginalized representations that are directly suppressed, either economically (through limited exhibition, production, and distribution) or by the state (p. 121). Yet, while the mass media may provide a location for feminist issues to be raised for larger audiences, the degree to which the issues and their representations in the mass media conform to the feminist struggle distinguishes them from their oppositional treatment in feminist media. For example, as the mass media frame the collectivist feminist struggle in terms of the individual, the reductionist tendencies in the incorporation process are at work. In question here is the degree to which the feminist struggle is represented, whether it is redefined as individual struggle, or, similarly, embraced as "women's experience" by alternative women's media.

As feminists continue to evaluate what it means to be activists in relation to the goals of the women's movement, this evaluation must also include an accounting for the women's movement media themselves. Responding to a panel at the second International Feminist Book Fair in Oslo in 1986, K. Kaufman questioned the relationship of feminist politics to women's media and women's culture. She asked if we, as feminist media producers, authors, image makers, readers and/or viewers, are being contained through our own participation/complicity? "Has the consumption of feminist culture—particularly in its avant-garde, alternative or progressive forms—become a passive and pacifying substitution for action toward substantive, structural change in women's status?" (Kaufman, 1986).

The question is crucial because it highlights the need for an ongoing, thorough evaluation of women's activities and projects in order to assess their efficacy for social change. Feminism is founded upon the assumption that women are a historically oppressed group, and that through a variety of means we must bring about fundamental changes in society, both ideological and structural, in order to eradicate the oppression of women. Feminist media were founded upon the assumption that if such social change is to occur, it is requisite that women establish various media formats to communicate through their own words and images, their own expressions of what feminist politics means. Insofar as knowledge and its production are fundamentally linked to the conferrence of power, feminist media workers have provided vehicles with which they produce and disseminate knowledge of their own and other women's lives (Kaufman, 1986, p. 13). However, if our research is to be consistent with the politics of the feminist movement, in which the structures and processes of women's subordination are to be made explicit, this research, in addition to feminist media production and consumption, necessitates an ongoing accounting for the radical, structural changes that feminism requires.

Further consideration is needed of the political impulses that motivate the formation of these media projects in the first place. This type of examination questions the ways in which the politics and struggles of our feminism(s) are defined. As feminism becomes increasingly involved in cultural politics, more rigorous theoretical distinctions are required to ensure that the question of how media representations work will be raised. Such an approach would continue to address the political utility of women's media projects and also serve the diverse groups within feminism.

NOTES

1. NOW initiated the process of "preferential balloting" for the election of its officers, in which each voting delegate indicates her first, second, third, and fourth choices of candidates for each office. When a majority vote (defined as the majority of all votes cast) is not reached for one candidate, the ballots for the candidate with the lowest number of votes are redistributed according to the second choices indicated on those ballots. The procedure of redistributing the ballots is continued until a count indicates a majority vote has been reached. Although this election process does not favor the candidate with the "most" votes, it does ensure that the eventual candidate selected will have been chosen in a process that is by definition more consensual, as this candidate may be the first, second, or third choice of a large number of NOW delegates (National Organization for Women, 1979, pp. 31-33).

2. Zillah Eisenstein (1981) labels this component the "progressive tendency" within liberalism (p. 231).

3. *The Woman's Journal* was first published from 1870 to 1890 by the American Woman Suffrage Association, until this organization merged with the National American Woman Suffrage Association (NAWSA). From 1890 to 1917 this journal was the public voice of the mainstream suffrage movement and NAWSA. Between 1917 and 1931, it was published as *The Woman Citizen* by the Woman Citizen Corporation as a result of a bequest from Mrs. Frank Leslie to Carrie Chapman Catt, president of NAWSA.

4. Casey Hayden and Mary King wrote an early memo addressing the inequitable status of women within the peace and liberation movements that was widely circulated among activists. Two months later a group of women walked out of the national convention for the Students for a Democratic Society and the following spring this memo was reprinted in *Liberation* (Armstrong, 1981, p.237).

5. Freeman argues that even in groups that have not been deliberately structured, informal leaders do emerge. The advocacy and implementation of structurelessness is, to Freeman, a method of masking power. Whereas the "structureless" style was appropriate for the consciousness-raising sessions characteristic of some parts of the early women's movement, Freeman asserts that this organizational style became problematic when groups were unwilling to change their structure as they reoriented their tasks toward more political activities (Joreen, 1973, p. 285).

6. The percentages of pages devoted to letters to the editor were as follows: *Good Housekeeping*, .7%; *Harper's Bazaar*, 0%; *Ladies' Home Journal*, 1.0%; *McCall's*, .8%; *Vogue*, 0%. These percentages are taken from a study by Rita Mookerji (cited in Mather, 1973, p. 199).

7. *Ms.* reported, for example, that in 1979 the monthly averages of reader contributions were 300 letters to the editors, 600 unsolicited manuscripts, 750 poetry submissions, 400 article suggestions, 200 submissions for the "Gazette" (a section covering news of the women's movement), 1,600 submissions to the "No Comment" section, and several hundred letters to specific authors or editors in response to their work. The *Ms.* letters to the editor are

now archived at the Schlesinger Library on the History of Women, Radcliffe College, 3 James Street, Cambridge, MA 021338 ("Schlesinger Library Acquires," 1982, p. 5).

8. I wish to credit Nina Gregg for reminding me of this important distinction.

9. A report on this study has been published subsequently in the *1989 Directory of Women's Media*. See Kranich (1989).

10. The *1988 Directory of Women's Media* (Allen, 1988b) lists many examples (Labrys Records, Lilyfem Records, Sea Friends, Whys Crack Records, Pleiades Records) as well as the artists each label represents.

11. WINGS may be reached at P.O. Box 6758, San Francisco, CA 94101-6758. The co-producers are Katherine Davenport and Frieda Werden.

12. This directory is published annually by the Women's Institute for Freedom of the Press, 3306 Ross Place, N.W., Washington, DC 20008.

13. Since the 1970s feminist film scholarship has had a significant influence on film theory (see, for example, Brunsdon, 1986; Kuhn, 1982). Research focusing on women's music includes a case study by Cynthia Lont (1984) of Redwood Records. By examining the women's music industry from a variety of perspectives (a recording collective, producers, critics, retailers, and so on), Lont was able to capture a more comprehensive picture of this cultural venture. Maida Tilchen's (1984) article is an overview of the contemporary women's music since its inception. In her study, Tilchen identifies four major trends in content, which she categorizes as separatism, innovative, political, and women-produced.

In addition to the studies mentioned in the text, research on women's publications include Rose Weitz's (1984) textual analysis of the *Ladder*, the first significant lesbian periodical in the United States, published between 1956 and 1972 by the Daughters of Bilitis, the first lesbian organization in this country. Weitz traces the development of lesbian identity through the definitions of lesbianism found in the *Ladder* over the 16-year period. A related study by Katie King (1986) investigates the contests for meanings within U.S. feminism by drawing on writing from U.S. feminists between 1968 and 1972. This semiotic approach examines how lesbianism has functioned as a constantly shifting sign in various histories of the women's movement. One additional study by Michel Brody (1985) is a history of *Lavendar Woman*, a Chicago newspaper that Brody helped found. Her study serves as a chronological record of the 26 issues published between 1971 and 1976, and includes 50 written pieces from the paper and interviews with seven former *Lavendar Woman* collective members.

Numerous studies exist about feminist art and criticism, among them Pollock (1988), Robinson (1988), and Parker and Pollock (1987).

REFERENCES

Allen, Donna. (1987, January-February/March-April) Yes, we still have pioneers—They're working for women's equal media outreach to the public. *Media Report to Women*, p. 20.

Allen, Martha Leslie. (1988a). *The development of communications networks among women, 1963-1983*. Unpublished doctoral dissertation, Howard University, Washington, DC.

Allen, Martha Leslie. (Ed.). (1988b). *1988 Directory of Women's Media*. Washington, DC: Women's Institute for Freedom of the Press.

Armstrong, David. (1981). *A trumpet to arms: Alternative media in America*. Boston: South End.

Armstrong, Louise. (1987a, February). The circle game. *Women's Review of Books, 4*, 9-10.

Armstrong, Louise. (1987b, March). The circle game (II). *Women's Review of Books, 4*, 9-10.

Barrett, Michelle. (1982). Feminism and the definition of cultural politics. In Rosalind Brunt & Caroline Rowan (Eds.), *Feminism, culture and politics* (pp. 37-58). London: Lawrence & Whishart.

Brody, Michel. (1985). *Are we there yet? A continuing history of Lavendar Woman, a Chicago lesbian newspaper, 1971-1976*. Iowa City: Aunt Lute Book Company.

Brunsdon, Charlotte. (Ed.). (1986). *Films for women*. London: British Film Institute.

Combahee River Collective. (1982). The Combahee River Collective statement. In Barbara Smith (Ed.), *Home girls: A Black feminist anthology* (pp. 272-282). New York: Kitchen Table: Women of Color Press.

Coward, Rosalind. (1980). "This novel changes lives": Are women's novels feminist novels? A response to Rebecca O'Rourke's article "Summer reading." *Feminist Review, 5*, 53-64.

Doughty, Frances, & Bunch, Charlotte. (1980). Frances Doughty talks to Charlotte Bunch about women's publishing. *Sinister Wisdom, 13*, 71-77.

Downing, John. (1984). *Radical media: The political experience of alternative communication*. Boston: South End.

Eisenstein, Zillah R. (1981). *The radical future of liberal feminism*. New York: Longman.

The Feminists. (1973). The feminists: A political organization to annihilate sex roles. In Anne Koedt, Ellen Levine, & Anita Rapone (Eds.), *Radical feminism* (pp. 368-378). New York: Quadrangle.

Ferro, Nancy, Holcolm, Coletta Reid, & Saltzman-Webb, Marilyn. (1977). Statement of purpose, *off our backs*. In Maurine Beasley & Sheila Silver (Eds.), *Women in media: A documentary source book* (pp. 117-118). Washington, DC: Women's Institute for Freedom of the Press.

Flora, Cornelia Butler. (1971). The passive female: Her comparative image by class and culture in women's magazine fiction. *Journal of Marriage and the Family, 33*, 435-444.

Franzwa, Helen. (1974). Working women in fact and fiction. *Journal of Communication, 24*, 104-109.

Freeman, Alexa, & Jones, Valle. (1976). Creating feminist communications. *Quest, 3, 3-12*.

Freeman, Jo. (1973). The origins of the women's liberation movement. *American Journal of Sociology, 78*, 792-811.

Freeman, Jo. (1975). *The politics of women's liberation*. New York: Longman.

Friedan, Betty. (1963). *The feminine mystique*. New York: W. W. Norton.

Frye, Marilyn. (1983). Some reflections on separatism and power. In *The politics of reality: Essays in feminist theory* (pp. 96-109). Trumansburg, NY: Crossing.

Glessing, Robert J. (1970). *The underground press in America*. Bloomington: Indiana University Press.

Hole, Judith, & Levine, Ellen. (1971). *Rebirth of feminism*. New York: Quandrangle.

Hooks, Bell. (1981). *Ain't I a woman: Black women and feminism*. Boston: South End.

Hooks, Bell. (1984). *Feminist theory: From margin to center*. Boston: South End.

Jaddou, Liliane, & Williams, Jon. (1981). A theoretical contribution to the struggle against the dominant representations of women. *Media, Culture and Society, 3*, 105-124.

Jaggar, Allison. (1983). *Feminist politics and human nature*. Totowa, NJ: Rowman & Allanheld.

Jay, Karla. (1986a, November). Power to the author. *Women's Review of Books, 4*, 5-6.

Jay, Karla. (1986b, December). Power to the author (II). *Women's Review of Books, 4*, 9-10.

Joreen. (1973). The tyranny of structurelessness. In Anne Koedt, Ellen Levine, & Anita Rapone (Eds.), *Radical feminism*. New York: Quadrangle.

Joreen. (1977). Voice of the women's liberation movement. In Maureen Beasley & Sheila Silver (Eds.), *Women in media: A documentary source book* (pp. 109-115). Washington, DC: Women's Institute for Freedom of the Press.

Kaufman, K. (1986, October). A world of writers. *Women's Review of Books, 4*, 13-14.

Kessler, Lauren. (1984). *The dissident press: Alternative journalism in American history.* Beverly Hills, CA: Sage.

King, Katie. (1986). The situation of lesbianism as feminism's magical sign: Contests for meaning and the U.S. women's movement, 1968-1972. *Communication, 9*, 65-91.

Kitchen Table Press to publish *Cuentos: Stories of Latinas.* (1982, January 1). *Media Report to Women*, pp. 1, 6-7.

Kranich, Kimberlie A. (1989). Celebrating our diversity/women of color periodicals: 1968-1988. In Martha Allen (Ed.), *1989 Directory of Women's Media* (pp. 86-89). Washington, DC: Women's Institute for Freedom of the Press.

Kuhn, Annette. (1982). *Women's pictures: Feminism and cinema*. Boston: Routledge & Kegan Paul.

Leamer, Laurence. (1972). *The paper revolutionaries: The rise of the underground press.* New York: Simon & Schuster.

Lont, Cynthia. (1984). *Between rock and a hard place: A model of subcultural persistence and women's music*. Unpublished doctoral dissertation, University of Iowa, Iowa City.

Mather, Anne Dudley. (1973). *A history and analysis of feminist periodicals*. Unpublished master's thesis, University of Georgia, Athens.

Mather, Anne. (1974). A history of feminist periodicals: Part I. *Journalism History, 1*, 82-85.

Moraga, Cheri, & Anzaldua, Gloria. (Eds.). (1981). *This bridge called my back: Writings by radical women of color*. Watertown, MA: Persephone.

Ms. staff. (1977). A personal report from *Ms*. In Maureen Beasley & Sheila Silver (Eds.), *Women in media: A documentary source book* (pp. 119-125). Washington, DC: Women's Institute for Freedom of the Press.

National Organization for Women. (1979). *The National Organization for Women policy manual: Administration*. Washington, DC: Author.

Parker, Rozsika, & Pollock, Griselda. (1987). *Framing feminism: Art and the women's movement, 1970-1985*. London: Pandora.

Pollock, Griselda. (1988). *Vision and difference: Femininity, feminism, and the histories of art*. New York: Routledge, Chapman & Hall.

Rich, Cynthia, Greenfield, Gloria, McGloin, Pat, & Snow, Deborah. (1980). Persephone Press. *Sinister Wisdom, 13*, 81-85.

Robinson, Hilary. (1988). *Visibly female: Feminism and art today: an anthology*. New York: Universe.

Rothschild-Whitt, Joyce. (1979). The collectivist organization: An alternative to rational-bureaucratic models. *American Sociological Review, 44*, 509-527.

Schlesinger library acquires letters to *Ms*. (1982, March 1). *Media Report to Women*, pp. 4-5.

Tilchen, Maida. (1984). Lesbians and women's music. In Trudy Darty & Sandee Potter (Eds.), *Women-identified women* (pp. 287-303). Palo Alto, CA: Mayfield.

Tuchman, Gaye. (1978). *Making news: A study in the construction of reality*. New York: Free Press.

Tuchman, Gaye, Daniels, Arlene Kaplan, & Benet, James. (1978). *Hearth and home: Images of women in the mass media*. New York: Oxford University Press.

200 women's media plan cooperation at national "Women in Print" conference. (1982, January 1). *Media Report to Women*, pp. 1, 6-7.

Weitz, Rose. (1984). From accommodation to rebellion: The politicization of lesbianism. In Trudy Darty & Sandee Potter (Eds.), *Women-identified women* (pp. 233-248). Palo Alto, CA: Mayfield.

WINGS radio service prepares for regular operation. (1987, January-February/ March-April). *Media Report to Women*, p. 6.

16

A Bridge to the Future

Re-Visioning Gender in Communication[1]

LANA F. RAKOW

Imagine you have been transported to a time in the future. As you fly around the country in your personal space vehicle, sizing up the state of things, you peer through windows into the offices and boardrooms of newspapers, magazines, public relations and advertising agencies, production houses, television and radio stations, and network headquarters. You notice that women and men are at work, writing, creating, designing, managing, delegating, deciding, buying, and selling. The scenario seems unremarkable to a transported earthling from the year 1989, though techniques and technologies have changed from the days you remember and business districts seem bigger, shinier, faster.

But something isn't quite the same. You can't put your finger on it. What's different about this picture? That's it! Look at how many women there are in those boardrooms and executive offices. In fact, they are working at all levels at these industries. And something else is different. The newspapers, the television programs, the advertisements—what these women and men are producing show women and men doing all kinds of things: shopping, working, caring for children, making business decisions, making news.

"So we managed to do it," you say softly—and proudly—to yourself. All those years of struggle and hard work finally paid off. Feminism did reach its goal, albeit at some rather far-off time in the future.

Or did it?

If you were to continue your air cruise, you might see other things that would not make you feel as good as seeing women well represented in

AUTHOR'S NOTE: I am grateful to Pam Creedon, Cheris Kramarae, Karlene Ferrante, and Kathy Cirksena for their comments on this chapter.

communication industries: poverty, homelessness, hunger, violence, unemployment, racism, anger, and discontent. Women still work "double shifts" at career and home, though more men are likely to have these burdens also. Black, Hispanic, and Native American women still make up the bulk of the poor and unemployed or underemployed; it is by and large their white "sisters" who have made it up the career ladder. Domestic abuse shelters still harbor a stream of women and their children, escaping from violent husbands and fathers. The incidence of sexual assault has not declined. Newspapers report a leak that the government is preparing to send troops to the latest global "hot spot" (despite "advanced" military technologies, world powers still resort to sending men—and now some women—into combat to reduce the risk of a full-scale, globally destructive war).

At this depressing sight, you are ready to go back to your own present. How could so many problems have been left unsolved, even when we were successful in getting women well represented throughout government and industry?

UNDERSTANDING THE PRESENT

Imagining future scenarios is a good exercise. It allows us to build a bridge between what we are fighting for today and what we want tomorrow to be. It shows us a possible outcome of the changes we are advocating. It makes clear the assumptions that underlie our present thinking. It helps us set our strategies and our priorities for bringing about a different world.

Few of us would say that this scenario for the future is what we had in mind. But might this be the future we are working toward, if we are not careful? Such a future is a possibility if we do not dare to make our critique of present conditions wide enough and deep enough. Let's look at some of the assumptions that underlie much of our present-day thinking that, if left in place, could produce this scenario.

Underlying our society are a structure and set of values that emphasize individualism, competition, the transcendence of property rights over other rights, hierarchy, the separation of public and private activities and moralities, and a reliance upon science for problem solving. Our gender system—of two distinct and hierarchically ordered groups of people—is not incidental to these ideas; in fact, the two are inseparably entwined.[2] The classical liberal ideas of the Enlightenment, mixing with nineteenth-century American notions of industrial capitalism and social evolution, produced a vision of society consisting of individuals (and eventually organizations, in the twentieth-century version known as pluralism) competing with each other for limited resources or rewards. The "best," of course, would win.[3] These individuals were assumed to be white and male, not surprisingly.

As industrialism was allowed to shape the structure of our economic and political system, these competing individuals came to be seen as occupiers of a public world of business and government. White women and women and men of color were excluded from the public sphere, with white women specifically consigned—in a "complementary" manner to the men in their lives—to the "private sphere" of the family, of nurturance, of caregiving.[4] People of color were relegated to a separate class upon whose backs the public and the private rested (in their roles as seasonal workers, maintenance workers, housekeepers, and nursemaids, for example). The split in values between the public and private spheres, then, came to define what being a woman or a man meant and still means, defined according to white standards. *Man* came to stand for rationality, competition, aggression, individualism. *Woman* came to stand for emotionality, nurturance, cooperation, community. Of course, none of this was or is biologically determined. In fact, at different times in Western history, *man* and *woman* have meant very different things.

Nonetheless, these values have been assigned to two different groups of people who occupy two different—and unequally valued and unequally powerful—regions of activity in society. As long as white women and people of color were denied the status of either "human" or "citizen," they could continue to be excluded from the public world of the "individual" or "normal" human. But people of color and white women have fought long and historic battles challenging those definitions, often, however, on the very principles of the system that has been oppressive to them. These are such principles as "equal opportunity." Despite the appeal of the phrase, it rests on the assumption of a society of individuals free to compete in a hierarchically ordered contest of winners and losers.

These are the principles that, left intact, could produce the scenario described above. It might be (some) white women who achieve some success at entering the white male domain of ownership, management, and leadership, or it might be (some) Black men. Regardless of which group makes some headway into the system, the system remains much the same, and *most* white women and people of color will not benefit.

On the other hand, can we envision a future based on those values historically relegated to the private sphere—cooperation and nurturance?[5] Here is the possibility for building a new world community with broad-based political participation and decision making, justice and fair treatment, dignity and purpose. And it is here that feminism has the most to offer, for feminism recognizes not that women have special virtues because of biology (women can be aggressive and competitive as well as men, they are just less likely to be because of prescriptions against it), but that the values relegated to women have been the values that are to be avoided, even ridiculed, by men because of their association with women (and, of course, men can be cooperative and nurturant as well as women, they are just less likely to have the training).[6]

Underneath any scenario of the future, then, is a social theory carried into the future. We must think ahead to where our critiques will carry us if they should come to pass. However, pointing out the shameful record of the treatment of white women and all people of color in news and entertainment industries—in employment and content—does not necessarily have to lead us to a solution of "equal opportunity," which would preserve a system of hierarchy. If we extend our critique to the structures and value systems of our society, we will recognize the need for deep and profound change.[7] In the remainder of this chapter I would like to suggest further critiques that we need to make and the possibilities we can envision for the future as they relate to both mass communication (as employers, industries, and cultural practices) and mass communication education.

THE PLACE OF MASS COMMUNICATION

Other chapters in this book document the record of women (mostly white women) as members of communication professions and as objects of media content. This is important evidence for us in documenting the treatment of women and the conditions under which we live our lives. Now what are we going to do with this information? We can suggest that women need more opportunities in the workplace, that they need to be treated like their male counterparts when it comes to hiring and promotion, that more women need to be portrayed in more diverse and less sexual ways in media content, but these are solutions belonging to an "equal opportunity" future. Instead, let me suggest some other solutions.

Rather than encouraging women to make their way within the industries as those industries currently exist—encouraging them to get their individual piece of the career success pie—why not encourage them to *transform* the industries they work for? Think a minute about the kind of mass communication systems that are supposed to be serving the needs of the people of this country. It is no news to any of us that mass communication is currently made up of large, wealthy organizations controlling technologies for the overriding purpose of making a profit. Is that *really* what we want our communication systems to do? Is that *really* the most important need we have for communication? Our communication systems *could* provide us forums for discussion and debate, for genuine dialogue rather than monologue, for the sharing of values and rituals orginating *from* us, not directed *at* us. They could provide us with a commonly achieved culture and a commonly arrived-at society. They could provide those of us long without "voice"—that is, the presence and weight of our participation in public discussion—the opportunity to have it. Here I share the sentiments of the Women's Institute for Freedom of the Press Associates' Statement that a means of communication must be available to all who need and want it and that changes in our structure of mass communication must come to include the voices of all those who are left out.[8]

Our critique, then, of the role of women *in* media industries *must also include* a critique of the media industries themselves. Do we really want some women to have a better shake in an oppressive system? What can women do who are in those systems to change them? I am not an optimist when it comes to believing that the mere presence of more women will have a substantial impact on media industries *unless* those women are feminists or are at least politically activated toward collective change. Women can take on the values of men (since none of these characteristics is biological) or some useful hybrid of masculinity and femininity, and some can achieve "success" in this way. But the ones who will pass through the fire will be those who are least likely to want to change the system. Changing from within will take change-oriented women working together, who—to make an understatement—will not have an easy time of it.

Another way that women can try to transform our communication systems is through activism on the outside of media industries—supporting and creating our own media to at least reach more women; challenging the "rights" of newspapers, broadcasters, and other industries; and changing the terms of public debate about communication (for example, questioning whose right to speak is preserved by broadcasters' assertion of First

Amendment protection or speaking out about the concentration of media ownership in fewer and fewer hands).

We have to see, ultimately, that the *content* of our media systems is integrally tied up with preserving a structure and value system that I have described earlier. It is here that definitions of such terms as *woman, man, Black, Asian, Hispanic* get constructed and displayed in particular ways.[9] It is here that public policy struggles over child care, welfare, pornography, poverty, and unemployment get played out. We must look to the content of our media systems, not only to see how few women are used as characters in prime-time television or how objectified women are in advertising or pornography, but also to see how our identities and our experiences are defined for us. The solution to media content, then, cannot simply be "more women characters" or "less exploitation of women's sexuality" or more hard news about women. In fact, we have seen that media industries can take these demands and produce characters, visual images, and news that are no more flattering, useful, unexploitative, or meaningful than they were before, but done in the name of the "new" and "modern" American woman. That is because the basic structure and purpose of the media industries have not changed, and women are not *freely* telling their own stories and experiences with complete access to the media as citizens and not as employees.

This is where research can come in. We need to move beyond content analysis, which documents the presence or absence of certain things, to a richer analysis of definitions of identities and public policy issues. We need to look at women's own stories and experiences, found in women's media and elsewhere. We need to document the ways in which women have been denied voice and the ways that they have resisted, successfully and unsuccessfully, attempts to silence them. The more rich evidence we have of a history of women's struggles and alternatives, the more documentation we have for changing the terms of the problem. To do this, researchers will have to go beyond the traditional, legitimated research methods of our field and search for new methods.[10]

We will have to think about the study of communication differently. Why continue to divide up the world into speech, interpersonal, organizational, and mass communication, and further into studies of radio, magazine, television, advertising, and public relations? Instead, let us think about the world from the perspective of women (or other subjugated groups) and see what the world of communication looks like from their vantage point. We would immediately see that the divisions are quite meaningless, especially if we are interested in the impediments to women's communication and their struggles and alternatives to those restrictions. We would have to look at efforts to restrict women's public speaking in the nineteenth century, as well as etiquette books in the twentieth that told women to be listeners, not talkers. We would have to look at the alternative kinds of cooperative, nonhierarchical organizations women have worked in, including those producing feminist and other alternative media. We would have to look at the role that women's media have played in helping women to organize and effect political change. We would have to look at how feminist media have defined women and their problems and experiences, and the kind of language used to do so. We would have to understand the lives of women at different time periods and how they have made sense out of or resisted media content.

THE PLACE OF JOURNALISM
AND MASS COMMUNICATION EDUCATION

Journalism and mass communication education is important for us to look at because its critique, too, needs to be extended. Mass communication education is a site at which white women and people of color experience a system that does not benefit them as it does white men, as chapters in this volume attest. Perhaps, however, journalism and mass communication education might be a site for helping to change society on our way to a different scenario than the one I have described.

Since 1977, white women have been the majority of students in journalism education, a fact that has been viewed with considerable concern. Men faculty and administrators seem most concerned that the perception of journalism as a profession may decline, and, more important, that salaries of journalists may as well, given the historic pattern of other occupations associated with women. Women faculty have pointed out the tremendous discrepancy between numbers of women students and numbers of women faculty and the discriminatory conditions that await these graduates.[11] And lurking behind these concerns is a future one: If journalism education is dominated by women, will communication professions become dominated by them, too?

Let us look again at the language that is commonly applied to this situation. Women *dominate* journalism education; will they *dominate* the industries? Of course, women *do not* dominate these areas, they are simply the majority persons in them. But herein may lie a point of optimism. What if women *did* dominate, that is, take control of them? We are back to my earlier suggestion that women need to transform the industries they work for and transform the terms of debate about mass communication. Why not seize upon the majority presence of women and make it a positive condition? Why train them to take up their places in media industries rather than to take them over? Why not train all those women in our education programs to change the world of communication and, in doing so, change the world? That which has been called, pejoratively, the feminization of journalism education and the feminization of the media could be made to take on a positive, political connotation if we commit ourselves to collective social change.

I recognize how startling such a suggestion might be to women—even feminists—who are communication professionals and educators. It will be even more threatening, of course, to men, for I suspect that lurking under their concerns about women becoming the majority of students and perhaps eventually professionals is a concern that women might *really* take over, if we were ever to assert our collective power. Perhaps they have known something all along that we are just coming to realize.

Yet I still anticipate objections from women to making journalism education political in such a way. But why? *Journalism education is already political.* It is already a collection of social practices, politics, and economics that trains certain people into taking up a particular vision of the world (whether they are trained as reporters, advertising media buyers, or public relations practitioners) that enables them to sell their services to large, powerful organizations that exist primarily to make a profit (despite how good individuals and professions may feel about the value of what they do). As a consequence, certain interests are served by our present system of journalism education and our present system of communication. Why not serve other interests? Why not serve *all* our interests? Why shouldn't women be the group to show us that our communication systems need major changes? To accept them as they are, and in fact to bolster them with the work and talent of our graduates, is already a profoundly political act.

If we do not seek the transformation of our education programs and of our systems of communication, what will become of our women students? If we are successful enough in our struggle to fight discriminatory hiring and promotion practices, and if we encourage their career success outlook, some may make it to the boardrooms. But what about all those left behind? There is only a limited amount of room at the top and on the way to the top. That is a consequence of living in a hierarchical, pyramid-shaped society. Will only white, middle-class women benefit from our efforts?[12]

And even for these women, what will they do about the "superwoman" dilemma—the collision between the myth that you can "have it all" with the reality that you will also have to "do it all" to have it? In this scenario of good careers for more women there is no solution to our culturewide problem of the split between the world of the workplace and the world of our personal lives of home and family. This returns us to the public and private spheres of my earlier discussion. A fundamental change will have to occur in reconciling the split between these two spheres, or women will continue to exist caught between impossible choices: to give preference to having a career rather than children, or to choose both and struggle under immensely heavy burdens. Making more and better child care widely available solves part of the problem, but it can do nothing about the time and energy demands put on a professional woman. Of course, another solution is for a woman to drop out of her career, and I think we will be hearing even more stories (from Ann Landers's columns to *Newsweek*) of women who are returning to the home. In such an event, we will not even see such small changes as women occupying more and better career positions.

We need to envision a different society if we are going to solve this one, and we do our students no favor if we do not expose them to solutions other than the above "choices."[13] For example, we will have to deconstruct the myth of motherhood and the mother-infant bond to realize how deeply we believe—a cultural belief, not rooted in biological necessity—that a child needs its *mother* (not other caring adults, even a father). We will have to debunk our cultural notion that having children is strictly a personal choice (one supposedly unaffected by public policy and the social and economic conditions of the society we live in), making a woman (and perhaps also a father) solely responsible for the care and well-being of that child, rather than accepting any communal responsibility for children. We will have to look at how other cultures organize child care to learn other patterns of community caregiving.[14] We will have to think about alternates to the nuclear family and the isolated, work-ridden household.

It soon becomes apparent that if we are genuinely to tackle the problems facing women—including graduates of schools of journalism and mass communication—we cannot simply apply a Band-aid labeled "equal opportunity." But where do we start with all that I have suggested needs to be done? The structure and content of mass communication need to change, as do the structure and value system of society. Schools of journalism and mass communication education could lead the way or they could continue to perpetuate the problem. What would such a curriculum look like that took social change rather than social stasis seriously? That took its women students seriously? That set its sights on a future scenario of egalitarianism, popular democracy, and community? That valued cooperation and nurturance over individualism and competition? Would we need a course in copyediting? Newspaper management? Advertising media buying? Public relations campaigns? Or would we need courses in how to let people speak for themselves? How to start a feminist newspaper? How to create social change? How the media could be used for democratic purposes? Of course, the objections that will rise up from industries and administrators at the suggestion of such changes would be embarrassing evidence of just how political the curriculum already is.

This chapter has been intended to be a bridge, in two senses. First, it was intended to make a connection between the present conditions of women's treatment in media industries and content, as described in the rest of this book, to what we can do and should look for in the future. Second, it was intended to make a connection between two kinds of feminisms, linking but challenging the assumptions that underlie a liberal feminist approach to questions about women and the media with a more radical feminist approach. I have raised what I think—and hope—might be some unsettling issues. We must not let ourselves be too timid in either our critique of the present or our vision for the future.

A RE-VISIONED FUTURE

Imagine, now, that you have been transported into a different future. Instead of your own space vehicle, you hop aboard a free public monorail that takes you quickly and quietly to any destination. Out the window you see small communities of people—of a range of colors from deep chocolate to olive to beige and a range of appearances and clothing; some appear to be women and some men, but others do not fit your categories. The environments they live in are human-scale and safe for children, who climb in and out of interesting forms and play cooperative games, under the watchful eyes of older children and adults who work nearby. Food is plentiful, growing in fields, stacked in fruit and vegetable stands. You catch sounds of music—a calypso beat drifts by from one direction, drums and chants from another—and laughter in between the conversation of people at work.

What appears to be a newspaper has been left on the seat next to you. You read the words of many people, who have written of their experiences and their concerns. A prominent announcement alerts community members to a meeting that evening, for a discussion of how many tools the locally owned plant should produce next year. Television and radio sets are not broadcasting advertising and entertainment created by large, unseen industries. Instead, local individuals, groups, and communities use the airwaves to communicate with each other, discussing problems, presenting their viewpoints, sharing their stories and art.

"Now this is a strange and different place," you remark to yourself. It is not completely idyllic, of course. There are disagreements that need to be worked out, through mediation if necessary, but most decisions are communally arrived at through discussion and compromise. Though several generations have passed between 1989 and now, some vestiges of selfishness, greed, and even violence remain. But you find yourself staring at a world that is at once egalitarian and richly diverse, a world that does not rank and tightly categorize people by race or gender; a world that provides materially for all its members; a world that treasures children and considers them not the property of one or two parents, but the responsibility of parents *and* the whole community; a world that is decided upon by all the people living in it, not by powerful organizations or a small group of powerful men; a world based on values of cooperation and community, rather than competition and individualism. Communication technologies are used not for private profit, but for political and cultural participation by members of the society.[15]

Now here is a scenario that has real possibilities. I'll throw my chips in with this or some related vision of the future any day. It might be criticized for being unrealistic or farfetched, but the future has a way of becoming what we imagine it to be. It is time for women to have *their* wishes for the future come true.

NOTES

1. Some readers may be troubled by the grammatical license I have taken with the noun *vision* in the title of this chapter. In doing so I am claiming the right to make the English language work in a useful way for women, as have the other authors in this volume (see Pamela Creedon's comments on this point in Chapter 1). For a discussion of how male grammarians historically have tampered with the language to produce a set of grammatical rules detrimental to women, see Dale Spender's *Man Made Language* (1980, especially pp. 147-151).

2. For more discussion of our gender system, see Lana F. Rakow (1986).

3. This is a simplistic version of a complicated historical process, obviously. Those unfamiliar with this version of our past might wish to refer to Richard Hofstadter (1955a, 1955b), Daniel Boorstin (1974), and Robert Wiebe (1980).

4. There has been a great deal of attention to this historical and contemporary phenomenon by feminist historians and sociologists. See Ann Douglas (1977), Barbara Welter (1976), Rosalind Rosenberg (1975), and Eva Gamarnikow, David Morgan, June Purvis, and Daphne Taylorson (1983).

5. I do not mean to romanticize the private sphere, however. Kathy Cirksena has wisely reminded me to point out the pathology of the private sphere that can be obscured by focusing on the positive values with which it is mythologically endowed. The pathology takes such forms as the economic and emotional dependence of women on men, the high incidence of domestic violence, and the expectation that a woman should subordinate her own needs to those of others.

6. This treatment of the subject bears my own, radical feminist, interpretation; other feminist interpretations will vary. For an introduction to one classification system describing different feminist political and philosophical differences, see Jaggar and Rothenberg (1984), though I disagree with their characterization of radical feminism. Jaggar and Rothenberg classify feminists into liberals, radicals, socialists, and women of color.

7. I am an optimist about the possibility of bringing liberal feminism—which I have been describing as associated with a belief in "equal opportunity"—to a more radical critique of patriarchy, sharing the sentiments of Zillah Eisenstein in her book, *The Radical Future of Liberal Feminism* (1981).

8. See Martha Leslie Allen (1988) for the statement and other information about the Women's Institute for Freedom of the Press (p. 68).

9. There has been little research on this phenomenon as it relates to people of color, with such interesting exceptions as Tom Nakayama's (1988) work on Asian Americans as model minorities and James Oliver Horton's (1986) work on antebellum Black men's construction in newspapers of the ideal Black woman.

10. For an introduction to some of the issues of methodology that feminists have been discussing, see Gloria Bowles and Renate Duelli Klein (1983) and Lana F. Rakow (1987).

11. Maurine H. Beasley and Kathryn T. Theus (1988) provide an in-depth look at the phenomenon of women students becoming the majority in journalism education.

12. This is certainly a perception that at least some Black women share. As a panelist said on a panel on "Strategies for Studying Black Women and the Media" at the 1988 AEJMC convention in Portland, Oregon, "After feminists accomplish their agenda, I'll still have racism to deal with." This woman must be familiar with the limited goals of only some feminists; nonetheless, her point should be well taken.

13. These are, of course, no real choices if we are not happy with any of the alternatives or if we have no involvement in constructing the consequences of any of them. I am indebted to Barbara Katz Rothman (1986) for her wise discussion of the myth of "choices" available to women now about childbearing.

14. I do not mean to imply that women do not love their children and want to spend time with them, or that they should not want to in the future. However, we must problematize our cultural notions of motherhood and family. See such feminist work as Barrie Thorne with Marilyn Yalsom (1982), *Rethinking the Family: Some Feminist Questions*; Katherine Gieve (1987), "Rethinking Feminist Attitudes Towards Motherhood"; Adrienne Rich (1976), *Of Woman Born*; Nancy Chodorow (1978), *The Reproduction of Mothering: Psychoanalysis*

and the Sociology of Gender; Patricia Marks Greenfield (1981), "Child Care in Cross-Cultural Perspectives: Implications for the future Organization of Child Care in the United States"; Cathy Urwin (1985), "Constructing Motherhood: The Persuasion of Normal Development," and William Ray Arney (1980), "Maternal-Infant Bonding: The Politics of Falling in Love with Your Child."

15. Feminist writers of utopias and science fiction have done more imaginative jobs than I have here of envisioning better worlds. For an introduction to such interesting novels, I recommend Charlotte Perkins Gilman (1979), *Herland: A Lost Feminist Utopian Novel*; Sally Gearhart (1984), *The Wanderground*; Marge Piercy (1986), *Woman at the Edge of Time*; and Dorothy Bryant (1976), *The Kin of Ata Are Waiting for You.*

What communication technologies would look like and how they would be operated in a better future world is intentionally left unspecified in this description, other than to suggest that they should be grounded in the purpose of providing members of the society political and cultural voice. Specific media arrangements should be decided upon by members of the society. The Union for Democratic Communications is one organization of mass communication researchers, educators, and activists interested in bringing about such a system of democratic communications. For a further introduction to these arguments see the first chapter, "Introduction: Towards a Communications Democracy" in Richard Bunce (1976).

REFERENCES

Allen, Martha Leslie. (Ed.). (1988). *1988 directory of women's media*. Washington, DC: Women's Institute for Freedom of the Press.

Arney, William Ray. (1980). Maternal-infant bonding: The politics of falling in love with your child. *Feminist Studies, 6*(3), 547-570.

Beasley, Maurine H., & Theus, Kathryn T. (1988). *The new majority: A look at what the preponderance of women in journalism education means to the schools and to the professions*. Lanham, MD: University Press of America.

Boorstin, Daniel J. (1974). *The Americans: The democratic experience*. New York: Vintage.

Bowles, Gloria, & Klein, Renate Duelli. (Eds.). (1983). *Theories of women's studies*. London: Routledge & Kegan Paul.

Bryant, Dorothy. (1976). *The kin of Ata are waiting for you*. New York: Random House.

Bunce, Richard. (1976). *Television in the corporate interest*. New York: Praeger.

Chodorow, Nancy (1978). *The reproduction of mothering: Psychoanalysis and the sociology of gender*. Berkeley: University of California Press.

Douglas, Ann. (1977). *The feminization of American culture*. New York: Knopf.

Eisenstein, Zillah. (1981). *The radical future of liberal feminism*. New York: Longman.

Gamarnikow, Eva, Morgan, David, Purvis, June, & Taylorson, Daphne. (Eds.). (1983). *The public and the private*. London: Heinemann.

Gearhart, Sally M. (1984). *The Wanderground*. Boston: Alyson.

Gieve, Katherine. (1987). Rethinking feminist attitudes towards motherhood. *Feminist Review, 25*, 38-45.

Gilman, Charlotte Perkins. (1979). *Herland: A lost feminist utopian novel*. New York: Pantheon.

Greenfield, Patricia Marks. (1981). Child care in cross-cultural perspectives: Implications for the future organization of child care in the United States. *Psychology of Women Quarterly*, 6(1), 41-54.

Hofstadter, Richard. (1955a). *The age of reform: From Bryan to F.D.R.* New York: Knopf.

Hofstadter, Richard. (1955b). *Social Darwinism in American thought.* Boston: Beacon.

Horton, James Oliver. (1986). Freedom's yoke: Gender conventions among antebellum free Blacks. *Feminist Studies*, 12(1), 51-76.

Jaggar, Alison M., & Rothenberg, Paula S. (1984). *Feminist frameworks: Alternative theoretical accounts of the relations between women and men* (2nd ed.). New York: McGraw-Hill.

Nakayama, Tom. (1988). *Foucault, race and contemporary communication studies.* Paper presented at the annual convention of the Association for Education in Journalism and Mass Communication, Portland, OR.

Piercy, Marge. (1986). *Woman at the edge of time.* New York: Fawcett.

Rakow, Lana F. (1986). Rethinking gender research in communication. *Journal of Communication*, 36(4), 11-26.

Rakow, Lana F. (1987). Looking to the future: Five questions for gender research. *Women's Studies in Communication*, 10, 79-86.

Rich, Adrienne. (1976). *Of woman born.* New York: W. W. Norton.

Rosenberg, Rosalind. (1975). In search of woman's nature, 1850-1920. *Feminist Studies*, 4(1/2), 141-154.

Rothman, Barbara Katz. (1986). *The tentative pregnancy: Prenatal diagnosis and the future of motherhood.* New York: Penguin.

Spender, Dale. (1980). *Man made language.* London: Routledge & Kegan Paul.

Thorne, Barrie (Ed.), with Yalsom, Marilyn. (1982). *Rethinking the family: Some feminist questions.* New York: Longman.

Urwin, Cathy. (1985). Constructing motherhood: The persuasion of normal development. In Carolyn Steedman, Cathy Urwin, & Valerie Walkerdine (Eds.), *Language, gender and childhood* (pp. 164-202). London: Routledge & Kegan Paul.

Welter, Barbara. (1976). *Dimity convictions: The American woman in the nineteenth century.* Athens: Ohio University Press.

Wiebe, Robert H. (1980). *The search for order, 1877-1920.* Westport, CT: Greenwood.

About the Contributors

Maurine Beasley, Professor of Journalism at the University of Maryland, received her Ph.D. degree in American civilization from George Washington University. She holds a master's degree in journalism from Columbia University and bachelor's degrees in both journalism and history from the University of Missouri—Columbia.

Carolyn Garrett Cline, Assistant Professor of Journalism at Southwest Texas State University, San Marcos, earned her Ph.D. from Indiana University. She earned both her M.A. from Indiana and her B.S. from Boston University, School of Public Communication, in journalism.

Judith A. Cramer, Assistant Professor of Radio and Television at Long Island University, Southhampton, earned her M.A. in communication from the University of Hartford in Connecticut. She earned her B.A. in sports information/journalism from Keene State College in New Hampshire.

Pamela J. Creedon, Assistant Professor of Journalism at the Ohio State University, earned her M.A. in journalism from the University of Oregon and her B.A. in English from Mount Union College in Ohio.

Carolyn Stewart Dyer, Head of Undergraduate Studies in the School of Journalism and Mass Communication at the University of Iowa, earned her Ph.D. in mass communication with concentrations in history and law from the University of Wisconsin—Madison. She also earned her M.A. in journalism from Wisconsin and her B.A. in government from Beloit College in Wisconsin.

Eric S. Fredin is an Assistant Professor in the School of Journalism at the Ohio State University. He received his B.A. from Oberlin College and his Ph.D. in mass communication from the University of Michigan.

Alice Gagnard is Assistant Professor at the Center for Communication Arts, Southern Methodist University. She holds a Ph.D. degree in communications from the University of Tennessee—Knoxville.

Larissa S. Grunig, Assistant Professor of Journalism at the University of Maryland, earned her Ph.D. in public communication from the University of Maryland and her M.A. in journalism, also from Maryland. Her B.A. in English and Spanish is from North Dakota State University.

Susan Henry, Professor of Journalism at California State University, Northridge, earned her Ph.D. in communications from Syracuse University. She completed her M.S. in journalism from the University of Illinois and her B.A. in English from the University of Connecticut.

Sammye Johnson, Associate Professor of Communication at Trinity University in San Antonio, Texas, earned her bachelor's and master's degrees from the Medill School of Journalism at Northwestern University.

Sue Lafky, Assistant Professor of Communications in the Department of Journalism in the School of Communications and Theater at Temple University in Philadelphia, earned her B.S. in journalism from the University of Oregon and her M.A. in journalism from Indiana University, where she is currently completing her doctoral dissertation.

Linda Lazier-Smith, Creative Director at CRE, Inco, an advertising and marketing communications agency in Indianapolis, is a former faculty member at Ohio State and Indiana universities. She earned her Ph.D. in mass communication with a minor in women's studies from Indiana University. She earned her M.A. and B.A. in journalism from Ball State University.

Paula Matabane is a Graduate Associate Professor in the Department of Radio, TV and Film, School of Communications, Howard University, where she also serves as Television Production Sequence Coordinator. She earned her Ph.D. from Howard, her M.A. from Stanford, and her B.A. from the University of Pennsylvania.

Carroll Ann Ferguson Nardone is a Mass Communication Instructor at El Paso Community College in Texas. She completed her master's degree in journalism at the Ohio State University.

Lana F. Rakow, Assistant Professor of Communication at the University of Wisconsin—Parkside, earned her Ph.D. from the Institute of Communications Research at the University of Illinois, Urbana-Champaign, in cultural studies and feminist studies. She received her B.A. in English and her M.A. in journalism and humanities from the University of North Dakota.

Jane Rhodes is a doctoral student at the University of North Carolina at Chapel Hill and an Assistant Professor of Communication Studies at the State University College at Cortland, New York. She received her B.S. and M.A. degrees from Syracuse University.

Linda Schamber, currently a doctoral candidate in the School of Information Studies at Syracuse University, earned her master's degree in journalism at the Ohio State University and her bachelor's degree in education from Ohio State.

Conrad Smith, an Assistant Professor of Journalism at the Ohio State University, received his bachelor's degree in physics and his master's degree in photography and cinema from Ohio State. He received his doctorate from Temple University.

Marilyn Crafton Smith, Associate Professor in the Art Department at Appalachian State University, is completing her Ph.D. dissertation at the University of Iowa School of Journalism and Mass Communication. She earned her M.A. in painting from New York University and her B.F.A. in graphic design from the University of Georgia.

H. Leslie Steeves, Assistant Professor in the School of Journalism at the University of Oregon, earned her Ph.D. in mass communication from the University of Wisconsin—Madison. She has a B.S. degree in forestry and wildlife management from the University of Vermont and an M.S. degree in agricultural journalism from the University of Wisconsin—Madison.

NOTES

NOTES

NOTES

NOTES

NOTES